THE CHURCH AND SOCIAL PROGRESS

THE CHURCH AND SOCIAL PROGRESS

Background Readings
for Pope John's
Mater et Magistra

BENJAMIN L. MASSE, S.J.

THE BRUCE PUBLISHING COMPANY

MILWAUKEE

[1966]

IMPRIMI POTEST:
    JOHN J. McGINTY, S.J.

NIHIL OBSTAT:
    JOHN E. TWOMEY, S.T.L., PH.D.
    Censor librorum

IMPRIMATUR:
    ✝ WILLIAM E. COUSINS
    Archbishop of Milwaukee
    March 2, 1966

To the Memory
of
Pope John XXIII

PREFACE

Although the selections offered the reader here touch on many of the points made by Pope John XXIII in *Mater et Magistra*, the coverage is not as complete or intensive as originally planned. As the work of assembling materials progressed, it became clear that if the book was not to assume encyclopedic proportions, some topics would have to be excluded or treated only tangentially. The job of selection was painful.

In an age when fiscal policy has achieved high importance, it was not easy to skip over Pope John's remarks on taxation, which raise pertinent questions of social justice. It was also hard not to pursue more thoroughly his treatment of the population problem. In view of the Pope's emphasis on the interdependence of nations in our shrunken world, to skimp the timely subjects of foreign trade and balance of payments was equally difficult. It was especially disconcerting not to be able to give more space to the growing concentration of economic power and its implications for competition and planning in our society. As for the relationship between government and private enterprise, which Pope John treated in a helpful, down-to-earth way, that merits a book by itself.

Nevertheless, what has been gathered together here may contribute in some way to a better understanding both of Catholic social principles and of their relevance to contemporary American life.

Since those principles are more or less common to all the major religious traditions in our pluralistic society, no one who strives to spread and apply them need have scruples about promoting a sectarian interest. It is part of our good fortune that there is no clash in the United States between the temporal goals of our society and the religious beliefs of our people. As can be seen in the war on poverty and the civil rights movement, the beliefs validate and reinforce the goals.

The old argument over the propriety of church pronouncements on socioeconomic questions has lost much of its intensity. The dispute now is not so much over the right and duty of churches to speak out on moral aspects of public issues as it is over the extent to which clergymen should leave their pulpits for active involvement in the social arena. That development should hasten the end of a confusing era during which churches were indicted with equal gusto for irrelevancy and for immersion in secular affairs.

So far as Catholics are concerned, Vatican Council II strongly ratified Pope John's concern for the modern world. Although the Council Fathers made few specific additions to the doctrine of *Mater et Magistra* and *Pacem in Terris*, they did give us, in the bulky Pastoral Constitution on the Church in the Modern World, an inspiring theological base for an expanded social apostolate. In the spirit of Christ, the council embraced the secular city.

To all the contributors and their publishers, I am very grateful. The contributors were magnanimous in permitting the editorial surgery that harsh requirements of space dictated. The reader will be rewarded if in every case he takes the trouble to study the selections unabridged in their original sources. This procedure, by introducing him to the rich periodical literature on the Church's social doctrine, will pay extra dividends. I can only hope that in no case have I distorted anybody's thought. If I have inadvertently done so, I ask in advance for understanding and forgiveness.

BENJAMIN L. MASSE, S.J.

America House
New York City

CONTENTS

THE CHURCH AND SOCIAL PROGRESS

CHAPTER 1

HISTORICAL FRAMEWORK

> While enormous riches accumulated in the hands of a few, workingmen in vast numbers found themselves contending daily with grinding economic hardships. Wages were insufficient, even in some cases at a starvation level; working conditions of the more exploited workers were oppressive and destructive of health, morality and religious faith. Especially inhuman were the working conditions that were often imposed on women and children. The specter of joblessness was ever present to the worker's mind. There was a progressive disintegration of family life.
>
> The inevitable consequence of all this was a feeling of resentment and a spirit of revolt among workers. They became receptive to extremist theories that were worse than the evil they aimed to remove.
>
> It was in such times that Leo XIII proclaimed his social message in Rerum Novarum.
>
> John XXIII in Mater et Magistra

The modern social teaching of the Catholic Church is a response to the struggle in Western society that started nearly two centuries ago and has kept much of the world in ferment ever since.

That struggle had its roots in the Industrial Revolution of the latter half of the eighteenth century and in the simultaneous rise of an economic doctrine that saw in the free pursuit of individual self-interest the secret of the wealth of nations. Though the new system generated a vast increase of production and brought about a rise in living standards, it also led to gross abuses that aroused consciences all over Europe.

One of the consequences of the moral revulsion from laissez-faire capitalism was a wild swing of the social pendulum. Overemphasis on the individualistic side of human nature quickly begot an exaggeration of its social aspect. Various types of socialism sprang up in Europe, and one of these, fathered by Karl Marx and Friedrich Engels, was soon engaged in a revolutionary attack on the capitalist system.

Since Marxian Socialism was a philosophy of life as well as an economic doctrine, the attack on capitalism became inevitably an onslaught on all existing institutions of society, including religion. The goal of justice, especially for the masses of propertyless workers, was consciously wedded to atheistic materialism.

Meanwhile, non-Marxist critics of economic individualism began drafting and advocating programs of reform. Among the critics were prominent Catholics in Germany, Belgium, France, and other European countries. When their ideas led to controversy with Catholic defenders of laissez faire, the issue eventually went to Rome for judgment. The result was Pope Leo XIII's *Rerum Novarum*. It decided the case in favor of the reformers.

Over the years, as Pope John noted in *Pacem in Terris*, the lines of this historic social struggle have become blurred. However static the theories may remain, there has been in practice an evolution in reaction to changing circumstances. This is notably true of capitalism, but it is true of socialism as well. In the Western world there is widespread interest today in economic planning, and this development is matched in the Communist world by recent advances toward a market economy. The deeper differences remain, however. They will undoubtedly persist until Marxian Socialists come to see that atheistic materialism was a nineteenth-century aberration that had nothing to do with the protest against laissez-faire capitalism.

Meaning of Liberalism*

THOMAS P. NEILL

Liberalism is a term of many meanings, often of no precise meaning at all. It is a word of high emotional rather than intellectual content. This is unfortunate, both because it creates confusion and because it divides persons and groups who might otherwise work harmoniously together in at least some areas of social and political action. . . .

Until recently the term enjoyed general good repute in America. Ex-

---

* From "Liberalism," *Social Order*, October, 1954.

cept for small classes of scholars — some theologians, some historians and the like — Americans looked on liberalism as an assemblage of humane attitudes and generous theories based somehow on the Constitution and the American tradition. For most Americans liberalism meant an open-minded approach to social questions, a willingness to study all points of view and to arrive at honest conclusions. It meant freedom from the hard cake of custom and from any "arbitrary" authority. . . .

Strong emotion engendered by the New Deal and by international politics since about 1935 (the Popular Front) gave liberalism a new meaning in this country. Opponents of the New Deal accused Roosevelt and his supporters of having stolen a "grand old word" as a label for a socialist program. This group, small in numbers, still claims that liberalism in its true sense belongs to those who would limit government in the interest of free enterprise. *Freeman* is the journal that best represents this point of view, which is also expressed bluntly in such business newsletters as *Industrial News Review* and more subtly in releases from the National Association of Manufacturers. No serious sociologist or historian uses liberalism in reference to this group unless he quickly explains the content of the term.

Liberalism is more generally used nowadays to refer to programs that give the federal government a larger role in economic and social life. (Supporters of such programs are referred to by *Freeman* as "pseudo-liberals" or "egg heads" or sometimes as "fellow-travelers.") Liberalism is used more generally and most frequently in a neutral, nonemotional sense, to refer to the thought of those who favor social reform by increased governmental regulation and operation of certain industries. It means, in this sense, the doctrine of those who would give the government an increasingly large paternalistic role over its citizens' lives. Thus liberalism is the label for theories favoring a "welfare state."

The Catholic position, when contrasted with these two extreme liberal attitudes, may help to clarify Catholicism's enduring view of liberalism. Catholic social policy, while generally midway between these conflicting views, is broad and tolerant. There could easily be different Catholics who would agree wholeheartedly with both extremes of liberal policy.

Catholic opposition to liberalism rarely concentrates upon social policies espoused by liberals. In almost all instances the point of controversy is rather the radically naturalistic view of man and society which doctrinaire liberals entertain. This has commonly been a characteristic of the liberal view, whether that be so "conservative" (to our way of thinking) as *laissez faire*, or so "progressive" as the position of many liberals today. It might not be correct to claim that naturalism is *always* the point of Catholic opposition, but it is certainly far and away the most common.

Liberalism is also used in an opprobrious sense to refer to secularist solutions which would exclude both religious groups and religious principles from any role in American social and political life. Those who use the term in this sense labeled defenders of the McCollum decision "liberal." These are mostly but not exclusively Catholics. They give it a more restricted and a harsher meaning than does any other sizeable group in America.

Here it is that confusion on the meaning of liberalism has unfortunate practical results. Americans who do not know the tradition of Catholic social thought read into Catholic strictures against liberalism a condemnation of everything they associate with American liberalism — which for many is everything distinctly American. Such people are doubly confused when, on further study, they find that the Popes and the great majority of Catholic social thinkers in America advocate many of the same measures they consider part of liberalism. Catholics, on the other hand, see in liberalism the bundle of anticlerical and antireligious attitudes and doctrines condemned by the Popes and by European bishops under the title of liberalism. They tend automatically, therefore, to associate such attitudes and doctrines with anyone who calls himself a liberal.

Some light is thrown on the meanings of liberalism by sketching the history of the use of the word. It seems to have been first used in Spain in 1811 to refer to the body of thought held by the proponents of the constitution adopted the next year. This Constitution of 1812 was modeled on the French Constitution of 1791, which epitomized the radical thought of the Enlightenment. Proponents of the constitution were anticlerical rationalists, children of the secularist thought of the Enlightenment. In this first use of the term liberalism, then, is included anticlericalism as an essential ingredient. Included also was a general hostility toward religion having any role in social or political life. Opponents of this group were the supporters of the Old Regime, clerical and lay, who condemned the constitution both as unworkable and as a document based on false theological and philosophical assumptions. . . .

Within a few years the Spanish term had appeared in Italy as *liberalismo* and in France as *liberalisme*. In each country the specific doctrines it stood for differed somewhat, according to the local political and social situation, but in every case liberalism in the Latin countries involved theological and philosophical principles as well as political and social doctrines. Liberalism appeared as a word in England sometime around 1830 to refer to the doctrines of the left wing of the Whig Party that was then campaigning for the reform bill of 1832. Liberalism in England was basically economic, secondarily political, and only incidentally was it tinged with philosophical and theological considerations.

The English liberalism of this period consists of the body of doctrine commonly associated with the names of Malthus and Ricardo, Bentham and Macaulay, all neatly summarized in the writing of Herbert Spencer, especially in his *Social Statics* of 1850. This is the liberalism that considered government an evil — which, with Spencer at least, might become an unnecessary evil in the more civilized future. It considered public education, free libraries, and other such state services a form of socialism and an unjust robbing of the rich (taxes) to support the poor. This is the liberalism that considered poor relief immoral and universal suffrage "the end of civilization." It accepted the "natural laws" of the economists that fixed wages at a subsistence level and condemned the working class never to rise from its providentially assigned lot in life. Anglo-Saxon liberalism did not become openly and violently anticlerical, as did its continental counterpart of the same period. Instead, it disassociated economic and political life from theological and moral considerations. . . .

English liberals were successful in putting most of their theories into practice. The Reform Act of 1832 and the Municipal Corporation Act of 1835 gave the middle class control of Commons and of local government; the repeal of the Corn Laws in 1846 and the remaining Navigation Acts in 1849 gave the merchant class something very close to free trade; the New Poor Law of 1834 was the last step in creating a free labor market, and a series of land acts put land into the market as a free commodity.

Thus classical liberalism was put into practice in England in the age of the Victorian Compromise (1832–1865). Liberals of this period were satisfied that their chief task was to prevent a reaction toward a stronger government on the one hand, or, on the other, a march toward universal suffrage. They opposed the Chartist Movement, for example, because of its dangerous demand for universal suffrage. They fought unions as being in restraint of free trade in labor. They opposed government regulation of working conditions as "unnatural" limitations on free enterprise. Classical liberalism was a doctrine which assumed a world of separate employers, distinct workers, and individual consumers, all freely competing in the open market to set the price of land, labor, and goods. Such a world was almost realized for a time, but the very nature of free enterprise soon created large corporations and threatened to create unions. The vote could not long be withheld from the working man. Most liberals bowed to the inevitable and tried to "educate" the laborer so that he could be trusted to vote intelligently — which meant he would subscribe to the truth of liberalism.

Thus liberalism began to change in England in the last half of the nineteenth century. There is no need for tracing the process of this change here. It is sufficient to note that by the end of the century liberalism in England meant social insurance for the workers, having the government protect the masses from Big Business, abandoning the *laissez-faire* concept of the state for something approaching a welfare state. There were all degrees of opinion on how far this process should go, but all liberals agreed that the state should take a positive role in achieving social justice.

Certain adherents of classical liberalism refused to accept the new liberalism. They likewise refused to surrender the title of liberalism, to which, indeed, they clung tenaciously and fiercely. The leader of this group was Herbert Spencer, and associated with him were such lesser figures as Lord Hartington, the Duke of Argyll, Bruce Smith, and George Goschen. These men organized the Liberty and Property Defense League, much like the American Liberty League of 1934, that set forth on a crusade to defend liberty and property from the attacks of the new "welfare" liberalism. Classical liberalism thus became conservatism in England at the turn of the century. The confusion of terms increased as each group laid claim to the title liberalism and accused the others of "spurious liberalism" or "blind conservatism."

This pattern of confusion was, for all practical purposes, duplicated in America in the twentieth century. As we have already indicated, almost all Americans considered themselves liberal throughout the nineteenth century. But a group of social thinkers and business leaders laid special claim — quite validly — to the title of liberalism. Led by Graham Sumner they transferred the classical liberalism of Herbert Spencer to America. This is the doctrine subscribed to not only by professors like Sumner and economists like David A. Wells, but also by business leaders like Andrew Carnegie. It was substantially the same *laizzez-faire* doctrine as regards the government, the same glorification of individual enterprise, the same appeal to "natural laws" in economics, the same belief that by his own efforts a man obtains what he deserves in this life as well as in the next. This is the liberalism which, in a modified way, is held today by the *Freeman* writers and the N.A.M.

We have seen that the term is more generally used in this country to refer to those who would solve more economic and social problems by state action. These are the social theorists and the politicians who, like the later liberals in England, carried on the fight against big business: the Populists, the Progressives, the Fair Dealers, the New Dealers, and their successors in this decade. These liberals look to the government for protection from big business. Again, there are all shades of opinion as to how many functions are to be allotted to the federal government and how much is to be left to local agencies of government or to non-governmental groups. But the general tendency of this kind of liberalism is toward increased regulation or replacement of business by the government.

Confusion in the use of the term in America was increased by Catholics — and by certain splinter groups — who emigrated to this country from the Continent. For them liberalism has still another meaning, one they learned from Continental Liberals and from papal pronouncements since the time of Pope Pius IX. . . . It meant the doctrines of Mazzini in Italy, Quintana in Spain, Rotteck in Germany, Michelet in France. This was a liberalism that had declared war on the Church (or perhaps the declaration of war was a mutual thing), and whenever it achieved power had despoiled the Church of its holdings, had dissolved religious orders, had excluded religion from education, and had systematically set about destroying the established religion of each country — which in the Latin countries was the Catholic Church. This is the liberalism which is flatly condemned by Pope Pius IX and his successors, which is written against by Louis Veuillot and Juan Donoso Cortés and is condemned not only for its war against the Church but also for its theological and philosophical errors.

Most Catholics, then, continued to understand liberalism in the continental sense when they came to America. The contents of the bottle were different in this country, but the label was the same — and it is natural for people to look at labels instead of analyzing contents. For this reason Catholics were stigmatized with the reputation of being anti-liberal. Moreover, the presence in this country of splinter groups from the Continent, such as the German "forty-eighters" (expelled liberals against whom Catholics continued their polemics) seemed to validate such an accusation. Catholic groups came to see liberalism as a doctrine dangerous to the very framework of American life as set forth in the Constitution. Most American liberals, on the other hand, thought that they were only seeking new ways and means for promoting the general welfare, which they considered the purpose of good government anywhere.

Can these three kinds of liberalism — 1. Continental liberalism, as viewed by Catholics; 2. Classical liberalism as expressed by Herbert Spencer and formulated in this country by Graham Sumner; 3. Welfare liberalism of the English liberals of 1906 and the American New Dealers — be seen to have anything in common? If they can, there may be some generic meaning in the term which would validate its being used with an appropriate adjective to designate the various kinds of liberalism that have existed in the past and still exist in the present.

First, let us see what is not consistently to be found in liberals — for many claims by its adherents and accusations by its opponents add to the confusion about its meaning. As we have already seen, liberalism is not an unchanging body of doctrines. It is not the same thing as democracy, nor does it hold a consistent view of liberty. Neither is it correct to equate liberalism with tolerance and with a sympathetic understanding of all points of view. Some liberals have, at one time or another, held all these views — but other liberals have held the contrary.

Liberalism has consisted of a bundle of more-or-less related attitudes, ideas and methods, rather than a set of clearly formulated doctrines. In the first place, it has always been opposed to the established powers of the time. In the age of classical liberalism's formation in England it was opposed to the mercantilistic state. On the Continent it was the established church and the royal regime. At a later date, when the government had been weakened by liberal victories, the power to be feared was big business. Opposition to religious authority has always been present in liberalism, sometimes as an active ingredient and sometimes latent. Even liberal Catholics find themselves forever fighting the temptation to anticlericalism, a temptation inherent in their position as liberal Catholics.

Liberals have consistently enthroned individual judgment, making it sovereign over revelation and tradition, social opinion and that complexus of factors — rational and nonrational — which we call a way of life. Contemporary liberals do not hold the same atomistic view of society or subscribe to the same individualism that classical liberals held.

But they do claim that each individual is still sovereign judge of right and wrong, and each is still the best judge of his own interests. In this respect, liberals have never outlived their earlier naive trust in man's unadulterated rationality. . . .

Sometimes implicitly and sometimes explicitly — especially on the Continent — liberals have developed a distinctive theory of human nature. Denying original sin, they make man innocently good. They account for evil on the grounds of ignorance and bad social organization. Because man's desires are good and full confidence is put in his unaided reason, liberals have consistently subscribed to a theory of progress that looks for some kind of near perfect state in the future. If man is to reach this state he must know the truth — which to liberals is a practical rather than a metaphysical thing. Truth, they believe, can best be reached by freedom of speech and press, by the right to put all shades of truth and error in the open arena. In the long run truth will survive and error will pass away, because all men are rational.

Throughout the nineteenth century, liberalism possessed other common characteristics associated in some way with the middle class: a reverence for property rights even at the expense of the rights of the human person; an identification with that system of production and distribution called "capitalism"; a loose affinity for certain brands of Protestantism as against the established Anglican, Lutheran, and Catholic religions and a frame of mind more congenial to the middle class than to the peasantry or the aristocracy; an empirical, scientific, mundane approach to reality. Contemporary liberalism has shed these characteristics as it disassociated itself from the middle class. For today liberalism cannot be identified with any single economic or social class. It is the doctrine of those who advocate change, and it may be subscribed to by "intellectuals," by wealthy men (like Marshall Field) who accept inherited fortunes with uneasy conscience, or by the large number of people who believe the socioeconomic system must be radically changed in order to give them their just place in society.

What, then, may be considered the proper use of the term liberalism today? If the word is to have any meaning at all, it cannot properly be applied to the heirs of classical liberalism. Groups like the N.A.M. and writers like John T. Flynn are best classified as conservative. Liberalism remains too broad a term for expeditious usage even when this group has been eliminated. It can be applied properly to all those who have scant respect for the traditional institutions we have built through the ages. Liberals look hopefully to the future, and they put a somewhat naive trust in anything new. In the empirical tradition, they are willing — even anxious — to try new solutions for old problems. Instead of relying on the accumulated wisdom of the past (the existence of which they would deny), they tend to put faith in man's intelligent use of the new technology to achieve a better world in the future. . . .

Of necessity most contemporary liberals look to the government for a solution of social and economic problems. For this reason they are frequently labeled "totalitarian" by their opponents — a label which fits some but not by any means all contemporary liberals. A closer look at today's liberals reveals that they have little else in common. . . .

Some liberals oppose adding to the central government's functions and powers. They favor solution of all problems possible by local government or by such independent groups as labor and capital. There are Catholic liberals — an heroic group, this writer believes — who by the nature of their position are doomed to the odium heaped on such a leader as Ozanam in the days of classical liberalism, but who are both soundly liberal and soundly Catholic. Catholic liberals can, with considerable justification but with some slight shading of things, look to the present Holy Father, Pope Pius XII, as their chief spokesman. These are thinkers who want to keep the political, social, and technological accomplishments of the past and to inform them in the future with true Christian principles. . . .

Socialism: Philosophy and Program*

GEORGE H. DUNNE, S.J.

What has to be understood about Socialism is that it has embraced two different things and in varying proportions: a philosophy about man and society, and a program for the economic reorganization of society for the purpose of assuring a just distribution of this world's goods. The philosophy was not essential to the program, nor was the program a logical derivative of the philosophy. There have been many socialist movements, of non-Marxist inspiration, which were largely or entirely innocent of the philosophy. But the main current of modern Socialism, which calls itself scientific as distinguished from utopian, has been

---

* From "Socialism and Socialism," *Commonweal*, November 23, 1945.

Marxist in character. It is one of the tragedies of modern history that the Fathers of this, the most influential kind of Socialism, insisted that philosophy and program were inseparable.

If the Fathers of Socialism had been content to built their program upon their generally sound intuitions about the social nature of man and the solidarity of the human race, there need never have been any serious conflict between Socialism and Catholicism. Unfortunately they were doctrinaires who liked to philosophize, and they were poor philosophers. Their speculations were unhappily influenced by the superficial rationalism in vogue in their day. They were further confirmed in their bias by the all too frequent association of various churchmen with reactionary persons and causes. As a consequence they developed a sophomoric attitude toward belief in God and formulated a doctrine about man and society which was materialistic, anthropocentric, and antireligious.

Obviously Catholicism could not join hands with that kind of philosophy, with that kind of doctrine. Catholicism's opposition to Socialism was an opposition to its philosophy about man and society. This is what must be understood about Catholicism. Otherwise the question of its relationship to Socialism will be lost in a miasmic fog of confusion.

The whole question is confused enough as it is. A major factor contributing to the confusion has been the tendency of Socialists to think of their doctrine in terms of program. Thus their views about marriage, about the family, about religious education, about religion itself, properly belonged to their philosophy. Yet Socialists have made these doctrinal views part of their social program and have really planned to impose them upon society. It was easy for them to indulge these fancies so long as they were a small minority party not charged with responsibility. But in the measure that they have been formed to assume responsibility and to deal with reality the doctrinaire character of these views has become more and more evident.

As a result, these features of Socialism have tended to seek their proper level, which is doctrinal rather than programmatic. It has become increasingly possible, therefore, to distinguish between program and doctrine and by program to mean chiefly the Socialist proposals for the economic reorganization of society. It is in terms of this development that it is correct to say that the hostility between Catholicism and Socialism was rooted in Socialist doctrine rather than in Socialist program.

The Socialist economic program, centering around the concept of community ownership of at least the major instrumentalities of production, is not the peculiar property of the Socialist Party. What is peculiar to the Socialist Party is its doctrine and its doctrinaire assumption that its economic program is inseparable from its doctrine. I have attempted in this article to keep this distinction clear by capitalizing Socialism and Socialist only when referring to the Party itself, or to its doctrine, or to its program but specifically as pertaining to the Party. Wherever reference is made simply to a program of social reform centered upon the ideal of community ownership, capitalization is not employed. Used in this latter way the word socialism includes, but is not synonymous with, the economic program of the Socialist Party, though not qua Socialist Party.

The fact is that long before modern theories of Socialism were born the Church had been familiar with economies organized along socialist lines. This was notably true in Spain during the later Middle Ages. These economies not only had not aroused the hostility of the Church, they had been encouraged by the Church and were developed under the leadership of Catholic monks and priests. There is no evidence that these programs aroused the slightest sense of surprise or shock in the Catholic environment of the times. There is every evidence, on the contrary, that they were regarded as natural derivatives in the economic order of the Catholic concept of the social nature of man, the social function of property, and the unity of man in the Mystical Body of Christ. They were surely far more native to Catholic soil than the philosophy and predatory system of utilitarian individualism, which supplanted them. This is why one of the ironies of modern times has been the spectacle of Catholics bitterly opposing certain measures of social reform deeply rooted in Christian tradition and instinct simply because they were also espoused by Socialists.

Catholics have not been altogether to blame for this. The blame is shared by the Socialists who, although there was no logical connection between the two, tied their program up with a doctrine that explicitly repudiated Christianity. Typical of their doctrinaire attitude was August Bebel's dictum: "Christianity and Socialism are like fire and water." In view of this attitude it is naive to ask why the Church regarded Socialism as a mortal enemy. It is also naive to expect Catholics always to distinguish carefully between the Socialist program and doctrine since the Socialists themselves so hopelessly confused the two. Because the doctrine was avowedly and militantly anti-Christian, it was easy to conclude that whatever pertained to the program was equally tainted. And because the utilitarians paid at least lip service to religion, it was easy for Catholics to succumb to the illusion that the economic philosophy to which they adhered was somehow or other identified with Christianity.

Because they were preoccupied with their antireligious doctrine, the Socialists themselves discredited the constructive features of their program. They dissipated energies, which might have been better spent in carrying on their fight for social justice, in a disastrous effort to secularize society and to substitute a shallow rationalism for the deepness of Christian faith. . . .

It was because of their foolish fascination with their antireligious doctrine, which tended constantly to become part of their program, that a Charles Péguy, who was socialist because he was at heart profoundly Christian, was forced to repudiate the Socialists because he was at heart profoundly Christian.

A major difficulty for Catholics in this whole question arises from the pronouncement of Pope Pius XI: "No one can be at the same time a sincere Catholic and a true Socialist." But here one must be extremely careful not to confuse labels with things. One can easily conclude from these words — as many have — that the hostility between the two is fixed and immutable and that even an effort to explore the possibilities of a rapprochement smacks of disobedience. Yet it is perfectly clear from the whole context of the discussion of this question in *Quadragesimo Anno* that what Pius XI condemns as irreconcilable with Catholicism is the Socialist doctrine about man and society, not the Socialist program of economic reform. He went out of his way to make this clear, pointing out that the Socialist "programs often strikingly approach the just demands of Christian social reformers." If this is true, then it follows that those who stand upon a program of Christian social reform will find themselves standing "strikingly" near to those who stand upon a program of Socialist social reform.

One would never guess that this were true from the tendency of certain Catholics, who have read the social encyclicals either superficially or not at all, to conclude that their Catholicism obliges them to stand as far removed as possible from anything that resembles the Socialist program. One would not be so annoyed by this were it not for their bland assumption that, in defending the stronghold of rugged individualism, of laissez-faire economics, of utilitarian philosophy, they are defending the citadel of the Faith.

The reasoning of these people, many of them too intelligent to be easily excused, is simple and fallacious. . . . They are victims of that most malignant of all intellectual diseases, the substitution of labels for things. It is an ancient disease, known to philosophers as nominalism, but it has become endemic in modern times. Given the nature of the disease it is not surprising that its victims are often condemning in the name of Pius XI measures explicitly defended by Pius XI. Such is the nature of this confusion worse confounded. . . .

Some will object that, altogether apart from the question of Socialist philosophy, there is an irreconcilable conflict between Catholicism and Socialism on the programmatic level because of the latter's denial of the right to private property. A number of things need to be said about this:

(1) The denial of the right to private property never properly belonged to the Socialist program but to Socialist doctrine. Having rejected Christianity and the Christian view of human history and human nature, the Fathers of Socialism had to find a substitute for Original Sin. They found it in private property.

(2) There is no Socialist party today whose program calls for the abolition of all forms of private property. While the Socialist program, because like all programs of social reform it is necessarily empirical, differs in detail from country to country, it may be said that in general it calls for community ownership of those industries and services which, either because of their gigantism or their intimate relationship to the common good, involve a degree of social ownership which cannot safely be left in private hands. If one could free oneself long enough from the intellectual toils of nominalism, it would not be altogether impossible to prove that what most Socialist programs aim at is the restoration to the disinherited masses of the enjoyment of their right to private property, a right of which they have been deprived by capitalism. One of the ironic paradoxes of recent times has been the spectacle of men defending in the name of private property a system which has been steadily driving more and more men into the ranks of the propertyless.

(3) The Catholic position on the subject of private property needs clarification. Despite the warnings of Leo XIII, Pius XI, and Pius XII, Catholics have a tendency to think of private property as an absolute right, as an end in itself, and as a primary principle of the natural law. They are confusing the right to private property with the right common to all men to a sufficiency of material goods to live a decent life. This latter is the absolute right, derogation of which is a violation of a primary

principle of the natural law. The right to private property is itself but a derivative of this primary principle and is valid only in terms of its relationship to the end it is supposed to serve. Property is functional in character and the right to private property is also functional in character. . . .

From this discussion I conclude that there is no insurmountable obstacle in the way of establishing peaceful relations between Catholicism and Socialism. It is of paramount importance to the interests of each and to the interests of the people of Europe that they do establish peaceful relations with each other. Only if these two forces are able to collaborate in a spirit of mutual understanding is there any hope of Europe finding a middle path between equally intolerable extremes of violence and tyranny.

If this desirable end is to be achieved, the old-line Socialist parties of Europe must rid themselves of the last vestiges of nineteenth-century doctrinaire mumbo-jumbo. To a considerable extent gradual evolution in this direction has already taken place. Pope Pius XI frankly admitted as much in *Quadragesimo Anno*.

It would be unrealistic to pretend, however, that this evolution has proceeded evenly in every country and has reached the point where all Socialist parties have so far purged themselves of doctrinaire influences as to remove any basis for Catholic misgivings. In this respect Socialism among Anglo-Saxon peoples seems to have advanced more rapidly than Socialism on the Continent. There is somewhat the same difference between Anglo-Saxon and Continental Socialism as between Anglo-Saxon and Continental masonry. It is because of this, as the *Osservatore Romano* recently pointed out to the Italian Socialists, that there is nothing inconsistent in the fact that the Vatican looks upon the victory of the British Labor Party with complacency while maintaining an attitude of reserve toward Italian Socialism. . . .

The Communist Manifesto*

NICHOLAS S. TIMASHEFF

If a great book is one that has dominated innumerable minds and launched a grand-style social movement, then *The Communist Manifesto*

---

* From "Karl Marx: The Communist Manifesto," *America*, April 24, 1948.

is one of the greatest. Through it was organized into a mighty social force the socialist movement, which, before its publication, had existed among only a few tiny and unrelated groups of intellectuals. Its words inspired some of the leaders of the Russian branch of the movement to seize power in the name of communism. He who wants fully to understand the tragic conflict of our day, which makes peace precarious and the survival of Western civilization uncertain, must know the *Manifesto*.

Among the great books, this is a surprisingly short one. It contains only 15,000 words, about 3,000 of which are devoted to a rather dull survey of the socialist literature and the political situation at the time of its writing. In later years, when new editions were prepared, the authors pondered whether they should drop or rewrite that portion. They decided they should not, since the *Communist Manifesto* had become an historical document. Only a few footnotes and a new Preface were added by Friedrich Engels, who survived his co-author Karl Marx by many years.

Except for the few passages just mentioned, *The Communist Manifesto* is one of the most forceful works of propaganda ever composed by man. Written and published in the midst of the social and political turmoil which immediately preceded the revolutions of 1848 in France, Prussia, Austria, Hungary, and Italy, the work reveals the goals of every social revolution to come in our day. The traditionalists, say the authors of the *Manifesto*, accuse them of the intention to abolish property, freedom, the family, the fatherland, the traditional culture. Yes, they continue, they really have these intentions. But in planning their revolution they merely want to legalize and make universal the trends which, in embryo, already prevail in bourgeois society (the term they use to designate the social system known today as the system of free enterprise). They want to abolish private property; the bourgeois have already abolished it for nine-tenths of the population. They want to abolish freedom in its bourgeois meaning — the freedom to buy and sell everything, including human labor. They want to abolish the traditional family; but there is no need to inaugurate the communization of women since it has existed since time immemorial and, in bourgeois society, means that bourgeois men have at their disposal the wives and daughters of the proletarians. They want to abolish the individual nations; the proletarian has no fatherland. They want to abolish the existing culture, for the ruling ideas of every epoch are the ideas of the ruling class and, with the passing of private property as a means of production, the ideas generated by the bourgeois must and will go.

The authors of the *Manifesto* recognized that their program was not new: others had already preached socialization of the means of production, the abolition of the traditional family, and so on. But, they asserted, for the first time in history a group of men were basing the order of the future not on dreams or speculation, but on the study of actual relations between men in the past and present. This order, they claim, is not a mere plan, but a scientific prediction. It will be realized, because the Communists expound the program of the proletariat, and the victory of the latter is inevitable. Why? Because in the midst of bourgeois society the proletariat is the only revolutionary class and, throughout history, the class representing a new order of production and exchange has always defeated the class representing an obsolescent order.

Moreover, the *Manifesto* ascribed to the proletariat the providential role of terminating one of the greatest social evils, the class structure of society and the exploitation of men by men. Class struggle, said Marx and Engels, has always been the general law of history. Through class struggle humanity had advanced from the ancient slave-holding society to feudal society and from feudal society to bourgeois society; and it will advance from bourgeois society to communist society.

In the earlier stages of development, says the *Manifesto*, the revolutionary class had its particular selfish interests, since it always owned something; therefore, revolutionaries carried out their revolutions in their own interests. The bourgeoisie has, however, accomplished something unprecedented; it has deprived the proletariat of everything except manual strength. The bourgeois pays the laborers just subsistence wages, enough for bare survival and reproduction. It cannot do otherwise because labor forms part of the means of production. In consequence, gaining victory, the proletariat cannot use it in its own special interest. It will gain victory for all men and create a classless society.

Ascribing to the proletariat this providential role was a masterpiece of propaganda. You can incite man to act by showing him that a certain action well serves his interest; but you can treble the force of his zeal by showing him that, acting in his interest, he will also advance the common good. Add to this the certainty of victory and the allegedly scientific — i.e., irrefutable — character of the reasoning, and you will understand the impact of the *Manifesto* on many members of the class to which it was addressed and on intellectuals aware of the many injustices and irrationalities of the social order around them.

In their later works, Marx and Engels lent much more precision and allegedly scientific background to the statements of *The Communist Manifesto*. But never did they again expound their views with the same force. Two examples will suffice.

A careful and well-trained reader can find in the *Manifesto* the hypothesis — later explicitly formulated by Marx in his *Critique of Political Economy* — that the social relations of production evolve independently of human will and, evolving, unilaterally determine all other phases of human coexistence, such as religion, morals, philosophy, art, literature, not to speak of political organization. But, in the *Manifesto*, the hypothesis is veiled and, in consequence, it is not exposed to obvious objections.

Moreover, one can find in the *Manifesto* the dialectical scheme of Marxism, the assertion that everything — including the social relations of production — develops according to the Hegelian triad: in other words, everything passes through the phases of thesis, antithesis, and synthesis. The cumbersome efforts made in the authors' later works to explain the history of mankind in terms of these triads make them exceedingly dull reading. In the *Manifesto*, the idea is present, but appears in concrete and readable form.

The Communist Manifesto is a great book because it proved forceful enough to convert millions of minds. But it is also a vicious book because it converts men to fallacy. Therefore one should know its basic weaknesses. By pointing them out, one is able to combat its appeal to those who do not see that the teaching of the *Manifesto* is a system of ideas incompatible with the principles of Christianity and sound philosophy. Those who see this incompatibility need no other grounds for rejecting the *Manifesto*.

Here are some points to be made in demonstrating the fallacy of the *Manifesto* to those who are on the verge of being persuaded. First, its scientific character is asserted, but is conspicuous by its absence. The reasoning is of the type which prevailed in the day of Marx and Engels and continued often to be used up to the end of the nineteenth century. It consists of an almost childish simplification and schematization of the enormously complicated social phenomena. The *Manifesto* is right when it asserts that, throughout history, there has been class struggle; but there is no valid reason for its declaration that class struggle is the cause, the only cause, of everything that happens in human society. It ignores the fact that, in addition to antagonism, there is, among men, evidence of much solidarity and cooperation; and that, throughout history, antagonisms between individuals and between social groups have been provoked not only by conflicting economic interests, but also by religious dissent and by emotions based on what we today call exaggerated nationalism.

Only by distorting facts and making bold and unsupported assertions are the authors of the *Manifesto* able to insist on the paramount importance of the economic factor as expressed in the class struggle.

Second, in analyzing what they call bourgeois society, the authors take it for granted that, in that society, labor can receive only subsistence wages. Such was approximately the situation when they wrote their book; and their charge was based on facts which Engels had previously published in a remarkable book on the state of the laboring class in England. Today, a century after the publication of the *Manifesto*, one knows their assertion that bourgeois society cannot do otherwise was wrong. He who would today write a book on the state of the laboring class in the United States and in the advanced countries of Western Europe (prior to the Second World War) could not but report an almost miraculous rise in the standards of living of the laborers. The bourgeois order is able to grant to labor a considerable participation in material achievements and in culture. Therefore, it is not necessarily doomed, as was asserted by the authors of the *Manifesto*.

Third, a strong argument against the *Manifesto* may be drawn from events in Russia. There, the communist revolution represented largely the application of the principles of the *Manifesto*; but today, thirty years after the event, few doubt that the division of men into social classes has reappeared. The top group consists of leaders of the political machine and the economic system; a second group is composed of fellow travelers among the authors, artists, etc.; a third group is the residue. The interests of the groups are conspicuously opposed to one another, and the new ruling class misses no opportunity to consolidate its privileges and transmit them to its progeny. It seems that, to make a human aggregation a going concern, a certain differentiation between organizers and passive participants in an organized effort is necessary, and that this differentiation must be further augmented by higher awards to the members of the active group than to those of the other. This is completely at variance with the teaching of the *Manifesto* which, in consequence, would incite men to undertake an impossible revolution and to abolish the very condition of social efficiency.

Concluding, one can say that *The Communist Manifesto* aims at impossible goals. Its pretensions to being scientific are utterly false. Its effect has been to unite into a mighty world union all the forces of evil. The fate of humanity depends on the ability of Christians to demonstrate, by words and deeds, the fallacy of this "great book."

Soviet Policy Today*

FRANZ H. MUELLER

Changes in post-Stalin Russia seem clearly to indicate a certain deviation from the command type of economy prevalent until about a decade ago. These changes can be observed not only in Soviet Russia itself, but in just about the entire Soviet bloc. Even the Chinese are about to substitute the carrot for the stick and to end the share-alike to prevent the starve-alike. In Russia, farmers are given more freedom. Livestock is gradually turned over from collective farms to individual peasants. State banks extend loans to farmers wanting to purchase cows and heifers for private income. It has been officially and publicly recognized that too much central planning had adverse effects not only in agriculture but also in the areas of manufacturing and distribution. . . .

The question we are now confronted with is whether such things as acceleration of consumer goods output, relaxation of restrictions against private plot farming, raising the morale of peasants to increase food supply, bonuses for successful managers, incentive wage scales, using the profit motive for a more efficient allocation of scarce resources, decentralization of detailed decision-making, greater reliance on the price mechanism than on turnover taxes, subsidies, and other direct control instruments, etc., do indicate a change of mind, a revision of goals, a new economic ethics. I do not pretend to know the answer, but I am inclined to think that this alteration of means is of a tactical and strategic nature only and is not intended to serve essentially different ends.

It is important to keep in mind that *some* of these tools were experimented with even before the death of Stalin, especially before the introduction, in 1928, of the so-called Five Year Plans. The use, for instance, of the price-market mechanism in the area of consumer goods distribution and of the allocation of manpower is not really something novel in Soviet

---

* From Dr. Mueller's comment on a paper read by Prof. Francis M. Boddy, "Ethical Aspects of Current Soviet Economic Policies," at the 23rd annual convention of the Catholic Economic Association, Chicago, Ill. *Review of Social Economy*, March, 1965.

lands. Compensation according to deed rather than need also is neither new nor does it represent a deviation from communist principles. In 1875, Marx predicted that it would not be until the advent of full communism that each could be rewarded according to need. Until then, he said, performance would have to determine wage rates and scales. Significantly, piece wages are more typical in the U.S.S.R. than in the U.S.A.

The desire to beat the capitalist world at its own game has indeed been strengthened ever since the rise of Khrushchev and it has not been lessened by his fall. But what is more significant is — as Carl Landauer, in *Contemporary Economic Systems*, has rightly pointed out — that even if the communists abandon the labor value doctrine, accept modern price theory, drop the imposition of production targets on enterprises, and so on, "economic processes would still take a different course in the Soviet Union as compared with a capitalist country having the same resources and inhabited by a population with the same individual and collective preferences." Why? Because "Soviet planners would in part substitute their own preferences for those of the consumers." Landauer agrees that while western countries have no planners as powerful as those in the Soviet Union, they can and do transfer "purchasing power from individuals to the state and use it for politically determined purposes," such as those of the defense industry and for public works. However, he says, in the West this can be done only to the extent approved by the representatives of the people. In other words, the progressive conformity of techniques on both sides of the Iron Curtain does not of itself involve a progressive approximation of goals. They remain totalitarian on the one side and democratic on the other. As a matter of fact, it is imaginable that it is exactly the increasing adaptability and versatility of quasi-Machiavellian systems, such as Soviet Communism, which would strengthen their viability and promote their advance. We must not forget that while Marxian theory may appear doctrinaire and inflexible, communist policy is, in a sense, "existential," and pragmatic. The readiness of any devoted Soviet leader to use and justify whatever means are available to accelerate the movement toward the communist aim of a classless society, with high material standards of living, seems quite compatible with dialectic materialism.

Both Hegelian and Marxian dialectics are somehow relativistic. Everything is seen as in a flux, that is, as engulfed in a dialectic process of continuous transformation, advancing from thesis to antithesis to synthesis. Since the synthesis is assumed to reconcile the conflicting forces

preceding it, Marxians have always acknowledged that the great and supposedly final synthesis, which will — once and for all — resolve all conflicts, namely mature communism, will embody elements taken from
capitalism. Communists availing themselves of the techniques of a market
economy thus need not feel that they compromise and make ideological
concessions. These techniques are sublimated, as it were, in the historical
process so that they can now serve higher ends.

Of course, we are not bound by their rationalizations. There is no
reason why such changes could not be interpreted as demonstrating the
indestructibility of the natural moral law and as proving that no ideology,
no movement, and no system can, in the long run, pervert and resist
nature or the commands of natural reason with impunity. . . . But if we
believe these recent trends in Soviet economic policy do represent a
victory of reason and human nature, we must beware of the notion that
our own system in its present form represents the final embodiment of
what is demanded by the natural moral law. Ours cannot claim to be
an *economia perennis*.

We should not lose sight of the fact that in the present stage of so-
called late capitalism, characterized by imperfect competition and by
monetary and fiscal policies and controls of hitherto unheard of dimen-
sions, our system too is undergoing tremendous changes. Paradoxical as
it may seem, these very changes may preserve our system, just as the
apparent metamorphosis of the Soviet economic system may sustain rather
than destroy it. It is in this connection interesting to note that while the
American ideology of capitalism rejects central planning as a syndrome
of totalitarianism, the United States does demand as a condition for
much of the aid given to underdeveloped countries "that detailed plans
be presented by the recipients as to how the aid would be used."

All this is not to suggest an impending ideological *rapprochement*
between the western world and the communist bloc. At present I see
no bridge between their respective standards of value. Yet I envisage
at least the possibility that once again the course of history may be
changed simply through the operation of what Wilhelm Wundt, in his
Introduction to Psychology, called the "principle of the heterogeneity
of purposes," according to which, as Hegel expressed it, "in history an
additional result is commonly produced by human actions beyond that
which they aim at and obtain — that which they immediately recognize
and desire" (*Introduction to the Philosophy of History*, Vol. 46, p. 165b).
Such unintended side-effects or by-products often, as Wundt pointed out,

inspire the "actor" or agent to a revision of his original designs or induce others to add new aims to the old ones.

The Soviet leaders obviously intended to liberalize economic procedures for no other purpose than to achieve more quickly what they believe to be the culmination of social justice: the classless and propertyless society. There is, however, at least a chance that success and prosperity *now* will help them discover that decentralized decision-making, equal opportunity, reward of achievement, multiplication rather than abolition of private property, and some kind of industrial democracy offer better prospects for the eventual emancipation of man and mankind from social injustice than any future social order based on the chimera of perfect equality.

Whether they do make this discovery, however, may well depend on the readiness of the "free world" to demonstrate in fact rather than in oratory that social welfare is the true and acknowledged end of their economic system — rewarding deeds *and* regarding needs!

CHAPTER 2

THE POPES SPEAK

> Though the Church's first care must be for souls, how it
> can sanctify them and make them share in supernatural goods,
> it is also solicitous for the needs of man's daily life, with his
> livelihood and education, and his general temporal welfare and
> prosperity.
>
> In all this it is but giving effect to principles that Christ
> Himself established in the Church He founded. When He
> said "I am the way, the truth and the life," and "I am the light
> of the world," it was doubtless man's eternal salvation that was
> uppermost in His mind; but He showed His concern for the
> material welfare of His people when, seeing the hungry crowd
> of His followers, He was moved to exclaim: "I have compas-
> sion on the multitude."
>
> Pope John XXIII in Mater et Magistra

The path that the Church must walk between its religious mission and a
related concern for the temporal order is a narrow one. By nature and
profession, the Church is not equipped to administer the affairs of state,
or to manage business corporations, or to direct labor unions. Nowhere
in the gospels does Jesus Christ instruct His disciples in the mechanics
of banking or the conduct of foreign trade. Though he warns them against
greed and an excessive concern for material goods, He utters not a single
word about fiscal policy or the gold standard.

On the other hand, the Church is committed to promote justice and
foster love. It must teach and enforce a code of conduct, as well as lead
its followers in the worship of God. In so doing, it cannot ignore an area
of life in which men spend most of their waking hours and where questions of justice are constantly raised. Just as the Church teaches what is
right and wrong in family life, so it must expound the ethics of the
marketplace.

This is not as well understood as it ought to be. Over the past few years, minorities in several affiliated bodies of the National Council of Churches of Christ have strenuously protested its involvement in the civil rights movement and the antipoverty program. Earlier they had complained about the council's pronouncements on other socioeconomic questions. These protesters have their counterparts in the Catholic Church, as at least two Popes, Pius XI and Pius XII, have publicly deplored. The social encyclicals of the Popes have not been universally acclaimed in Catholic circles. In too many cases they have not even been read.

This is a great pity. It may even be a tragedy. Admittedly, the Church cannot offer a system of Christian economics — in any strict sense of those words — as a divine answer to man's temporal aspirations and perplexities. It can provide, however, basic truths about human society and the human nature Christ redeemed, about natural resources and God's design for them, about the management of earthly goods and their relation to man's eternal destiny. These moral guidelines can help men to conduct their affairs in a way becoming children of God.

Such are the truths that the modern Popes, beginning with Leo XIII, have set down and applied in their social teachings. In doing this, they have not strayed from the path charted by Jesus. On the contrary, they have given a Christian witness to the troubled world of our times.

The Church in the Temporal Order*

ALBERT LE ROY, S.J.

On June 1, 1941, Pope Pius XII broadcast a message to the Catholic world on the occasion of the fiftieth anniversary of the publication by Pope Leo XIII of *Rerum Novarum*. . . .

That encyclical has, in fact, always been regarded as the Charter of the Catholic social movement. Not that it actually gave rise to the movement, or was the unprepared outcome of some kind of spontaneous generation. . . . Before the encyclical appeared members of the clergy and the laity alike had been moved in most European countries by the sad state to which the working classes had been reduced. Faced with the grave new problems created by the Industrial Revolution, they had tried to find a

---

* From "The Fiftieth Anniversary of the *Rerum Novarum*," *International Labour Review*, October, 1941.

solution in conformity with the doctrine of the gospel. Bishop von Ketteler in Germany, Gaspard Descurtins in Switzerland, Albert de Mun in France, Cardinal Manning in England, Baron C. de Vogelsang in Austria, to mention only a few names, had preached against the crying abuses of the times and had championed a social order founded on justice. In the United States a still more forceful voice had been raised, that of Cardinal Gibbons, Archbishop of Baltimore, in the resounding case of the Knights of Labor. . . .

But even though the Catholic social movement had already shown its vitality before *Rerum Novarum* was published, the fact remains that the encyclical gave it a new impulse. It has given rise to an abundant literature, devoted solely to commenting on and spreading its doctrine. Special chairs have been dedicated to it at Catholic universities and seminaries; numerous congresses, social weeks, and study circles have been held to delve more deeply into its teaching; Christian trade unions, the specialized Jocist and Jacist youth movements (*Jeunesse Ouvrière Chrétienne* — Christian Workers' Youth Movement; *Jeunesse Agricole Chrétienne* — Christian Rural Youth Movement), mutual aid societies, employers', engineers', and handicraftsmen's associations of all kinds have no other aspiration than to put into practice the principles laid down in Leo XIII's document. Pope Pius XI himself, when he published *Quadragesimo Anno* in 1931, linked it up directly with *Rerum Novarum*. Far from wishing to make innovations, and still less, corrections, he pointed out that the new encyclical aimed merely at advancing on the road already mapped out, at explaining and settling points under discussion, and above all at interpreting the immutable doctrine of the Church in the light of new needs.

From *Rerum Novarum* to the Message of June 1, passing through *Quadragesimo Anno* and the encyclical *Divini Redemptoris* on atheistic Communism, the line is unbroken. The ever-recurring problems springing from the evolution of economic and social conditions will always be examined and judged in the light of the same principles, those which Leo XIII laid down once for all, or — to speak more accurately — those which he thought it advisable to bring to mind again, since they are as old as the gospel itself. It is the facts that have changed; but the doctrine in its integrity was established twenty centuries ago. It is complete, and it suffices as a rule for man's every activity; what remains is to apply it in the manner called for by the needs of the times.

It would therefore be a mistake to look on the encyclicals as a source of ready-made formulae giving an answer to every question, and to believe that they only need to be copied word-for-word to bring about an economic and social order infused at once with the breath of life. Their aim is both more modest and more elevated. They lay no claim to forming a complete system and to giving an answer in technical matters, since these lie outside the competence of religious authority.

Even though the Church claims the right to survey all human actions, and even though she can very truly say that nought that is human is alien to her, this does not mean that she proposes to exceed her own proper domain. Economic and social affairs concern her only because they are closely bound up with the moral and spiritual side of things. She can never agree that any man — and a Christian even less than others — may divide his life into two halves: his private life, subject to the prescriptions of moral law; and his public or business life, where so-called economic laws reign ineluctable and supreme. The Church recognizes only one morality, and this, she affirms, should govern man's every activity. When she pronounces judgment on the various conflicting schools of thought, she is in fact guided ultimately by spiritual considerations alone. If she finds that the measures they propose are unacceptable, she is not thereby asserting that such measures would fail to secure the production of a sufficiency, or even of the greatest possible amount, of wealth, but only that they are opposed to certain spiritual values which the Church cannot renounce. Man does not live by bread alone. The economic and social order must be such as to secure his bread for every man, but at the same time it must respect those other values which are the inalienable prerogatives of human nature. "Economic science is guided by its own principles. The laws of economics determine what aims are unattainable or attainable and what means are therefore necessary" (Q.A.). But these particular aims are "subordinate to the supreme aims of man" and must be in complete harmony with them.

This is the angle from which the Church regards the social question. Hence it is the object of the encyclicals to determine those essential principles neglect of which lies at the root of the evils afflicting the modern world and which must be reestablished in full if a remedy for these evils is to be found. The object, as Leo said, is only to prevent any "mistake as to the principles which truth and justice dictate" for the settlement of the social question. Practical measures are left to the free initiative of governments, groups, and individuals, and may vary widely in character.

Interpreting Papal Documents*

W. J. SMITH, S.J.

The phrase "papal documents" refers to quite a wide range of documents. These include encyclical letters (that is, letters sent by the Pope to the hierarchy of a country or of the world), addresses given to some group of people visiting the Pope, addresses broadcast by the Pope from Vatican Radio — any published statement, in fact, which the Pope intends to use as a means of teaching something to the faithful throughout the world. This intention of providing universal teaching is sometimes formally expressed at the time of speaking or writing, but it usually becomes clear when the statements are published in the *Acta Apostolicae Sedis*, the Vatican's official periodical, in the section reserved for the Holy Father's solemn and universal — though not necessarily infallible — pronouncements.

Such papal pronouncements are made about a great variety of topics; but in this article only those are considered which deal with political, economic, and social topics.

In these matters, as in those of a directly religious nature, the Church claims an authentic divine mission; she must study the temporal affairs of men and set out her judgment of the way Christian faith and morality should be applied there. Her purpose in doing this is to assist those people whose right and duty it is to seek solutions for practical problems to find them — in conformity with the teachings of Christ. However, she does not claim the right to direct men to choose any particular lawful solution from among several that may be available. Nor does she claim that she herself is able to tell men with certainty whether or not any given practical proposal will actually produce the political, social, or economic effect hoped for.

One further preliminary remark must be made, namely, that it *is* necessary to provide some principles by which a reader may understand the varying degrees of obligation imposed upon him by different documents or by different parts of the one document. For there are varying degrees. . . . The content can range from statements with the full weight of papal

---

* From "How to Interpret Papal Documents," *Advocate* (Melbourne), June 15, 1961.

authority behind them to mere "timid suggestions"; and, unfortunately, this fact is sometimes not recognized by inexperienced readers. . . .

The principal types of propositions found in papal documents may be divided into two basic and quite distinct categories.

The first category includes propositions which, without any possible doubt, are intended to express absolute truths or universal values that are valid for any time or any circumstances. This first category divides naturally into two classes of propositions.

The first of these classes takes in statements which express some element of the deposit of faith. Thus, the Christmas Messages of Pius XII contained many statements about the mystery of the Incarnation, and the Pope used these as a starting point for his discussion of temporal problems.

The second of these two classes includes all those statements which express unchanging truths or values of the natural order. The human mind is capable of arriving at these without the aid of revelation, but it reaches some of them only with difficulty, and there is no little risk of error on the way. It is because of this fact that such truths are given frequent expression in papal writing. They figure largely in *Rerum Novarum* itself, examples being the statement that a human person must not be treated like a machine, that human labor must not be bought and sold like mere merchandise, that man has a right to the possession of property.

The first category of propositions, with its division into two classes, constitutes papal teaching in the strict sense of the word. The propositions themselves, which are not found in great profusion, are in the form of broad general principles, occupy a fundamental place in the documents in question, and demand the assent of Catholics.

The second main category contains assertions that are directly related to the needs of a particular time and refer to particular circumstances.

They make up the greater part of papal writing on economic, social, and political themes. They are definitely not the affirmation or reaffirmation either of sections of the Christian revelation or of elements of the natural law. Rather they represent an attempt to make such doctrines or principles effective in given circumstances. Normally, the claim is not made for them that they are the only possible way of applying absolute truths — although they may be in some situations.

A good example would be Pius XII's Christmas Message of 1941. It was an application of the general principle that we should love one another, and it set out a series of steps by which a true and permanent peace might be set up at the close of hostilities. One of these was a proposal for progressive disarmament. No doubt someone else could well have formulated a disarmament plan in different terms and on a different basis — or even have questioned the need or the possibility of disarmament.

This second main category of propositions has several important characteristics, and it will be well to bring these out.

First characteristic: these propositions can be set out as judgments or proposals or directives.

They can take the form of doctrinal or moral judgments about concrete circumstances, judgments made in the light of the first main category of propositions as discussed above. Thus, in Rerum Novarum, Leo XIII judged that the treatment given to the workers in the nineteenth century was immoral because it attacked their human dignity.

They can take the form of concrete proposals or directives made so that unchangeable truths may be applied in given circumstances. To use the example of Rerum Novarum once more, Leo XIII stated in that encyclical that when work for wages provides the sole source of income for a worker, such wages must be at least high enough to provide an honest, industrious worker with the means for a frugal living.

Second characteristic: this second category of propositions should not be applied, whether as judgments or directives, outside the circumstances to which they are related.

Thus, while Leo condemned as unjust the wage system of his time, he did not thereby condemn the wage system as such. And when he stated that workers should receive a living wage, he was not referring to workers outside the capitalistic industrial situation — e.g., workers living under the tribal system of Africa.

Third characteristic: propositions in the second category can refer to activities, or to institutions, or to ideologies which are all subject to internal change. They do not necessarily apply to these same activities, institutions, or ideologies after a period of such internal change.

For instance, the free enterprise system criticized by Leo XIII is different in many ways from the free enterprise system of the present day, although the one we know has developed from the system of Leo's time. His criticisms cannot all be rigidly applied to the present system — nor can all his criticisms of the European socialism of his time be applied to present-day European socialism.

Fourth characteristic: the bearing that assertions and proposals are intended to have on the consciences of the faithful is usually to be gathered from the manner in which these are expressed.

Assertions vary from statements solemnly expressed as certain to others for which clearly nothing more is claimed than simple probability. Proposals range from strict orders to earnest counsels to simple suggestions.

For example, when Leo XIII wrote that "nothing would be more desirable [for the settlement of industrial grievances] than that a committee should be appointed composed of reliable and capable members . . . whose duty would be . . . to settle the dispute," he was clearly not giving any peremptory command. Just as clearly, Pius XI was claiming much more than simple probability for the validity of the following judgment from *Quadragesimo Anno:* "It is your chief duty, Venerable Brethren, and that of your clergy, to seek diligently, to select prudently, and train fittingly these lay apostles, among workingmen and among employers." The clergy could not, with clear consciences, disregard the directive contained in this statement.

Fifth characteristic: No matter what is the tone or manner of their utterance, there is an area of greater uncertainty about some propositions in this second category than about others.

This is because assertions, directives, or proposals directly based on the findings of scientific investigations in the fields of economics, politics, and sociology have a direct relation to the validity or adequacy of the investigations themselves, or of the interpretation of their findings. The only guarantee Catholics have in this regard is that action taken on the basis of such technical calculations will not bring the universal Church to ruin. There is no guarantee that it will bring the result hoped for.

Because propositions in this second category are so closely related to contingent circumstances and because they are "not the affirmation or reaffirmation of either sections of the Christian revelation or of elements of the natural law," the importance of distinguishing them from such general propositions is clear. Sometimes it is not easy to do this. For example, there are a number of condemnations of "revolution" in papal documents of the last century — e.g., the condemnation made by Gregory XVI in *Mirari Vos* — and it is difficult from the text itself to decide whether or not these are directed against revolution as such, or have a narrower target. Only by an examination — not without difficulty — of the historical circumstances in which the Popes issued these condemnations can one now see that the revolutions condemned were not all revolutions, but specifically the "liberal" revolutions of those times. This fact is emphasized by more recent papal statements in support of "just revolutions" — e.g., Pius XI's *Firmissimam Constantiam*, which was published in May, 1937, on the occasion of disturbances in Mexico.

Further difficulties arise also from the way in which the Latin language, in which the documents are often written, lends itself to abstraction and generalization, and from the fact that the writers themselves are men of their own time and are influenced by the intellectual and social habits of that time. They speak, too, without knowledge of the cultural and social evolution that makes later times different from their own. Thus a writer who dealt with international law topics in the nineteenth century did not have before him the experience of the League of Nations and the United Nations Organization, and his statements could not be based on the breadth of experience now available.

The social teaching of the Popes who have followed Leo XIII, while it shows considerable reliance on Leo's ideas, is also inspired by a desire to elaborate, or complete, or adjust in some ways what Leo wrote. This factor should also be kept in mind, for it means that a later statement is usually much more than a reiteration of earlier teaching.

The solemnity of the terms employed in the documents must also be studied. For example, Pius XI in *Casti Connubii* condemned birth prevention with such a tone of supreme authority that there is no possibility that the Church will ever go back on this judgment.

All this may seem a very complicated approach to what are often treated as quite simple pronouncements; but the fact is that papal documents normally need such an approach precisely because so many of them have considerable depth of meaning. It is possible, in fact, to do a good deal of harm by treating them as simple, as open to a facile interpretation, and as capable of being used in brief quotation to bludgeon opponents. On the other hand, they are not so vague that they can be used quite honestly by all comers for their own party purposes. To those who are prepared to make the often rather difficult effort of interpretation suggested in this article, papal teaching on social, political, and economic topics can be a revealing guide to understanding the modern world.

In the face of these and other no less important difficulties of interpretation, it will be useful to observe the following rules of procedure:

The meaning of words should be investigated with a good deal of care — e.g., the meaning of the word "revolution" in nineteenth-century documents.

If possible, the sources used in the preparation of the document should be investigated. These can throw light on the meaning of words, on the historical and scientific presuppositions of the document, and therefore on the type of judgment or directive contained in a passage in question.

The documents must be "placed" in the historical and local context of their production. Thus, certain statements about European trade unionism have little reference to trade unions in Anglo-Saxon countries.

The documents must also be considered against the totality of Catholic teaching as it has unfolded over centuries. Referring again to the condemnation of "revolution," it would be a mistake to read the nineteenth-century statements without relating them to the relevant teaching of St. Augustine and St. Thomas Aquinas on the subject of resistance to tyranny.

The teaching of a Pope who has reigned for a fair period of years often shows a certain continuity and development, and this factor should be taken into account in reading any new document issued by the same person.

The Contributions of Leo XIII and Pius XI*
PHILIP TAFT

The modern world is continually faced with the need of deciding basic economic policy. Not only must we evolve institutions that will assure equity and justice; we must here and now avoid anything that looks like a major depression. Serious industrial dislocation and wide unemployment would not only cause great distress but would weaken and perhaps even destroy our power to resist infiltration by totalitarian groups.

While the present generation faces the grim task of defending society and its traditions against corrosion from within and attack from without, the problems themselves are not new, and guidance on these questions can still be found by non-Catholics as well as Catholics in the papal encyclicals, Rerum Novarum and Quadragesimo Anno. Despite their age, these documents have a vitality and freshness absent in many contemporary pronouncements on social issues. Not only do they accurately diagnose the economic maladies of our time, but the remedies prescribed have been found effective in the past and are sufficiently potent to be helpful in the present.

* From "The Popes Point the Way to Social Justice," America, April 22, 1950.

Rerum Novarum

Rerum Novarum appeared in 1891, soon after the modern Socialist movement had established itself upon an international basis and was for the first time attracting to its standards large masses of industrial workers in continental countries. The spread of Socialist ideas could be primarily traced neither to the attractiveness of its doctrine nor the logical cogency of its arguments, but to the unbearable burdens imposed upon the wage earner by aggressive and expanding capitalism.

While modern industrialism raised living standards, it also encouraged sprawling city-slums, overwork, and the brutal exploitation of the young and the weak. These conditions were justified by a theory of laissez-faire whose tenets received an unenthusiastic reception among industrial workers. Instead they began to turn toward socialism. Germany witnessed the formation of the first modern Socialist party in 1863, inspired by Ferdinand Lassalle, who outlined his program in his Open Letter. Within the next twenty years, Socialist parties were functioning in every European country that allowed free political activity.

The causes for the spread of radical doctrine among the industrial population were clearly perceived by the Catholic Bishop of Mainz, William Emmanuel von Ketteler, who recognized the evils of modern industrialism and insisted that the Church take the lead in eradicating them. His Christianity and the Labor Question not only attacked evils but prescribed remedies. The view that society should leave economic problems to the free play of economic law was challenged, and the theory that nothing could be done to mitigate the hardship of the worker rejected. Bishop von Ketteler's work was carried further in Germany, and similar movements were inaugurated in other European countries. All were founded on a belief that unregulated industrialism was not only guilty of inhuman treatment of the worker but, by its excesses, it was driving the worker into the arms of the revolutionary legions clamorously appealing for support.

Out of this awakening among Catholic social pioneers grew Pope Leo XIII's Rerum Novarum. It addressed itself to the social and economic problems raised by a laissez-faire capitalism, and prescribed a broad program for their solution. The encyclical showed that between the demands of the rugged individualist for no interference with the working of economic law and the revolutionary theorist for complete government control over economic resources, a third road was available — one of orderly, gradual adaptation to change.

One notices this feature of *Rerum Novarum*: it is a reformist and not a revolutionary document. Its approach to social problems is pragmatic, not doctrinaire, simple and direct rather than devious and complicated. Evils exist, a remedy is presented. Although the encyclical dates from the nineteenth century, it reads today like a current document, for our world has learned at the price of much suffering that complete and "one-shot" remedies for complex social problems are an illusion, that man is too limited, fallible, and stubborn to find an easy, complete answer to the problems that beset him.

The tone of *Rerum Novarum* should be described as "reformist," in the sense that it is more concerned with the eradication of evils than the transforming of institutions. The Pope sees the modern worker exposed to many evils and oppressions. He rejects the remedies offered by the Socialists of his time. He suggests as an alternative a program of reform, of guaranteeing the worker the right to organize, of placing a floor under wages, a ceiling upon the hours of labor, of protecting the young and weak against exploitation. He is intent on applying ethical principles, but to the existing order.

In examining the economic system of his time, Leo XIII did not deal with abstractions, as do the Marxists and the economic liberals, but with the impact of the new industrialism on individual men and women. He insisted that the poor, who contribute by their labor to the welfare of the community, must not be neglected; that the prizes must not be monopolized by the strong and powerful. *Rerum Novarum* emphasized, therefore, the necessity of establishing those legal safeguards for the worker which have since been partially or entirely adopted in Western Europe and the United States. Government policy, said the Pope, must be so arranged "as to produce . . . public well-being and private prosperity."

The argument in behalf of such measures is based upon the inequality of bargaining power between employer and employee. The right of workers to form associations for the advancement of their interests is affirmed, and "every precaution should be taken not to violate the rights of individuals, and not to make unreasonable regulations under the pretense of public benefits." This warning directed against governments controlled or influenced by the wealthy classes is even more applicable to the contemporary totalitarian regimes, which in the name of public interest either subordinate or destroy every expression of individual or group independence. *Rerum Novarum* outlined the methods by which the workers' welfare and dignity could be protected. It also chastised those who accepted the then dominant belief that an overweening lust for gain was a high social virtue.

The view that economic activity must be the servant and not the master of man was a blow at both the insatiable demand for even greater profits, and the theorists who insisted that society and the great variety of its institutions only reflected the changing aspects of economic activity.

Quadragesimo Anno

The forty-year period between the publication of *Rerum Novarum* and *Quadragesimo Anno* witnessed the expansion of the labor movement, and the introduction of many reforms envisaged in the earlier encyclical. It also saw a division of world socialism, with the extreme wing setting up a movement of its own under the name of communism. *Quadragesimo Anno* was issued when the doctrine of *laissez-faire* in economic affairs had lost most of its appeal, and when the economies of Europe and the United States were in the throes of a severe crisis. The automatic adjustments and the optimum distribution of capital and labor by the market had failed to solve the severe difficulties engulfing most of the world.

Whatever the explanation may be, the greater significance of trade unions and of government in economic life could not be denied. Limitations on the use and even ownership of property had taken place in virtually all parts of the world. The subordination of property rights to the needs of society had been increasingly accepted. Control upon the use of wealth in behalf of the community was no longer regarded as interference with the legitimate rights of property, a view excellently expressed in *Quadragesimo Anno*:

> However, when civil authority adjusts ownership to meet the needs of public good it acts not as an enemy, but as a friend of private owners; for thus it effectively prevents the possession of private property . . . from creating intolerable burdens and so rushing to its own destruction.

Reform is justified not only on moral grounds, but as the most effective protector of the institution itself. Certainly the "New Deal" and "Fair Deal" programs were based upon similar assumptions. Inferentially the encyclical recognizes that the institution of private property is in danger not only from those who would overthrow it, but from those who insist upon continuing the injustices that arise as a result of unrestricted use.

The pronouncements with respect to labor are more explicit in *Quadragesimo Anno* than in *Rerum Novarum*, owing to the changes that had taken place in the interval between their publication. The latter was in a real sense a pioneer statement of a more sure if less spectacular road to social and economic progress than the one offered by extremist doctrinaires.

Quadragesimo Anno advocates a wage policy that will allow the worker to earn an adequate amount for the proper support of his family. However, the wage policy must be sufficiently flexible to take into account the position of the single enterprise so that wages, considering also the basic needs of the worker, will not be so high as to cause unemployment. The Pope recognized that while such decisions can be made only by examining particular conditions, a policy that leads to unemployment is not merely harmful to the individual but socially dangerous as well. No specific wage policy is laid down, and the great diversity in the condition of individual businesses is recognized.

The test of a wage policy, in addition to minimum levels, must be its effect on employment — a good modern view. Severe unemployment, said Pius XI, is a dreadful scourge; it causes misery and temptation to the laborer, ruins the prosperity of nations, and endangers public order, peace, and tranquillity the world over. In a few simples lines, the dangers inherent in widespread unemployment are eloquently expressed. In the discussion of wages, the emphasis is on common good rather than on individual or group advantage. While minimum wage standards should be observed, the Pope recognized that the rates paid for different occupations and grades of work must be related. Otherwise there is not only a tendency for some groups to profit, but distortion in the wage structure may cause unemployment.

The Pope shows an awareness of changes in corporate organization, and his view — that "immense power and despotic economic domination is concentrated in the hands of a few, and those few are frequently not the owners, but only the trustees and directors of invested funds, who administer them at their good pleasure" — might have been taken out of the report of the Temporary National Economic Committee. The concentration of economic power is not only a threat to domestic order but to international peace. Few secular documents contain as sharp an assault upon *laissez-faire* competition, nor is it often stated in language as direct and simple.

In dealing with socialism the Pope recognized the changes that had taken place since the 1890's, and some of his observations foreshadow the evolution of the "Third Force" which has played an important role in stemming the Communist tide after World War II. After World War I the Socialist movement became divided into hostile factions. The seeds of this division had long existed, for in the Socialist camp were found extreme revolutionaries as well as moderate reformers. The victory of Bolshevism in Russia in 1917 ended the artificial unity. Extreme Socialists began to call themselves Communists, while the moderate Socialists retained their old name.

From the beginning the Socialists opposed dictatorship, the one-party state, and suppression of minorities. Moreover, Pope Pius XI recognized that their emphases upon human dignity and moderate reform rather than revolution "often strikingly approach the just demands of Christian social reformers." While still critical of some of the doctrines advocated by Socialists, the Pope saw the reasonableness and the utility of many of their demands. "For it is rightly contended that certain forms of property must be reserved to the state, since they carry with them an opportunity of domination too great to be left to private individuals without injury to the community at large." While specific criteria are not laid down, the Pope states that some types of industry might have to be nationalized. The test in this instance is not that nationalization is in itself desirable, but that private controls over some areas of economic life allow some people too much power over others.

Conclusion

Both *Rerum Novarum* and *Quadragesimo Anno* show a keen insight into the problems of their time. Both encyclicals stress reform by moderate means. While they denounce the doctrines of *laissez-faire*, they see great evils in the complete subordination of the individual to an all-powerful state. The method of achieving improvement in economic relations is through groups such as trade unions, and laws directed against specific evils. There are no all-embracing panaceas, but readers of the encyclicals, irrespective of religion, can find there eloquent appeals in behalf of justice and human dignity. In *Quadragesimo Anno* the Pope sensed the crucial issue of the century: whether men are to remain free or be swallowed up in a new slavery. He extended the hand of fellowship to all men desirous of correcting the evils of our industrial society and at the same time holding fast to the traditions of human liberty.

Pius XII and the Social Order*

BENJAMIN L. MASSE, S.J.

To say that Pius XII's socioeconomic teachings reflected two great and dominating concerns is very likely an oversimplification. Yet that statement contains so much truth that it can serve, perhaps, as a unifying principle for the remarks that follow.

The Pope was deeply concerned, first of all, that Catholics take seriously to heart the corporative, or occupational-group, system which Pius XI had described and recommended in *Quadragesimo Anno*. In an address to Italian employers on January 31, 1952, he called this system — known popularly in the United States as the Industry Council Plan — the "chief part" of that encyclical. He was greatly concerned, in the second place, that economic life in our highly organized, technological age be *human*. He did not want the individual to become a cog in a wholly mechanistic order, whether that order was imposed by an omnipotent state, or by huge, anonymous aggregations of private power. Though these themes do not exhaust the Pope's teaching, they are, I believe, a key to understanding it.

While the Holy Father had indicated early in his reign that *Quadragesimo Anno* was to remain the basic charter of Catholic socioeconomic doctrine, there may have been some question here and there about the emphasis he wished to place on the occupational-group system. In certain Christian trade-union circles abroad, there was a feeling that Fascism had so compromised the vocational order that a fresh approach was needed if the Church's teaching was to have some impact on the postwar world. Any doubts that existed about the Holy Father's attitude on this point were quickly dissipated by his celebrated letter to the 1946 meeting of the French Semaine Sociale at Strasbourg.

The subject of that meeting was the nationalization, or socialization, of large private enterprises. This was what many Europeans had in mind when they talked of the *réformes des structures*, which were widely thought necessary to satisfy worker aspirations for a better life than was known in prewar days. A solid bloc of French Catholics not only accepted the need for nationalization but right after the war had started

---

* From "Pius XII and the Social Order," *America*, November 1, 1958.

working to bring it about. In their fight for social justice, nationalization had assumed a dominant place.

The Pope was neither indifferent to the plight of the workers nor ignorant of their desires for a new and just social order. Several times during the war he had referred with sympathy to the aspirations of workers and had called them legitimate and justified. But in his letter to the Semaine, he thought it necessary to flash, if not a red light bringing traffic to a halt, at least an amber light warning it to proceed cautiously. In Catholic social teaching, there was a place for nationalization, but that place must not be exaggerated. Wrote the Holy Father:

> Our predecessors and We Ourselves have more than once touched on the moral aspect of that measure [nationalization of enterprises]. It is evident, however, that, instead of diminishing the mechanistic character of life and labor in common, nationalization, even when it is licit, is rather in danger of further accentuating it; and that, in consequence, the advantage which nationalization brings to the profit of a true community, such as you understand it, is very much to be judged with care.

But if large-scale nationalization is not the way, by what means can workers be fully integrated into modern industrial society? How can they achieve some control over their destiny, and their rights and dignity be safeguarded?

The Pope answered in the familiar terms of *Quadragesimo Anno*:

> We think that the setting up of corporative associations or units in all the branches of the national economy would be much more beneficial to the end which you pursue, and more beneficial at the same time for the best output of the undertakings. . . . There is, moreover, no doubt that, under present circumstances, the corporative form of social life, and especially of economic life, in practice favors the Christian teaching concerning the person, the community, labor and private property.

It is interesting to observe that events soon confirmed the Pope's estimate of nationalization. In a number of cases, notably in Great Britain, many workers and union leaders quickly became disillusioned with public ownership. Though the workers, for instance, theoretically owned the coal mines which employed them, their relationship to management was no more "personal" and satisfying than it had been under private enterprise. If anything they had less freedom of action than in the bad old days.

The controversy over co-determination afforded the Holy Father another opportunity to reaffirm his faith in the occupational-group approach to modern industrial life.

On May 7, 1949, addressing the International Union of Catholic Employers, he noted that the drive for co-determination was powered both by a desire to emphasize the mutuality of interest in the worker-employer relationship, and by the need of giving the workers some stake and voice in the enterprise. He applauded the goals of this drive but expressed reservations about the means. With Pius XI he agreed that the wage contract, though not unjust in itself, might well be "somewhat modified by a partnership contract." This would enable workers to become "sharers in ownership or management or to participate in some fashion in the profits received," as was stated in *Quadragesimo Anno*. But the Pope insisted that workers could not demand a share in the "economic decisions" of management *as a natural-law right*. He went on to insist, in the words of Pius XI, that the occupational-group plan was "a practical and timely prescription" for expressing the mutuality of interest between workers and employers.

On January 31, 1952, the Holy Father spoke in a similar vein to the Italian Catholic Employers Association. Again admonishing those preoccupied with co-determination, he said that, while thus engaged,

> they pass over more or less in silence the chief part of the encyclical *Quadragesimo Anno*, which contains that social policy embodying the idea of an occupational, corporative order of the whole economy.

The Pope's insistence on occupational groups may be said to reflect his conviction that only through restoring an organic character to economic life could class warfare be abolished, workers be integrated into the system, and private economic activities duly subordinated to the common good. Failing such a reform, the only alternative seemed to be the almost unrestricted growth of the state, even in democracies, as the only agency capable of giving a necessary unity and coordination to the wealth-making pursuits of its citizens.

Pope Pius XII's second great concern, that social and economic life remain *human*, appeared early in his reign. In an address on Christmas Eve, 1941, he noted that the human spirit, alienated from God, had attempted to fill the void by striving to surpass all "previous accomplishments in the attainment of riches and power." In economic life, the consequence was the "domination of great, gigantic enterprises and trusts"; in social life, the "uprooting and crowding of masses of people in the centers of industry and commerce." As a result, the "relationship between men in their social life took on a character that was purely physical and mechanical"; and the bond holding them together, giving what unity there was to society, was external force, not the great social virtues of justice and charity, and a wise system of laws.

On March 11, 1945, addressing a large group of workers in Rome, the Pope again referred to the danger from huge monopolistic enterprises — "the economic tyranny of an anonymous conglomeration of private capital." But he warned, too, of abuses of trade-union power. Democratic values could also be endangered, he said, "by the preponderant power of organized masses, ready to use their power to the detriment of justice and the rights of others."

Two years later, on July 16, 1947, he decried reforms that would reduce the worker "to the state of complete subjection to the bureaucratic clique holding political power." Any program for improving the lot of workers, the Holy Father insisted, would be a "mechanism without a soul" unless it respected "the human person in all men. . . ."

It was this concern of the Holy Father for the human person that led him on many occasions to champion the cause of the small producer and craftsman. In a broadcast on September 1, 1944, he deplored the excessive concentration of economic goods because, as a result, "we see small and medium holdings diminish and lose their value to human society." On a number of occasions during the postwar years, he returned to this theme. Typical is this extract from an address on October 20, 1947:

> The Church wishes to impose a definite limit to the subordination of man to the machine. Small craftsmen as a class may be regarded as a militia chosen to defend the personal dignity and character of the workers. For more than a century they have had to fight for their existence against great industrial enterprises.

The Pope had, if anything, an even higher regard for the farmer, especially for the farmer who cultivated a family-sized holding. In an address to the International Catholic Congress on Rural Problems, on July 2, 1951, he referred to complaints that in our modern, technological society, with its assembly lines and big organizations, labor had lost "the personal and social sense of human living." For this evil, he said, there was no simple remedy. Nevertheless, it is true "that the work of the farm acts as a powerful defense against all these disorders." And to make sure that he was not misunderstood, that he was not talking about "factory-farming," he added: "We are thinking here first of the family-type farm."

Not that the Holy Father was opposed to invention and technological progress. On November 15, 1946, he exhorted members of the Italian Farmers' Federation to be ready "to employ methods that represent a real progress compared with the past." He did not wish to deny, he said on another occasion, "the utility, often the necessity, of larger farm enterprises." And a number of times, notably in Christmas Eve addresses in 1941 and 1952, he expressed similar appreciation of technological gains and noted the contributions which large-scale industrial enterprises had made to material progress.

What the Holy Father thought important to emphasize was that technological advancement and economic efficiency must not be considered ends in themselves. Before accepting, with a kind of fatalism, mechanization and the bigness in industry and agriculture which it encouraged, he wanted men to stop and ask themselves what the effect of these changes would be on individual dignity, on family well-being, and on all those values which are essential to a really human society. Pope Pius XII was not opposed to change. He merely wished to make sure that change was subordinated to man, and not the other way around.

Like his predecessors, Leo XIII and Pius XI, the Pope was not free from criticism. Accused by some of diverting the Church's social teaching into too conservative channels, he was censured by others for his radicalism. His insistence on freedom of access to the world's raw materials, his warm pleas for liberal immigration policies, his exhortations to wealthy nations to help the "have-not," underdeveloped countries were not universally applauded. There are still Catholics, alas, who want no relaxation of our strict U. S. immigration laws, and others who persist in labeling as "operation rathole" the same foreign-aid programs which the Holy Father on more than one occasion publicly praised. As was the case with Leo XIII and Pius XI, the passage of time will confirm the inspired wisdom of Pius XII and the rumbles of criticism will be only echoes of history. In developing the Church's social doctrine for our age of automation and nuclear power, he enriched the entire world.

Significance of John XXIII*

JOHN F. CRONIN, S.S.

It may seem strange to find in *Mater et Magistra* an opening to the left. In terms of European politics, the purpose of the encyclical was quite the opposite. To the European Christian Democrat, the tone and

* From "Mater et Magistra: Catholic Social Teaching Updated," *Social Order*, September, 1961.

direction of this document are such as to give the center political parties a powerful appeal to workers and farmers. The Church has stolen the thunder of the Marxist left by offering generous and understanding programs of social reform.

Because of this approach, the encyclical is as much pastoral as doctrinal. Those who were looking for innovations in the development of doctrine will not find them here. In the treatment of the problems of developing nations, there is no explicit discussion of land reform as a needed element of change. While the encyclical shows awareness of new ideas in the area of property rights, it does not find these new factors an occasion for modifying the traditional concept of private property.

On the other hand, Catholics who sought a shift to the right will find little comfort in this majestic document. The thesis that the welfare state is a direct road to communism does not seem to have occurred to Pope John XXIII. He has no desire to return to the days of rugged individualism, with the state standing by impotently in the face of exploitation, unemployment, and destitution.

He confronts the modern world, with all its complexity, with a sincere desire to accept and Christianize all that is good in it. It is a world characterized by intense social activity. Within the confines of individual states, there is a wide variety of social-welfare programs. There are also measures of economic control, especially those designed to iron out the business cycle.

Outside of state boundaries, we find an immense apparatus of international social, economic, and political bodies. They are engaged in seeking to promote peace and the development of nations that hitherto have lagged behind in economic growth. The Pope specifically mentions the Food and Agriculture Organization of the United Nations. He also notes the work of the International Labor Organization, of the same body.

All these intense social activities are accepted and indeed approved as a necessary part of modern life. There are no nostalgic sighs for a simpler society. There is no call for a return to patterns based upon the best elements of the medieval social system. *Mater et Magistra* does not outline any specific blueprint of social reform, although it does summarize the concept of social order presented in *Quadragesimo Anno*.

Accordingly, we must characterize the new encyclical as realistic, moderate, and progressive. Within the confines of subsidiarity, it allows for much social experimentation. There is a deep optimism in the Pope's approach. When, for example, he calls for greater labor participation in business management and also in national and international political life, there is implicit trust in the wisdom of labor and its leaders. The acceptance of "socialization" likewise assumes that modern states will show adequate political wisdom.

While the encyclical is rich in detailed observations and judgments, its lasting greatness may be found in its total approach rather than in details. It portrays an image of the Christian which is truly noble. There is nothing of small-souled nit-picking; no petty fears or criticisms; no trace of isolationism or negativism. Candor forces us to confess that such elements exist within the Church. We have always had our integralists and heresy-hunters. But John XXIII rises above the purely negative and proposes in grand outlines the majesty of a Christian concept of society.

This approach is especially evident in two of the major topics treated: socialization and aid to developing nations. Socialization, as defined in the encyclical, refers to a wide variety of social activities that characterize modern society. These include social-welfare action by the state, but the social aspect of the private sector is also analyzed.

Socialization has its dangers.

> It restricts the range of the individual as regards his liberty of action and uses means, follows methods, and creates an atmosphere which makes it difficult for each one to think independently of outside influences, to work on his own initiative, to exercise his responsibility, to affirm and enrich his personality.

It can create the organization man.

But it need not reduce men to automatons. It is a process subject to the control of man's free will. Hence it is possible to Christianize it; to remove the negative aspects and to enhance its advantages. Two requirements are involved here: that those invested with public authority have a "sane view of the common good," and that intermediary bodies

> enjoy an effective autonomy in regard to the public authorities and to pursue their own specific interests in loyal collaboration between themselves, subordinately, however, to the demands of the common good.

What this means in detail is noted in various passages of the encyclical. The Pope assumes that a central economic body, whether a central bank or a branch of government, will exercise needed monetary controls to prevent inflation and deflation. He assumes a proportional system of taxation. He refers to social insurance, subsidized housing, and government assistance to agriculture. All these developments, sometimes referred to as the welfare state, can be an acceptable part of modern society.

The encyclical treatment of world problems is equally great-souled. The Pope notes that nations are economically and politically interdependent:

> The different political communities can no longer adequately solve their major problems in their own surroundings and with their own forces, even though they be communities which are notable for their high level and diffusion of culture . . . political communities react on each other. It may be said that each succeeds in developing itself by contributing to the development of the other.

It is true that the major outlines of a Christian approach to world problems can be found in the numerous addresses of Pope Pius XII. But they are gathered together, expanded, and issued in an even more solemn form in this encyclical. What Pius XII explained in general terms, the present Pontiff often makes quite specific:

> It is obvious that the solidarity of the human race and Christian brotherhood demand that an active and manifold co-operation be established among the peoples of the world. They demand a co-operation which permits and encourages the movement of goods, capital, and men. . . .

Undoubtedly the reference just given is to the European Common Market. But it is given in the form of a general principle precisely because Europe is not the only area that could benefit by economic cooperation and the free movement of capital and labor. If the total output of a nation is low, then social-welfare programs are more devices for sharing poverty than for sharing wealth. Economic and political action are needed to build up the productive base of nations and regions:

> More and better production corresponds to a rational need and is also an absolute necessity. However, it is no less necessary and conformable to justice that the riches produced come to be equitably distributed among all members of the political community. Hence effort should be made that social progress proceed at the same pace as economic development.

While the context of the quotation just given is that of aid to developing nations, the principle is equally applicable to nations that already have an industrial base, yet are afflicted with great pockets of poverty. They need both economic growth and social progress.

But the fact that industrial nations have internal needs should not blind them to their obligations to the really poor and underdeveloped people. Several separate statements make this point:

> We are all equally responsible for the undernourished peoples.
> The solidarity which binds all men and makes them members of the same family requires that political communities enjoying abundance of

material goods should not remain indifferent to political communities whose citizens suffer from poverty, misery, and hunger, and who lack even the elementary rights of the human person.

Therefore it is necessary to educate one's conscience to the sense of responsibility which weighs upon each and every one, especially upon those who are more blessed with this world's goods. . . .

Among the more specific measures urged are technical assistance and the providing of educational opportunities for advanced study. The Pope also notes with approval the role of private enterprise in providing capital "in countries on the way to development." While endorsing much that has already been done,

> we cannot excuse ourselves from pointing out that the scientific, technical, and economic cooperation between the economically developed political communities and those just beginning or on the way to development needs to be increased beyond the present level and it is our hope that such a development will characterize their dealings during the next decades.

Another caution in the encyclical concerns the dangers of weakening the political independence of nations as a result of foreign aid and of undermining the spiritual values in native cultures through an excessive emphasis on the material and technical. The references to a "new form of colonialism" seem primarily aimed at Iron Curtain countries, but the West can also be on its guard in this matter. And undoubtedly we have made our share of mistakes in the matter of trying to impose our culture in carbon-copy fashion on other peoples.

These warnings apply particularly to the efforts to spread contraceptive birth control measures as means for meeting the population problem. The encyclical outlines accurately the arguments given by demographers in connection with population growth. Yet it is basically optimistic that the problem can be met. It notes that at the present moment, viewed on a world scale, there is enough food for all. Moreover,

> God in His goodness and wisdom has diffused in nature inexhaustible resources and has given to man intelligence and genius to create fit instruments to master it and to turn it to satisfy the needs and demands of life.

It is true that there are areas in which deficient economic and social organizations are barriers to such progress. But here:

> the true solution is found only in the economic development and the social progress which respects and promotes true human values, individual and social — an economic development and social progress, that is, brought about in a moral atmosphere . . . and in the co-operation, on a world scale, that permits and favors the fruitful interchange of useful knowledge, of capital, and of manpower.

Pope John's treatment of international matters breathes a spirit of Christian brotherhood. It offers a humane alternative to the selfish spirit that has produced such noxious fruits as isolationism, colonial exploitation, and economic imperialism. We are definitely our brothers' keepers. The achievement of world peace and prosperity is to be found in good works and incessant and sacrificing activity.

In the area of labor problems, the main papal concern is twofold: a just wage for the worker, and a greater degree of labor participation in the enterprise, as well as in national and international economic decisions.

The encyclical outlines the complex demands of the common good in regard to wages. It notes that wage levels should be set so as "to provide employment to the greatest number of workers, to take care lest privileged classes arise, even among the workers. . . ." It is also considered desirable that employees of medium-sized and large-sized enterprises "be able to participate in the ownership of the enterprise itself." This is advanced as one method of preventing inequitable distribution of income produced by such firms.

Another reason for worker participation in the enterprise stems from the demands of human dignity:

> an innate exigency in human nature which demands that when men are engaged productively in activity, they have the opportunity of employing their own responsibility and perfecting their own being. Wherefore, if the structures, the functioning, the surroundings of an economic system are such as to compromise human dignity . . . or if they systematically blunt in them the sense of responsibility, or constitute in any way an impediment to expressing their own personal initiative, such an economic system is unjust, even if, by hypothesis, the wealth produced through it reaches a high standard and this wealth is distributed according to the criteria of justice and equity.

To say that the above is a strong passage is an understatement. A productive economic system that pays its workers well is still unjust, if it blunts in them the opportunity to exercise initiative and develop personality. To avoid this danger, small business and firms consisting of craftsmen should be protected and encouraged. Cooperatives can help such persons and all workers on family-type farms. The warm papal endorsement of cooperatives is particularly significant, since previous social encyclicals and addresses did not give much attention to them.

In the same context of developing personal initiative, Pope John goes far beyond Pope Pius XI in endorsing worker participation in the activity of the enterprise:

This means that the workers may have their say in and may make their contribution to the efficient running and development of the enterprise.

The authority of management must be safeguarded, but workers are not to be

> simple and silent performers, without any possibility of bringing to bear their experience, entirely passive in regard to decisions that regulate their activity.

When workers are organized into unions, they should not confine their activities merely to collective bargaining. The reason for this is that decisions affecting individual plants are made by public authorities "or by institutions that act on a world-wide, regional, or national scale." Hence it is appropriate that in such bodies

> the workers also or those who represent their rights, demands, and aspirations should have their say.

In the American context, these passages on labor are particularly significant. Some of our publicists of the right have been portraying the Vatican as opposed to the union shop, demanding Christian unions in the United States, and generally eager to curb the activities of organized labor. By contrast, *Mater et Magistra* takes a totally positive and constructive attitude toward workers, their rights and aspirations, and toward the trade unions that represent them. While it lauds Christian unions, it also has words of praise for Catholics in "other professional groups and associations of workers." And in the same context it praises the work of the International Labor Organization. . . .

A class of workers given special consideration in the encyclical is the almost universally afflicted class of farmers. The Pope deplores the fact that so many workers leave the farm and immigrate to the city. While he lauds the moral and spiritual values of farming, especially in the family-type farm, he also notes the necessity for economic and social changes to make farming attractive and profitable.

There are numerous detailed suggestions, such as social insurance as a means for redistributing income in favor of farmers, price regulation, progressive taxation, credit unions and cooperatives, education and other means to increase efficiency of production, and even political action by farmers. Governments should see that roads, health services, educational facilities, and the like be such as to make rural living attractive to modern workers. . . .

Although the encyclical goes to great length in treating private property, the summary here will be comparatively brief. It is reported that there were divisions of opinion on this subject on the part of experts consulted by the Holy See. Undoubtedly some urged the view that property is no longer the main source of security in more developed nations. Pensions rights and social security are more important to many persons. Likewise the skill and experience of the worker are more productive for him than are property rights.

While these points are duly noted, the Pope insists upon the basic character of private property as the sound foundation of social order. He reiterates the insistence of Pope Pius XI that the social as well as the individual character of property be considered. And he makes his own the views of his immediate predecessor that an effective distribution of property is an imperative need. Thus understood, property is a source of freedom, initiative, and security. . . .

Many more points could be noted in commenting on *Mater et Magistra*.

The main point, and in this we rejoice, is that Catholic social thinkers now have clear and definite guidance, as well as warm inspiration, in facing the complex problems of the modern world.

CHAPTER 3

OWNERSHIP, PRIVATE AND PUBLIC

It is not enough to assert the natural character of the right of private property, including productive property; strenuous efforts also must be made to see that the ability to exercise this right is extended to all social classes.

In modern times there is an evident tendency toward a progressive transfer of property to the state or other agencies of public law. The explanation of this trend is to be found in the ever-widening activity which the common good obliges public authorities to undertake. But even in these circumstances the principle of subsidiarity is to be faithfully observed. Accordingly, the state and other agencies of public law should not extend their ownership except where evident and real needs of the common good dictate it.

Pope John XXIII in *Mater et Magistra*

In considering the ownership of productive property, it is helpful to distinguish between effective ownership and nominal ownership.

An effective owner may be defined as one who manages his property or actively supervises those who do. A nominal owner neither manages his holding nor exercises authority over its direction. Many farmers and most small businessmen are effective owners. Almost all corporate stockholders are nominal owners.

One of the most perplexing aspects of our capitalistic system is that only a small and dwindling minority of Americans are effective owners of productive property. Although a considerably larger minority are nominal owners, the vast majority of our people are wholly dependent for their livelihood on wages, salaries, and insurance payments of various kinds. They no longer associate their security exclusively, or even mainly, with ownership of productive property.

This development has led some Catholic social scientists to question the Church's insistence on widespread ownership as one of the chief answers to the "proletarian question." In *Rerum Novarum* Pope Leo deplored the division of society into a small capitalist class and a mass of propertyless workers. In insisting on a living wage, he held out the hope that workers would be able to save something and acquire a modest property. Both Pope Pius XI and Pope Pius XII reaffirmed this teaching, and even expanded it. They proposed that workers be encouraged and helped to acquire ownership in the businesses that employed them. Pope John weighed the arguments for deemphasizing ownership, found them not without merit, but concluded that they were not convincing. "Today, more than ever," he wrote in *Mater et Magistra*, "the wider distribution of private ownership ought to be forcefully championed."

In this country the trend is strongly against any expansion of effective ownership. The number of independent farmers continues to decline, and since 1940 the number of business firms, though growing in absolute terms, has barely kept pace with the growth in population. If there is to be any wider distribution of ownership of productive goods, it will have to take the form of nominal ownership. This strongly suggests the need of assisting the employees of big businesses — the dominant form of private enterprise in the United States — to acquire stock in the corporations that hire them. Although some progress has been made in this direction, it has been too small up till now to have had any significant effect on existing patterns of ownership.

None of this means that the average employed American has a proletarian mentality. The contrary is true. Besides his job, which he regards as a form of property, he more often than not owns the home in which he lives and possesses all the consumer durables — from refrigerators to automobiles — which are the badge of the middle class.

Mrs. Murphy's Property*

WILLIAM J. DAVIS, S.J.

Of the many witnesses to come before the Senate Commerce Committee, testifying against the public-accommodations section of the 1963 civil rights bill, perhaps none was more eloquent or forceful than

---

* From "Mrs. Murphy's Private Rights," *America*, October 19, 1963.

Governor Farris Bryant, of Florida. In a packed Senate Caucus Room, he told the Senators that he came "to argue the case for freedom."

Customers are free to trade where they please, but this civil rights bill would deny owners a like freedom. If a customer can walk into a store, look over the owner or the merchandise, and then decide not to buy, for any reason whatsoever, or even for no reason at all; if he can base his decision even on the looks of the storeowner — then "the owner of the property ought to have the same freedom." So runs the argument of Governor Bryant, and so runs the argument in the minds of many reasonable men who seem genuinely concerned about federal interference with the rights of property owners.

To resolve the apparent conflict between civil rights and property rights, it is necessary to take a second look at our traditional view of private property. Just what rights, for instance, does the now famous Mrs. Murphy have in the running of her boardinghouse?

For Mrs. Murphy, and for Americans generally, the right of ownership is an unassailable absolute. "I earned this property. It's mine. I can do with it as I please." Some such expression of absolute ownership, including use, rises spontaneously to the lips of most Americans. Even those who cannot justify this right philosophically know that it is somehow guaranteed as God-given and inalienable, and the presumption is one of absolute independence in the ownership of property. The defenders of Mrs. Murphy contend that she (or her family) built her establishment independently and that she therefore can expect to do as she pleases with it. They decry government interference as an infringement on her right to own and dispose of her property freely.

Their argument begins with the fact that this property was gained by private initiative. Was it really? Did the Murphys mill the boards that built it? Did they smelt the steel that fashioned the tools that drove the nails? While the building was under construction, who grew the wheat and ground the flour and ran the railroads and provided the thousand and one other services that the Murphys used? And even more fundamentally, who settled the land and built a society and maintained law and order, so that this building could be constructed? "Private" initiative, in any absolute sense, is a myth.

But if Mrs. Murphy could not originally acquire her boardinghouse without the aid of society, neither can she now maintain it "privately." How can she keep it safe from thieves? How can she be assured that the commodities she needs to run it will not skyrocket beyond her means through the action of monopolists? How can she be assured that the food she buys for her guests will not poison them? And finally, how can she be secure from those today who have sworn to "bury her"?

The point is obvious. The individualist's exaggerated view of private endeavor is one of the greatest hoaxes ever to slip into the stream of conventional wisdom. No one owns a boardinghouse, or anything else for that matter, without being in partnership with a tremendously complex, cooperating, interrelated organism known as society. Like it or not, we are interdependent. And if property cannot be gained independently or maintained independently, then neither can it be used in total independence.

To say that owners have the right to do whatever they please with their property, irrespective of society, is simply false. St. Thomas Aquinas, while defending the right to acquire private property, makes it very clear that this right does not carry with it the right of indiscriminate use. The disposal of private goods must be in accord with the primary destiny of all goods — service of man. As Ambrose Farrell, O.P., puts it: "Ownership of every kind is a stewardship carrying with it social obligations."

Traditionally, we have emphasized the fact that man's very nature demands a measure of independent ownership. But what we must bear in mind, while insisting on this "natural" right, is that man's nature is a social nature and demands a concern for society even in his ownership. It is not as though man has independent rights to which are added a few social riders. The fact is that the right itself is essentially colored by man's social nature.

The social character of private property, therefore, is not a sort of afterthought of only relative importance. It is of the very essence of private property. . . .

This is not to say, as Saint-Simon, Comte and their camp followers said, that society is the real owner of all property. Individuals are true owners, but society has a vested interest in their ownership. Especially those "private" businesses that draw constantly from the public must, in turn, recognize the rights of the public. If they do not, then public authority must intervene.

Some might object that government intervention is bad. In a sense it is; it's *too* bad. In fact, in a sense it is tragic, because it is an indication that we as individuals have not recognized and fulfilled our social obligations. Because of our failure, government intervention becomes necessary and its desirability is no longer the question. And if there is danger involved (as there admittedly is) in such intervention, we have no one to blame but ourselves for failing to act on the individual or local level. . . .

Exaggerated individualism has traditionally blasted all social reforms with bromides about freedom from interference, private rights, private initiative, and creeping socialism. But the ironic truth is that no one makes social reforms more necessary than does the individualist. Numerous social problems calling for government regulation are the direct result of his laissez-faire principles. Granted, for instance, that I can do as I please with my property, then naturally enough I can shift the location of my plant without regard to employee dislocation; I can hire and fire without regard for collective bargaining; I can engage in rack-renting, in real-estate speculation, and in a host of other activities that result in social harm. Discrimination against Negroes caps a long list of abuses resulting from the liberalist view of "the sanctity of private property."

In fact, even the various forms of collectivism, which the individualists so universally fear, frequently follow from this same false premise of the absolute nature of private property. Given the assumption that ownership carries with it the right to use things as the owner pleases, then the only way to correct misuse is by a change of ownership. And so the various collectivist systems conclude that the state must become sole owner if society is to benefit properly from material wealth. . . .

In correcting abuses, however, we must not make the mistake of the collectivists. Government intervention must itself be controlled by strict limits. The day will never come when the right to ownership will be justly absorbed by the state. It will remain as long as man is man. The forms that ownership takes may need constant readjustment by social authority to bring them in line with their essential purpose, but that authority cannot swallow up the basic right.

Obviously, if individuals and lesser organizations realize their responsibilities, the state need not and ought not to step in; but when we on the lower level fail, then it is the responsibility of the government to see to it that community rights are not trampled on by individuals. In *Quadragesimo Anno* Pius XI insisted, while reiterating the warning to leave to subordinate groups as broad a control as possible, that public authority has not only the right but the duty to make adjustments in the matter of ownership. His words bear quoting at length:

> It follows from what We have termed the individual and at the same time social character of ownership that men must consider in this matter not

only their own advantage but also the common good. To define these duties in detail when necessity requires and the natural law has not done so is the function of those in charge of the state. Therefore public authority, under the guiding light always of the natural and divine law, can determine more accurately, upon consideration of the true requirements of the common good, what is permitted and what is not permitted to owners in the use of their property. (N. 49)

A Catholic can hardly deny the right of the state to intervene in the use of property for the common good, as indeed the state already does by a number of accepted practices, such as lawsuits to redress injuries, zoning laws, and eminent domain.

The attitude we should take toward such intervention was well expressed by Mayor Ivan Allen Jr., of Atlanta, Georgia, testifying before the Senate Commerce Committee in favor of the civil rights bill. Asked about federal intrusion into businesses in his city, he replied that such government actions as child-labor laws, certain labor laws themselves, wage-and-hour acts, and the like can hardly be considered "intrusions" since, for the most part, they have been "for the benefit of most of the people of the country."

Finally — and this question brings us back to Mrs. Murphy — when should the government act? Obviously, too much government interference will create more evils than it corrects; but too little is equally harmful. When the state moves, it must keep all aspects of the common good in mind. Property has a social aspect, but it also has a private aspect. The state must preserve both. When a business is small and relatively more private, as we will presume is the case with the Murphy boardinghouse, the state should not interfere directly, even though Mrs. Murphy may be unjustly drawing profit from the public without realizing her social obligations to that public. But in the case of those businesses that substantially affect the common good, the state can and should interfere whenever there is serious abuse. . . .

In conclusion, therefore, let me return to the problem posed by Governor Bryant. He has shrewdly appraised the civil rights issue as a struggle "between conflicting demands for freedom." But are the demands for freedom equally justified on both sides, or are owners demanding freedoms that were never theirs? Those who make private property an unassailable absolute stretch property rights beyond reason. And if they have their way, they will not only destroy an important civil rights bill; they will strip social authority of the very possibility of effective reform.

There is no solution to "the conflicting demands for freedom" if we accept the individualist assumptions about the nature of ownership. The solution Governor Bryant suggests — to allow the owners the freedom to continue to make errors — is intolerable when so large a portion of the public, indeed, when the whole nation, is suffering from those errors. The Communist or Socialist solution — to make the state the sole owner — is likewise intolerable in view of man's nature. This conflict can be resolved only by admitting that our right of ownership bears within it social responsibilities which should be promoted by the reasonable, controlled, and limited intervention of social authority.

Public Ownership*

LEWIS WATT, S.J.

In the matter of ownership, every Catholic moralist would maintain, with Leo XIII and Pius XII, that the right to private property is fundamental to every just economic and social order, and that the Christian conscience must condemn as unjust any social order which either explicitly denies the natural right of private ownership of means of production as well as of consumption goods, or in practice prevents the citizens from exercising that right. Not only is it a stimulus to effort and enterprise if personal industry is rewarded by private ownership, but in this way there is secured to the citizen that independence which he requires in order to fulfill the moral responsibilities which God imposes upon him.

So far the most extreme individualist would find no cause for disagreement; but of course that is not the whole of the Catholic doctrine about property. To avoid misunderstanding, Pius XI in *Quadragesimo Anno* insisted strongly on the fact that the institution of private property has a social as well as an individual aspect; that its natural purpose in the designs of God is not merely to enable those who, in one way or another, have become property-owners to support themselves and their dependents and to develop their natural capacities, but also to benefit the community as a whole. That is why the state is charged with the duty of ensuring that the property-system does not operate to the detriment of society, and of so adapting it to contemporary social conditions

* From "Pope Pius XII on Nationalization," *Month*, September, 1947. Also in *Catholic Mind*, March, 1948.

that it gives the maximum of advantages to the citizens as individuals and as a society. This well-established Catholic principle has been more than once reiterated by Pius XII. . . .

In his world broadcast at Whitsun, 1941, he said that the system of private property (which, of course, includes private trading, gifts *inter vivos*, and succession) ought to be regulated by public authority with a view to enabling the institution to achieve its natural purpose; and he makes the important point that the economic prosperity of a country cannot be correctly measured unless account is taken of the degree to which wealth is diffused among the citizens. Broadcasting at Christmas, 1942, he again referred to laws about property:

> The laws (of the state) regulating private property may change, and may grant a more or less restricted use of it; but if such provisions are to contribute to social peace they must protect the worker from a condition of economic dependence and servitude irreconcilable with his rights as a person. Whether this servitude is imposed by the might of private capital or by the power of the state makes no difference to its results. Indeed, under the oppression of a state which dominates everything and regulates the whole of public and private life, forcing itself even into the domain of ideas and beliefs and of conscience, this loss of freedom can have even greater consequences, as experience proves.

The allusion to totalitarian systems is unmistakable. Later he said:

> The dignity of labor demands not only a just wage, sufficient for the needs of the worker and his family, but also the preservation and improvement of a social order in which all classes can attain to the secure ownership of at least a modest amount of property.

The Papal emphasis on the worker's right to property, both here and in the social encyclicals, is no doubt chiefly due to the fact that the Church considers the existence of a propertyless proletariat a grievous disorder in modern societies; but it also serves as a reminder that her defense of the right of private ownership does not mean that she stands in the ranks of the "haves" against the "have-nots."

This was particularly clearly expressed in the famous broadcast of September 1, 1944. After rejecting as obviously incompatible with the Christian conscience any social system which is founded upon the denial of the right of private property, or in practice nullifies it, Pius XII brought under the same condemnation systems which, while nominally recognizing the right, are based upon a totally false idea of what it really is. If, for instance, by "capitalism" is meant a system which concedes to capitalists an unlimited right to do what they like with property, irrespective of the welfare of the community, then that system is condemned by the Church.

Having said this, the Pope describes in three trenchant paragraphs the main abuses of the modern property-system: excessive concentration of economic goods accompanied by the quasi-impossibility for the worker of acquiring *effective* property of his own, the gradual elimination of small and medium ownership, the economic and political domination of immense wealth and the resultant development of a multitude of people without secure means of living, without genuine interest in the things of the spirit, no longer aspiring after true freedom, ready to hand themselves over to any political party which promises food and tranquillity. . . .

It is quite evident that Pius XII was fully awake to economic and social developments, and that nothing could be more mistaken than to think of him as merely repeating, in an unenlightened sort of way, that private property is a natural right. Social institutions necessarily partake of the general mutability of human affairs, and, as Pius XI once remarked, even those we are accustomed to regard as completely fixed and static change substantially, for better or worse, in the course of centuries.

History, he observed, confirms what reason teaches us: that nothing human is immutable. The form of family life, the constitutions of nations, the organization of industry, the methods of production, the system of private property, all undergo changes. We must face this mutability of human institutions with equanimity, went on Pius XI, and prepare for it with enlightened insight.

Pius XII took the lead in this task. In that striking broadcast of September 1, 1944, the Pope warned the world that future social and economic policy could not long succeed in developing the true fruitfulness of social life and the normal productivity of the national economy if it failed "to respect and protect the vital function of private property in its personal and social value." What that means is more fully explained by his earlier statement that, in the designs of God, private property ought to be an element of social order, a stimulus to initiative and industry for the purposes of this life and of the next, an instrument of human freedom and dignity. These are the essentials of any sound property-system, and, as we have seen, they postulate a wide distribution of ownership.

When the actual distribution is such as to be an obstacle to them (and we have already seen what the Pope thinks of distribution of property in modern society), it is for the state, in the interests of the common welfare, to intervene. It should protect and encourage small and medium ownership in agriculture, in the various crafts, in commerce and industry, and cooperative unions should be set up to secure the advantages of large-scale enterprise. The Pope takes into account the fact that sometimes large-scale enterprise may be manifestly more productive than these other forms of organization, and in such cases recommends (as *Quadragesimo Anno* did) that the wage-contract be combined, so far as practicable, with some kind of partnership agreement, a suggestion likely to meet with greater favor now than before the War.

It is at this point in the broadcast that we meet with a brief reference to nationalization. If concentration of wealth is such as to nullify the benefits which the institution of private property should ensure, the state, failing the practicability of less drastic remedies, can proceed to expropriation, paying appropriate compensation. It is clear that the Pope does not mean "expropriation of all private owners," or even "of all owners of capital," because he advocates a better distribution of private property, not its abolition. Expropriation is merely a weapon to be used by the state in the last resort when some great concentration of capital blocks the way to just distribution. . . .

A further opportunity was afforded to the Pope of giving his views about nationalization when the Italian Workers' Association held a congress in Rome in March, 1945. He received in audience a delegation from it on March 11, and in an address laid down the Catholic principles which they should follow. Speaking of "what is today called the nationalization or socialization of industry (*azienda*)," he stated the conditions necessary to justify it. It can be accepted by Catholics only in cases where it is seen to be really necessary for the general welfare; which is to say, when it is the only really effective method of remedying some abuse or of avoiding a wastage of the nation's productive forces, and of ensuring that they are coordinated and directed to the advantage of the national economic interest. The purpose must be the regular and peaceful development of the national economy in order to promote the material prosperity of the entire people, a prosperity such as will be a sound basis of cultural and religious life. . . .

On July 10, 1946, Pius XII sent a letter to M. Charles Flory, the President of the *Semaines Sociales de France*, which appears to have caused in France more surprise and discussion than one would have expected, in view of his statement to the Italian Workers' Association just quoted and available to anyone in the official journal of the Holy See, *Acta Apostolicae Sedis* (1946: p. 315). "The letter has provoked, particularly in France, lively commentaries of differing interpretations. Through these it was easy to see the play of political parties and political speculations which, distorting the Pope's teaching, accused him, *inter alia*, of condemning the nationalization of enterprises outright and as such." So wrote the *Osservatore Romano* in a leading article on September 27, 1946, which proceeded to quote with approval the long explanation of the Papal letter by A. de Marco, S.J., in the *Civiltà Cattolica* of September 7, thus giving that explanation a semiofficial character. . . .

The *Civiltà Cattolica* article states that "according to the social thought of the Church, and this must be emphasized, the nationalization of enterprises is, in particular instances, not only licit but also opportune, and hence a suitable policy to be put into effect," and it cites the address to the Italian Workers in March, 1945. In other words, it continues, according to the Church, nationalization is one of the means, but neither the only nor the primary means, at the disposal of the state for the purpose of ensuring that productive property fulfills its social function and serves the public welfare. Recourse must be had to it *if and insofar as* other means, less radical and violent, have been shown by experience to be insufficient, in any particular case, to secure the effective subordination of private property to the national interests and to the just distribution of the products of industry.

Nationalization is appropriate in the case of an industry which, by its monopolistic character or by the nature of its product, is an instrument of exploitation in the hands of the private capitalist or in some way imparts to the whole productive system a direction contrary to the general welfare. As possible instances, the article mentions the big banks, transport, armament manufacture, some branches of the chemical industry, and others which, in given circumstances, are of particular national importance or resist the demands of public welfare. On the other hand, the mere fact that the state has the duty of exercising control over the production and distribution of wealth is not sufficient to justify nationalization of an industry, either morally or economically. The state has various other methods of performing its duty, such as fiscal policy, part-ownership of share-capital by the state, control over financial operations (*la disciplina dei finanziermenti*), legislation for the workers to share in profits and management so far as this can be done without prejudice to industrial efficiency.

Even when nationalization is morally legitimate, the article continues, it is not without its disadvantages. These may be outweighed by considerations of the public interest, but they do exist nonetheless. In large-scale modern industries the worker is a cog in the productive machine, and, we may add, the growing importance of personnel managers is a clear sign that employers are coming to realize the need for countering the depersonalization of the great mass of employees. Nationalization of an industry tends to increase this depersonalization because, no matter how fervently they are assured that the factory, mine, railway, and so on, where they work belongs to the nation, employees know, or soon discover, that their employer is the state, that abstract and impersonal reality, armed not only with economic power, but with political power, too. They become, to a certain extent, militarized. . . .

In view of this authoritative article it would be quite unjustifiable to interpret the Papal letter to M. Flory as an outright condemnation of all nationalization of property, even if the letter itself, with its phrase, "even when morally licit," were not clear enough to any careful reader, as it certainly is. The letter is obviously not to the taste of those who maintain that nationalization of an industry can do nothing but good; and still less is it acceptable to those who would like to see the state extend its ownership and control of the means of production, distribution, and exchange as fast and as far as possible, i.e., to collectivists. . . .

The Pope has, then, made the Catholic attitude toward the nationalization of enterprises quite clear. Like his predecessors, he firmly rejects the idea that there is something antisocial about the private ownership of any means of production, with the logical corollary that the state should take over the whole, or the greater part, of industry. . . .

Yet it must be stressed that the Pope fully recognizes that nationalization may sometimes be necessary to avert worse things. It is not for him to decide whether the actual circumstances of any particular country are such as to justify the expropriation (with compensation) of private capitalists, or what the precise amount or the form of compensation should be. There may well be room for differences of opinion among Catholics as to whether or not proposals for the nationalization of this or that industry (including the compensation to be paid) comply with the moral principles set out by the Pope. But all will agree that the organization of a nationalized industry ought to be such as to enable all engaged in it to feel that they are cooperating as intelligent persons and free men, and not as mere servants of the state. It would be fatal to the hopes of a better social order to acquiesce in the idea that the mere fact of nationalization will introduce justice and charity into an industry, or into its relations with other industries and the community at large.

Development of Natural Resources*

MARK J. FITZGERALD, C.S.C.

Throughout history the standard of living for any country has invariably depended on the natural resources available, in addition of course to the ingenuity and application of its people. The written record of man on earth goes back about sixty-two centuries. In all save the last century and one-half of that time industrial power has been supplied by man or beast. Now we are in a position where in our country fossil fuels and hydropower provide over ninety percent of the energy used in production. Moreover, technological developments in the last decade or two have increasingly placed tremendous demands on our natural resources to supply the needs of new industries relating to electronics, synthetic fibers, jet propulsion, and high speed fuels. In view of all these circumstances, normal prudence should warrant a careful appraisal of our resource situation as we move further into the second half of the twentieth century. . . .

Oddly enough the mineral we consider to be in most abundance may be at the top of the critical list of resources. It is true that on an overall basis the United States has enough water to assure indefinitely an increasing standard of living for its citizens. The practical difficulty turns on the geographical aspects and the availability for particular uses. So intense have these factors become in recent years that this resource, frequently taken for granted, is gradually becoming a national problem of awesome proportions.

With the prospect of rising population and greatly intensified demands for water because of industrial developments, underground water tables in most sections of the country are falling to lower levels. The seriousness of this decline becomes apparent when it is realized that underground sources provide the water for springs and wells, which perhaps serve fifty

---

* From "Natural Resources and Public Policy," *Review of Social Economy*, March, 1958.

to seventy-five percent of the population, both for domestic needs and on a growing scale for irrigation.

The arid states of the Western plains form only one area confronted with the dropping water table. The problem extends from Maryland and Virginia right across the Southern states. It is apparent now in southern Illinois, and has a serious aspect west of Mississippi and Missouri. There is uneasy realization at last that underground storage of water represents perhaps the total rainfall of only a half century and therefore is subject to exhaustion or to such declines in levels under intense use as to become practically unattainable. . . .

Contamination of rivers and streams by industries and cities is a serious cause of reduction in the supply of usable water. Moreover, it endangers national health, and gravely disturbs the natural economy that exists for water, soil, forests, and wildlife. Application of treatment processes to meet this hazard, while increasing absolutely, is failing to match the growing scope of the problem. Farmers and stockmen incur enormous loss each year, not only from the harm to cattle which drink such water, but from the financial outlay necessary to secure safe water for livestock. Even otherwise desirable industrial locations are rejected because upstream cities or plants have made the water supply at lower river points unfit for industrial use. If pollution of waterways continues in this unregulated fashion, the toll exacted of public health, land values, and outdoor recreation will be very great indeed. . . .

There is cause for concern that the quantities of copper, lead, zinc, and oil we have taken from the ground in the past half century are decidedly greater than present known reserves. In Michigan today the copper mines are a mile below the surface and they are regarded as the deepest throughout the world. Obviously at this depth, such copper mines make poor competition for low-cost districts in other areas.

Our natural gas supply, presently being extracted on a huge scale from the chief concentration in the Southwest, is commonly regarded as seriously limited and it may be the scarcest of all our major sources of energy. In ten or fifteen years the production of oil in the United States may begin to decline and there is fear that . . . the world production of oil will fall behind the demand for it. Interestingly enough, the diesel engine has tended to lighten the use of our enormous coal deposits while it greatly increases the drain on our much more restricted oil reserves.

One of the most precious resources is topsoil. Yet a solid hundred million acres of cropland have been made unfit for further cultivation.

Again, another hundred million acres have been subjected to various degrees of damage. The significance of this vast area becomes apparent when we consider that originally in this country there were about 500 million acres adaptable for growing foodstuffs. Combining both the ruined and damaged acreage, we have an area larger than the states of Ohio, Indiana, Illinois, Wisconsin, and Missouri. Unfortunately, each year we add 400,000 more acres to the hundred million spoiled for cultivation. Though man can rejuvenate topsoil, only nature can produce it and perhaps at a rate of less than one inch every five hundred years.

In the face of our mounting population and the rapidly rising need for natural resources, we should heed the warning that the fastest way to get a shortage is "to let the land go down." Destruction of the sod by unjustified plowing has been the fate for millions of acres, especially in the drier grass country. Though profitable cultivation was not possible there, the soil was exploited nevertheless. In many areas the land has been literally mined of its resources by overgrazing of cattle and by wanton overdraughts on declining underground water basins. Reckless deforestation has made disaster areas of a number of our watersheds by increasing the hazards from floods and soil erosion. Each day mountain-size quantities of eroded topsoil flow into the Mississippi delta because of our wasteful land practices over the years. . . .

After years of wasteful cutting, projected estimates for timber needs are now disturbingly in excess of our capacity to meet them. Using the lowest reasonable estimates, our forests will face in 1976 a demand of twenty-seven percent beyond that of 1952, and seventy-three percent more by the year 2000. Already, timber items which as late of 1939 were in substantial domestic surplus are now in deficit and therefore must be partly imported. As a consequence we have become the world's greatest importer of timber products. . . .

Despite this timber scarcity, wasteful cutting practices are still in use. A direct loss of one-fourth of the timber occurs in initial logging operations. At the lowest calculation only about thirty-seven percent of the original forest product meets the intended purpose. Further, there are millions of acres near the Great Lakes of once abundant timber country which have remained partially or entirely unproductive since the earlier onslaught of timber cutting. One finds it hard to understand why deforested states east of the Great Plains continue to spend millions of dollars annually for timber imports while a vast acreage of idle and eroding hill country in those states remains unused for timber growth and is a dangerously unsolved economic problem in land use.

We might well reflect on some of the comments by men who have devoted years to studying the problems of our natural resources. One such observer has stated that we are responsible for the greatest destructive exploitation of natural resources that the world has ever experienced, and, as is our wont, we have performed the feat in the shortest space of time.

There are serious grounds for us to ask what the posterity of this nation will think of our resource practices when the United States becomes as old as the present Britain, Italy, or France. Already there are tragedies of stewardship confronting us. Besides the gutted timber land of the Great Lakes states, we have a dozen dust bowls, and 500 polluted rivers. Many natural resources have a definite limit and can be depleted with dreadful finality. Present abundance is no rational basis for indifference and recklessness toward the future security of our natural wealth.

Only in recent decades has the realization come that the imposing achievements of the private enterprise system may encounter future reverses because of disregard for basic natural assets. The laws of nature do not adjust themselves to the so-called laws attributed to market economics based on a quick profit in the short run. Nevertheless, proposals for long-range conservation of resources frequently are met with the question of how much additional profit will accrue to owners of land by the adoption of such measures. There is a tendency to forget that natural resources are for the well-being of all society, and their present owners have an obligation to use them with as little waste as possible.

Strangely enough, despite this obvious relation of cause and effect, some people even today view remedial restrictions on land as "morally repulsive." On the contrary, a sturdy sense of stewardship may well hold such a negative attitude as unjustified when we recall that our soil has been subjected for decades to torture and wastage on a shocking scale, with few serious governmental restraints. A more responsible approach might come to bear if there were deeper realization that true economic wealth is in the land rather than in any monetary form. . . .

Notable cooperation has come from industry in several areas towards combating the problem of renovating our rivers. Some oil refineries have adopted processes of purification which return water to rivers and lakes in a cleaner condition than when it was originally pumped out. With industrial leadership and support, the Raritan River in Northern New Jersey will soon run clean again after a half century. Extensive purification plants and sanitary construction both by municipalities and industries are under way along the river's entire course. The renovated Schuykill River is already bringing returns in the form of an economical water supply for municipalities all along its path.

The slow progress of conservation should not provoke too much surprise since conservation in this country can only be traced back about two generations. Yet in sheer self-defense as a nation we cannot afford to let unregulated private use frustrate or make impossible long-range public service use of our resources. The real struggle here is not between federal and state jurisdictions, but between the public interest and short-run selfish advantage, which remains persistent and powerful. In the balance is a whole gamut of priceless goals: the security of watersheds, the control of stream flow, the regulation of erosion, and the preservavation of the life-giving layer of topsoil upon which our whole economy depends. These goals recognize that the title of ownership does not carry with it the absolute right to exploit natural resources in a manner injurious to the welfare of society. . . .

The unwelcome truth, so far as we view the national picture of resource conservation, is that all too little is being done to change men from miners of soil into faithful stewards of the land. Coordinated comprehensive programs for conservation of natural resources will not flourish unless the public becomes increasingly aware of the problem by thorough presentation of the profound issues at stake.

CHAPTER 4

WORK AND ITS REWARD

The principles expounded by Pope Leo XIII first and foremost concern work, which ought to be valued and treated not just as a commodity but as something that bears the stamp of a human person. For the great majority of men, work is the only source of livelihood. Thus, the question of fixing a wage for labor cannot be left to the mechanical play of market forces. It must be determined by standards of justice and equity.

It follows [also] that if the organization and operation of an economic system are such as to compromise the human dignity of those who engage in it, or to blunt their sense of responsibility, or to impede the exercise of personal initiative, such an economic system is unjust.

Pope John XXIII in *Mater et Magistra*

The American labor market is one of the most perplexing phenomena of our times.

More people are gainfully employed than ever before. They are earning more money and working in better conditions than anyone thought possible even a quarter-century ago. Yet, despite the vast growth in production and employment since World War II, the economy has not been able to provide jobs for all those able and willing to work.

This has been notably true of younger workers. As a consequence of the high birth rates that prevailed after World War II, an extraordinary number of young people have entered the labor market in the 1960's. Many of them have been unable to find work. Whereas the overall jobless rate in recent years has been between five and six percent of the labor force, for teen-agers it has been more than twice as high.

Meanwhile the number of women workers has grown spectacularly. They are now a third of the labor force. More than half of them are married, and nearly two-thirds are thirty-five years of age or over.

In another important respect also the composition of the labor force has changed. Ever since the turn of the century white-collar jobs have been increasing faster than jobs in general. By 1956 the number of white-collar workers had come to exceed the number of blue-collar workers, and the margin is growing. The spread of automation has contributed to this trend.

The economic and cultural implications of all these changes and the problems they are spawning have become the subject of much study and considerable controversy. Is technological progress, embracing everything loosely summed up in the word "automation," mainly responsible for today's unemployment? What weight should be given to economic growth, to education and training, to area redevelopment, to increased labor mobility as solutions to joblessness? Have we reached the point in technical proficiency where working hours must be reduced in order to accommodate all who want to work? If so, what challenges will increased leisure present? Will women continue to be attracted in great numbers to the labor force? Is a new pattern of family life emerging? Finally, must the traditional imperative of a family living wage be sought in part outside the wage system?

In the world of work, questions come easily to mind. The answers are harder to find.

Christian Concept of Work*

GIACOMO CARDINAL LERCARO

Before giving the Christian concept of labor based on divine revelation, I shall touch briefly on certain secular concepts. The contrast should help clarify Christian teaching.

The nineteenth-century "liberal" current divorces morality from economics and makes economics autonomous. Economic gain is the sole judge of productive activities; work is only a piece of merchandise. It has a price, is bought and sold and contracted for, like anything else on the market.

In this theory, labor is dehumanized and looked at in terms of crude commercial value. The capitalist sees it solely as a means of enrichment;

---

* From "To Christianize Labor," *Aggiornamenti Sociali*, June, 1961. Also, in English translation, in *Catholic Mind*, February, 1962.

the employee solely as his means of survival, his way of obtaining his daily bread. Such a dehumanization of labor creates a state of slavery. True, this is a modern slavery, without chains or lashes, but it is no less destructive of the human person.

Parallel to this concept of "labor-merchandise" is the view of those who uphold technocracy as a way of life and see labor only under its productive aspect. In this theory, too, every thought of the worker's person or his human needs simply disappears. Only one thing matters: *maximum production*, and to this the whole organization of business is geared.

Evidently, though these two views start from different presuppositions, they come down to one thing: a materialistic concept of life. Economics without morality and the primacy of technology are the expressions of a fundamentally materialistic mentality. . . .

These secular concepts of labor are not only theoretically stated; they are put in practice and have created two worlds of labor — the capitalistic and the communistic, opposite, yet converging in their materialistic premise. Their common consequence is the devaluation of man's dignity. . . .

The Christian concept of labor arises from the nature of man, who is God's creature, destined by Him to enjoy one day the very happiness of God.

Even in the natural order, man is superior to other things, being created to subdue and subject them to himself. He cannot be made their slave. In turn, man is naturally directed toward God, His knowledge, His praise, His service. Hence, far from debasing man, work elevates him, makes him free, and gives all his activities an intrinsic dignity.

The fact that man is elevated to the supernatural life of grace does not destroy, but elevates, this profound natural reality.

In the framework of this view of man, Christian teaching interprets labor as first of all a human activity. . . .

As a human activity, labor becomes a means of perfecting man through the development of his God-given energies and capacities. "There is need for labor," says LaPira, "because the human being is so structured that he cannot develop or reach his perfection without labor." The precept to labor bound man even in the earthly paradise, when nature obeyed man and offered him well-being. "The Lord God," says Genesis (2:15), "took man and placed him in the garden of Eden to till and keep it."

Man's intelligence, will, and physical power were to find their full development in the conquest of this wondrous kingdom assigned by God to man. Man was to achieve the joy of discovering more and more clearly the imprint of God on things and the image of God in himself.

This aspect of labor did not cease after sin had damaged the divine plan, even though after that labor took on a painful note, and created things became hostile to man and his work. Though tiring and often arduous and monotonous, work still has its happy function of perfecting man. . . .

It is the task of the Christian conscience to overcome all ideas that tend to brutalize labor and to alleviate as much as possible the need for work that is too monotonous or too uninteresting.

As Pope Pius XII said (March 27, 1948), to workers, "The most antihuman and antisocial tactic is to make work hateful. Work does often involve fatigue, even harsh, painful fatigue. But in itself it is beautiful and ennobling, since it furthers the work begun by the Creator by producing."

These words of Pius XII introduce us to another aspect of work: labor as the developing of God's creation, the perfecting of matter brought to the useful service of man and his needs.

Here we should stress the meaning of the divine plan. It offers man the means of life, much as it offers man the means of grace. But for both life and grace, man's collaboration is called for. This gives man an enrichment of life and of merit. . . .

The Creator is seen as ever greater in the vastness and variety of His works, in the wisdom of the laws that rule them. Moreover, His goodness appears ever greater in the very profusion of creation, which man investigates and discovers and makes useful by his own work. Labor is thus a cooperation with the Creator. By it, the work of God comes into closer and more profitable contact with man, new levels of reality are discovered (new continents, for example, and new space) as well as new energies (heat, electricity, nuclear energy), and new means are found to make such energies useful to man and subject to his service.

This is not to say, of course, that man's work makes something out of nothing; however, it does bring into evidence realities which were equivalently nonexistent for man before the intervention of human work. . . .

Fulfilling the conditions by which each one can lead a truly human life should be the task of everyone. Indeed, how much each of us owes others in his inheritance of knowledge, of conveniences, of the goods by which we live, the clothes we wear, the house we live in, the train we travel in, and the like. Everything around us is a gift, a service of others done for us. Each of us can give some service and each of us has the right and duty to do so. . . .

Even if this is done anonymously, is this not a noble form of love? Thus we see labor as a service given to our brothers. Our Lord has said that the love of the Christian must ever be modeled on His own love: "Love one another as I have loved you." This is the very commandment that He called "His own" — the "new commandment."

But how did He love us? "The Son of man came not to be served but to serve," he asserted. The Church has not hesitated to condemn those who assert that manual labor is incompatible with the life of perfection.

But the religious nobility of labor is put in a new light by Christian teaching when we see it inserted into the plan of the Redemption. We can say, in perfect truth, that labor has the mark of sacrifice — or rather, it ought to have when it is understood in a Christian way.

We realize this when we remember that the Word of God, having taken on our flesh and having been offered from His conception as a victim of praise and of expiation to the infinite majesty of the Father, wished, even before His members were nailed to the altar of the Cross, to sacrifice them in daily fatigue and humble work. Before pouring out His blood, He poured out His sweat for us.

Work has, because of man's sin, an expiatory character of sacrifice. By the loss of grace, the harmony of man's faculties was lost as well as the spontaneous submission of other things to man. This involved a rebellion of the lower faculties against the higher, of all things against man. Labor — the transformation of things — thus became a duty of sacrifice and sorrow. . . . From the day of man's fall, the earth ceased revealing its secrets to him. . . .

Thus, labor normally has a note of expiation in the fatigue that accompanies it. But when this is understood and accepted, it can be linked with the sacrifice of Christ.

However, this sacrifice implies the praise of God, too. For it is the completion of creation, the development and use of God's gifts in us and about us. . . .

We need to reflect and deepen our realization that human work contributes to the reestablishment of that first harmony of things, of that primeval order, by eliminating distress, achieving the submission of nature, tempering the forms of human suffering and sorrow. This will, of course, not bring paradise back to earth. But it will help lessen the disorders in things.

All this, after man's fall, is done only by sacrifice. As the Redemption of Christ was worked by the Cross and the offering of blood, so the redemption of the subhuman world — the completion of the human Redemption — will be done in suffering, "in the sweat of your brow."

Thus labor is understood both as the joyous expansiveness of mankind, the happy conquest of riches and treasures of nature, and as a painful and harsh sacrifice directed to resubjecting subhuman reality to the service of man. In fact, labor has both aspects: the first, joyous, comes from nature and is the work of the Creator; the second, painful, comes from sin and its consequences.

If we stress exclusively one or the other aspect, we lapse into error. The classical world saw labor only as suffering, and considered it unworthy of a free man. The stress of the ancient philosophers, like Plato and Aristotle, was on the supremacy of wisdom rather than on work. Labor remained in a lower order, at the service of the wise man.

It was Jesus the Worker — the Son of the carpenter — who established the principle of the dignity of work. . . . The Christian knows that labor is both a joy and a hard reconquest. To him, it is a cooperation with God's creation, but also an expiation and sacrifice. But it is a fruitful sacrifice, so long as man is inspired by Christ and united with the sacrifice of Christ.

Automation Arrives*

BERNARD J. OFFERMAN

The stages of technological development, usually termed the mechanization and mass-production phases, spanned the period from the simple hand-tool era to the familiar integrated mass-production industries of today. Mechanization through the application of power involved the extension of man's skills to the capacity of machinery. Mass production evolved later as a method of organizing production for increased efficiency.

Automation, on the other hand, takes men away from the machines and the assembly lines. Electronic sensing devices are replacing human effort and judgment, either eliminating or greatly reducing the direct application of human energy, skill, intelligence, and control. These self-

---

* From "Present Solutions Only Cushion the Job-effect Left by Automation," *Social Order*, December, 1963.

correcting mechanisms require only initial starting, periodic maintenance and repair, and sporadic adjustment. Developments such as these comprise the revolutionary aspect of automation.

The category of jobs most seriously affected by automation are the traditional production or operative positions — machine tending, material handling, routine machine work, and processing jobs. It is in these areas chiefly that the work force is being severely reduced.

At the same time, a smaller number of essentially different jobs requiring distinctly new and higher skills are being created. Equipment designing, maintenance, repair, production scheduling, coordination of highly integrated mechanisms, systems analysis, programing, and engineering are occupations now reflecting either entirely new job classifications or more refined developments of traditional jobs.

There are also upgrading and increased complexity in the job classifications that are retained. Through the integration of separate processes, the lines of jurisdiction among the old recognized trades are becoming blurred. Various skills are being combined in broader and more complicated job classifications. For example, the work done by die workers, machine repairmen, millwrights, welders, pipe fitters, tin-smiths, and hydraulic specialists may be absorbed into one key classification. Many of the skills formerly required in these occupations are exercised through the new mechanisms, but these in turn require the supervisory understanding and control of specially trained operators.

It seems that the unskilled and semiskilled occupations will largely disappear through "silent firing" (nonreplacement of retiring personnel), layoff, and the upgrading to skilled positions. It should also be noted that the potential for automation is even greater in the office than in the factory. Electronic computers and related equipment now performing routine office operations will eventually be further developed to serve as fundamental tools for gathering data for managerial decision, communication, and control.

Automation has greatly enhanced the value of the capital investment in equipment and makes the economic decisions of a company more crucial. Commitments of funds are so large that company planning and execution have to be highly rational.

Automation itself aids in the decision process by making available an increased quantity and a higher quality of information. This fact, along with the speed with which data are obtained, promotes efficiency and wisdom in managerial decisions.

Production in the aggregate and per man-hour is enormously increased. The great boost in productivity is due not only to the greater efficiency and capacity of the servomechanism but also to less obvious factors — reduced downtime, a continuous operation of plants, uniformity of product, and the removal of the human variable from the scene.

The economic framework within which automation must be approached today is not a very encouraging one. While total employment is at the highest level in history, unemployment, since the late 1950's, has been persistently high. . . .

Automation erodes over 300,000 jobs each year. But this figure does not tell the whole story. Many other jobs disappear as an indirect result.

A third fact to consider is that each year over one and a half million young men and women are joining the work force. This figure is climbing steadily, and it is estimated that during the ten-year period ending in 1970 some twenty-six million people will have entered the labor market.

The startling increases in labor productivity in recent years contributes further to the uncertain employment picture of the future. All these factors clearly illustrate the pressing nature of the unemployment problem.

Many of the solutions proposed to solve the problems occasioned by automation have been directed at lessening its harmful effects. Until recently this approach has been emphasized in most government and union programs.

Retraining of workers whose skills have become obsolete, broadening of seniority units, preferential hiring of displaced workers, negotiation of new job classifications, efforts to increase the mobility of labor, and various types of compensation for hardships attendant on technological change are halfway measures that have succeeded in affording the worker only patchwork protection. They merely help to forestall or at best cushion the more harmful effects. Unfortunately, they are not solutions to the basic problem — not even in the short run.

The key task, then, confronting us today is to discover ways to offset or at least mitigate the problems attending technological changes. Only in this way will we be able to look toward an increasingly automated future with any measure of confidence and optimism. . . .

Automation: The Human Element*

L. C. McHUGH, S.J.

Too much of our reaction to the erosive effects of automation on human values is concerned with partial and limited solutions. We ought also to be doing the bedrock thinking and planning that are needed for our future, if a runaway technology is not to become an ever-recurring threat to human welfare. Perhaps our sociologists, ethicians, and theologians should be working hard to elaborate a good theory on the essential nature of technology and its basic functions in relation to man's own nature and destiny. For if man could rightly comprehend the promise and the threat of technology to man's vocation on earth, perhaps labor and management, and public and government, as well as scientists themselves, could develop the proper guidelines for its use and control.

A modest starting point for such a view on modern technology was given us by Pope Pius XII in his Christmas Message of 1953. Let me give a paraphrase of some parts of that document.

Technology has brought man's domination of the material world to a pitch of perfection never before known. Yet in this sense religion has no difficulty in commending its magnificent achievements and potential. When man was first created, God told him to increase and multiply and subjugate the earth. What a long and hard road lies between the Garden of Eden and today, when the marvels of technology can permit man to say that in some sense he has fulfilled the divine injunction!

On the other hand, without a doubt, this very mastery of nature can pose a grave spiritual threat to man. In some of us, reliance on technology leads to a sense of independence and self-sufficiency that ill becomes the featherless biped who was created somewhat lower than the angels. In its apparent power to give us knowledge and proficiency unlimited, in the endless vistas of accomplishment that it dangles before us, modern technology puts before man a future so vast as to bewitch and blind the unwary, and to encourage a false conception of life and of the world which the late pontiff labeled the "technological spirit."

In what does that spirit consist? In this, that what is most prized in life is the leverage that can be drawn from the forces of nature. What is

---

* From "Automation and Man," *Catholic Mind*, December, 1963.

technically feasible is valued over all other forms of human activity, and the ultimate perfection of earthly culture and happiness is identified with clever manipulation of the forces in the universe.

Once man is infected with this technological spirit, he becomes intoxicated at progress, he grows infatuated with the machine. He effectively imprisons himself in matter and time, but no matter how deep and extensive this matrix may be, it is too confined to make a satisfactory home for the soul of man, made as he is in the image of God, and capable of finding rest nowhere but in Him. Woe to the man who makes technology a substitute for religion, and sells his soul for a mess of gears and transistors.

It is not that technology itself requires as a logical conclusion the denial of religious values. It actually leads to their acknowledgment if man, beholding the beauty of God in the technological process He has made possible to His creature, turns back to glorify Him in His works. But the technological spirit does tend to put man in a frame of mind that is unsuited for seeking, finding, and accepting truths and goods of the supernatural order.

What man needs, therefore, as he grows in technological power, is a sound growth in religious knowledge and practice, so that he may assess technology rightly and accord it its fitting place in a hierarchy of values. All too often, however, as Pope John XXIII noted in his long encyclical, *Mater et Magistra,*

> our age is marked by a sharp contrast between immense scientific and technical progress and fearful human decline. This is shown by its monstrous masterpiece of transforming man into a giant of the physical world at the expense of his spirit, which is reduced to that of a pygmy in the supernatural and eternal world.

But this blindness to higher values is not the only harm that results when technology is accepted as something autonomous and an end in itself. There also follows a series of profound repercussions on the way modern man lives and even on his social relations.

Thus, for instance, an unbalanced view of technology tends to exercise a degenerative influence on the idea of work; it comes to be regarded as a degrading occupation that is to be done away with forever. At the same time leisure is given a new value that makes it a good in itself, rather than a part of an ordered rhythm in life, while at the same time technology offers no program or motivation for any moral and creative use of the leisure it makes possible.

Because of the moral weakness of man and his strong inclination to indulge his lower nature at the expense of his higher faculties, the cultivation of technology for his own immediate ends and rewards presents a dangerous, and perchance the central, temptation for modern man, as W. Norris Clark, S.J., has noted in "Technology and Man: a Christian Vision" (*Catholic Mind*, April, 1963). Clearcut realization of the hierarchy of human values and firm moral self-discipline, both on the part of individuals and social groups, are therefore essential if man is to handle safely the powerful but ambivalent weapon of technology.

Nor can technology run rampant be free of harmful influences on the social relations of man, even in his family life. For where the family is penetrated by the technological spirit, in the estimation of Pius XII, the family loses its bond of unity, and is deprived of its warmth and stability. It remains one only to the extent demanded by the exigencies of mass production. No longer is the family a work of love and a haven of souls. It is a desolate depot of manpower for mass production, or a mere lot of consumers to keep the economy running. Thus it is that a kind of dehumanization and depersonalization overtakes mankind, when life falls too far under the sway of an economy managed by a few technocrats and their array of magic black boxes.

On balance, if I may reflect the thoughts of Father Clark once more, there is room for a cautiously optimistic view of technology among men who accept the Fatherhood of God and the religious truth that man is made in His image.

In this view, technology, as a partial aspect of reality, is to be evaluated in a context that affirms the prior value and good of man; it is not to be judged as a self-sufficient whole exclusively in terms of its own dynamism and laws. Man must always be at the center of our attention when we focus on technology, and we will judge the worth of its achievements by what it contributes or can contribute to the welfare of man as an individual and a social being. We dare not allow technology to be an end in itself, nor will we accord it the privileged status of a sacred cow, nor will we suffer it to work out its intrinsic potential without let or hindrance. We will bend it to our will and tailor it to our legitimate needs. "This conviction," Father Clark insists, "must be firmly held and acted on by the leaders of our society, from the government down, and impressed by appropriate control from above, if necessary, on the decision-makers within technology itself, if they are not able or willing to see its necessity under their own initiative."

Given this proper hierarchy of values, this measured structuring of technology, and the august role of man as the steward of the material creation under God, then we can say that technology has an important role to play in the drama of man's history. First, it can help liberate man from servitude to matter, by freeing his physical and mental energies for more characteristically human levels of working creativity and action. Secondly, it becomes the instrument whereby the liberated spirit of man can turn back to the material world and dominate it in a new way, making it the medium for new forms of self-expression and self-realization. And under this aspect nature no longer looks like a juggernaut that rolls relentlessly on, all oblivious to human goals and dreams. Rather the material world, again to quote Father Clark, becomes a "great plastic network of forces, open to its very depths to the creative molding power of the human mind and will, and inviting by its very malleability the re-creative touch of man.". . .

Mankind has lived through one industrial revolution that was unplanned and for centuries unregulated. It mechanized the Western world, and gave us many blessings — at the cost of enormous human loss and pain. Now we stand at the threshold of another such revolution, which will have a tremendous impact on far larger numbers of men in far less time than the first. Let us begin to think and work at once, so that its benefits are available as soon as possible, while its adverse effects are buffered, checked, and eliminated. This task can be accomplished, if we are willing to learn from history. If we are not, then, as the modern cliché runs, we shall be condemned to relive it, with incalculable hurt to the fabric of civilization.

Women in the Labor Market*

FRANCIS X. QUINN, S.J.

The average woman worker of today is a 40-year old married woman. Her counterpart of the 1920's was only 28 and single. Employment of women has expanded: one-third of today's labor force is feminine. If teen-agers and "plus 65ers" are excluded, one out of every three women is working. When the U. S. Women's Bureau was established forty-one years ago, only one-fifth of our workers were women, and less than one

---

* From "Women At Work," *Social Order*, February, 1962.

out of four women worked. Today the female work force has increased from 8¼ million to more than 22½ million and there is no decline in view. . . .

The influx of wives into the labor force, particularly those who return to work after their children reach school age, is indicative of a mounting drive for gainful employment where child care does not require a woman's presence at home. More and more, the typical work pattern for women is to remain in employment continuously, except for a break of 10–15 years in the childbearing period. The back-to-work movement among mothers of older children accounts in large part for a rise in the average age of working women from 26 years in 1900 to 32 years in 1940, to 37 years in 1950 and to 40 years in 1960. Even young mothers are going into the labor force with more frequency. More than 18 percent of the mothers of preschool children now work, compared with 7 percent in 1940. The labor force today includes approximately 6½ million women with children under 18; and 2½ million of this group have at least one child less than 6 years old. . . .

An analysis of women workers in 1960 reveals:

1. That more than half of all women workers are married women who are living with their husbands.

2. Five million women workers have children between the ages of 6 and 17 years only. Almost 3 million women workers have young children under 6 years of age; many of these women also have children 6 to 17 years of age.

3. In 4½ million families (1 family in 10) the family head is a woman. Half of the women family heads are in the labor force.

4. Of some 29 million women who worked at some time during 1959, about 14 million either worked at part-time jobs or worked at full-time jobs for half of the year or less.

5. Of a total of over 22 million employed women workers in April, 1960, clerical jobs accounted for 6½ million. Between 2 and 3⅓ million women were employed in each of four other broad occupational groups — as factory and other operatives; service workers (such as waitresses, beauticians, and practical nurses); professional and technical workers; and private-household workers. . . .

Disparity in earnings of the two sexes has existed since women took up employment outside the home. The first jobs open to women in large numbers were low-paying and frequently menial. A study sponsored by The Twentieth Century Fund revealed that earnings of women as distinct from rates of wages paid had been "half those of men and earnings of Negro women half those of white women." Latest census figures support those general observations.

Men make a better overall wage showing even in occupations in which the majority of workers are women, such as teaching and library science. Women's wages lag behind those of men in all industries; the gap is widest in industries which customarily employ large numbers of women. Women are having less trouble finding jobs but they show relatively little tendency to advance to higher levels of responsibility and remuneration. . . .

Lack of firm attachment to the labor force supports employer prejudice against promoting women to more important jobs. This affects the prospects not only of the casual employee but also of skilled workers determined to get ahead. In industry it tends to discourage employers from investing the money required to train a young woman who will have to give up the job when she marries and has a baby or who may have to leave town because her husband is transferred to another location.

To complete our profile, let us take a brief look at the educational attainment of women workers.

Chances that a woman will seek paid employment tend to increase with the amount of education she has received. For example, more than half of the American women with a college degree were working in 1959, in contrast to less than one-third of the women who had left school after the eighth grade. The relationship of educational attainment and employment was almost as strong for married women living with their husbands as it was for single women. The percentages of married women in the labor force were: 43 percent of the college graduates, 34 percent of the high school graduates, 28 percent of the elementary school graduates, and 18 percent of those with less than five years' schooling. Among single women, the percentages of workers varied from 83 percent of those with the most education to 27 percent of those with the least.

The amount of education obtained by a woman influences strongly the type of job she can obtain. In 1959 fully 78 percent of the employed women with college degrees had professional or technical jobs and another 12 percent were clerical workers. Of the remaining women almost half were included in the broad group of managers, officials, and proprietors, those who range from high-level executives to part owners of small businesses. Of the women workers who had one to three years of college training, 32 percent had professional or technical jobs in 1959 and 41 percent had clerical jobs.

For women workers who had finished high school but had not attended college the greatest employment opportunities were in the clerical field. Five of every 10 were service workers, such as waitresses, practical nurses, and hotel workers; another one out of ten were operatives employed primarily in apparel factories, laundries, textile mills, and food companies.

Most of the women workers who had received from one to three years of high school training were divided among three major occupational groups: service, operative, and clerical. Of the women who had not graduated from high school, almost none were employed in professional jobs.

Among employed women with an eighth-grade education or less, service workers predominated, operatives being the second largest group. Clerical and sales jobs were filled by significant proportions of the women who had graduated from eighth grade but by only small proportions of those with fewer years of schooling. . . .

Although the popular concept of women as marginal workers — the supplementary rather than the primary source of support for families — persists to an appreciable degree, it is generally taken for granted today that a girl on completing school will take a job at least until she marries. To these we offer the words Pius XII addressed to the Federation of Italian Women, October 14, 1956: "Because of this temporal goal, there is no field of human activity which must remain closed to woman; her horizons reach out to the regions of politics, labor, the arts, sports; but always in subordination to the primary functions which have been fixed by nature itself."

Why Women Work*

JOHN L. THOMAS, S.J.

The availability and widespread acceptance of women's employment outside the home proceed on assumptions that seriously challenge traditional conceptions of women's place and function in marriage and society. To be sure, in agrarian preindustrial societies, women worked hard in field and garden; at the beginning of the industrial revolution they followed men into mines and factories or toiled long hours at "sweated" piecework in the home; but gradually a pattern developed, among upper-class, urbanized groups, according to which men attended to all outside

---

* From "Why Women Work," *Social Order*, February, 1962.

activities while women remained at home either to care for the children and household or merely as ornaments. It is this well-established pattern that is currently being challenged and since there is a tendency to underestimate the complexity of the cultural forces involved, it will be worthwhile to enumerate briefly the major social factors that are operative in maintaining the present situation.

In the first place, widespread industrialization and urbanization have resulted in many more jobs for women; that is, there are more opportunities in clerical work and the service trades, while mechanization and technical advances in industry have made it possible for women to engage in employment hitherto reserved almost exclusively to men.

Accompanying these changes in the world of work have come vastly expanded educational opportunities for women, serving both to prepare them for remunerative employment, and to focus their interest on nondomestic pursuits. At the same time, the century-long feminist movement, with its goal of "emancipating women," considerably modified traditional conceptions of women's proper sphere of activity, thus enlarging their expectations and creating a general climate of opinion receptive of change in this area.

More importantly, there have been profound changes in our family system.

1. The industrial revolution introduced a shift in emphasis from the extended to the nuclear or the conjugal type family, with the result that unmarried, widowed, separated, or divorced women are now expected to be self-supporting or, at least, can make no clearcut, direct claims on their relatives for aid.

2. The economic contributions of wives in the home become greatly limited under urban conditions.

3. Childbearing, health care, household gadgets, diet, increased formal education of children, and so on, place a heavy financial strain on the modern family.

4. Our open-class social system, geared to competition and upward mobility, tends to measure success on the basis of conspicuous consumption and on the acquisition of material goods.

5. The accepted pattern of relatively early marriage usually means that couples start with few savings, so that both are expected to work, at least for a time.

6. Since girls are trained primarily for jobs, their premarital work experi-

ence frequently tends to give them little preparation or inclination for domestic pursuit.

7. The widespread knowledge and availability of contraceptives has made family limitation both possible and acceptable.

8. The concept of equality in marriage has lead many husbands to expect and many wives to assume the obligation of contributing to the financial support of the family by seeking employment outside the home.

9. Changes in the family cycle, marked by early and restricted child-bearing, the "bunching" of desired pregnancies in the first few years of marriage, the resulting earlier onset of the "empty nest" and increased life expectancy explain the high incidence of older married women in the work force.

Moreover, these changes have occurred in a society that does not clearly define the statuses and roles women are expected to assume. In theory, modern young women are presented with several alternatives — career, glamor girl, homemaker — but, since the majority eventually marry, they find themselves in practice trying to combine homemaking and a career. Such ambivalence is bound to leave women dissatisfied and insecure. . . .

Granting that the full significance of work in the world of women can be understood only in terms of the total social context we have briefly described, our next question is to ask why women work. Generally, for the same reasons that men work: because they need money, wish to contribute to the welfare of their families, or find employment outside the home both interesting and rewarding. In some cases women work because they are facing real, current needs; in others, they are trying either to anticipate future needs or to raise their family's standard of living. . . .

For better or worse, we must face the fact that we are no longer living in a culture that clearly defines what is expected of wives and mothers and consequently prepares and socially rewards them accordingly. Unfortunately, although this indicates a startling transformation in American society, we have only limited information concerning its possible implications. A priori, we may safely conclude that the change will affect the traditional, dominant position of men, as well as the structure and quality of marriage and family relationships. There can be little doubt that the growing independence of women in marriage is related to the possibility of seeking outside employment. At the same time, there is solid evidence that the relatively high standard of living enjoyed by many upper-lower and lower-middle class families is made possible by the employment of wives and mothers. In this connection it is relevant to note, as several recent studies indicate clearly, that it is the working wife who is most likely to be a consistent user of contraceptives.

Of more immediate interest, concern for the welfare of the children is usually uppermost in most popular discussions of working mothers. We may reasonably assume that employment outside the home will modify parent-child relationships, yet it is difficult to discover the full effects of the resultant adjustments, inasmuch as family patterns vary considerably in this regard and we lack adequate knowledge of how the needs of growing children should be met. The age of the child, the hours that the mother is out of the home, the kind of cooperation received from husbands, relatives, and so on, must also be taken into consideration. Little research has thus far been devoted to this problem; the few studies now available deal only with the immediate, short-term effects.

However, we have some information concerning the provisions made for the care of children while the mother is away from the home. Of the roughly two million children under six years of age whose mothers were working full time in 1958, approximately two-fifths were taken care of by relatives other than the parents, including older children in some cases. Another fifth were looked after by their own fathers or mothers, who either worked different shifts or whose working conditions were such as to permit the children to stay with them. About one-fourth were cared for by neighbors or other nonrelatives and only about five percent were placed in "group care centers," such as day nurseries, nursery schools, settlement houses, and so forth. Of the roughly three million children between six and twelve years of age whose mothers were full-time workers, a fair percentage were expected to take care of themselves, while the others received some supervision from adults or older children.

As has been indicated, current knowledge of the relationship between the employment of mothers and child development is not only limited but also speculative in character. Compared with past patterns of parent-child relationships, perhaps the most significant element in the current change is not so much the reduction in the total amount of time that working mothers devote to caring for their children as the relatively longer periods of continuous separation between mothers and children resulting from employment outside the home. In the past, the average busy housewife probably devoted little time to the special care of her children, yet in contrast to the contemporary employed mother, she was always working near them and was available when needed.

To recapitulate briefly, we are witnessing a profound transformation in women's orientation to the world of work. Although the vast majority enter marriage and marry relatively young, many no longer regard their work in the domestic unit as the sole means of contributing to the welfare of their families. Most American women work before marriage or until their first baby arrives and a good percentage rejoin the work force as soon as their youngest child is in school. Prepared by training, experience, and social expectation to seek employment outside the home, modern women have been gradually redefining their statuses and roles in marriage, the family, and society.

For the most part, this transformation has proceeded unnoticed and unchallenged, though it should be obvious that such basic changes in the position of women logically involve a series of assumptions concerning the nature of woman, her relationship to men, the significance of her functions in bearing and rearing children, and her expected contributions to society. In our rapidly changing, pluralistic society these assumptions tend to remain unformulated or implicit, for when there is no agreement on the nature of man, primary concern focuses on immediate, ad hoc adjustments to change and there is little awareness that such practical programs of action necessarily involve the application of accepted premises of values to a set of social facts.

On the other hand, we should avoid the error of those official "viewers with alarm" who tend to evaluate all changes in terms of criteria derived solely from the past. The increased opportunities for education and employment now available to women obviously question traditional conceptions of male dominance and the subordination of women in marriage and the family, yet it should be equally obvious that past formulations neither represent the ultimate in Christian outlook nor are wholly applicable under present conditions.

To resolve the present confusion, therefore, we need more facts, a more adequate understanding of their personal and social implications, and a serious reappraisal of the nature and significance of masculine-feminine complementarity in the light of Christian principles. . . .

Theory of the Family Wage*

REV. JAMES G. MURTAGH

The question of a just remuneration of labor is the most important and the most difficult problem in social theory and practice. Since the rejection of the inhuman "Iron Law of Wages," three principles of approach have been advanced:

The first is *equal pay for equal work*. According to this principle, two men doing the same work with the same degree of skill should receive the same wage. This in practice penalizes the married man with a family.

The second is *to each according to his needs*. This principle embraces wages and family allowances of various kinds and has come more and more to the forefront in social thought and policy.

The third is the *family living wage*. There is not a fundamental contradiction between this and the previous principle, because the ideal family wage includes the objectives of the principle of *each according to his needs*. As a matter of history, however, it has been more honored in theory than in practice, and has seldom moved out of the pages of books and the halls of learning, and been applied in the labor markets of the world.

The family living wage is the fundamental Catholic social principle on wage justice. A man and his family have a natural right to obtain a reasonable living from the world in which they live, that is, from the goods and services produced in society. For the masses of men, this can come only from their wages for work. Pope Leo XIII laid down the principle of a "living wage." Pope Pius XI developed it as a "family wage." Pope Pius XII often reaffirmed the teaching of his predecessors. But the Popes lay down broad sociomoral principles and naturally do not attempt to indicate how a family living wage is to be achieved in economic and administrative practice in different countries. It is left to Catholic moralists and sociologists to expound and develop the principle and to suggest concrete methods for its realization.

It is a problem bristling with complexities, as the first half of the twentieth century has abundantly proved. As the late Monsignor John A. Ryan said in his classic work *A Living Wage* (pp. 177–178):

---

* From "Toward a Family Wage," *Advocate* (Melbourne), September 9, 1954. Also in *Catholic Mind*, January, 1955.

The determination of complete justice in the field of economic distribution is bewilderingly difficult. According to the view of the writer, the order of importance among the various causes of distributive justice is as follows: 1) the needs of the worker; 2) the cost of preparation for tasks requiring skill of any kind; 3) the legitimate risks of necessary business enterprise; 4) the proportion of individual energy expended by the worker; 5) the disagreeableness of the work; 6) the productivity of labor; 7) the productivity of property, whether land or capital.

Today, Catholic commentators on the encyclicals generally, if not unanimously, teach that a family living wage is a matter of strict (or commutative) justice. All agree, following Pope Pius XI, that it is demanded by social justice. But when it comes to the question of ways and means, the commentators have not been very helpful, at least for framing practical social policy. Since World War II, however, a younger generation of sociologists, mainly in Europe, have departed somewhat from the traditional exposition of the family wage doctrine and now make a distinction between an *absolute family wage* and a *relative family wage*.

An *absolute family wage* means a wage adequate not only for the worker but for his family. Every normal adult worker, married or single, is entitled in strict justice, in ordinary circumstances, to receive such a wage for his labor.

A *relative family wage* means a standard base wage, paid to an individual adult worker, supplemented by marriage allotments and family allowances when he marries and has a family.

Generally speaking, it may be said that commentators whose approach to the wage problem is primarily and almost exclusively moral adhere to the principle of an *absolute* family wage. On the other hand, commentators whose approach is not only moral but socioeconomic recommend a *relative* family wage, at least in society *as it is today*.

But even those who hold to the *absolute* family wage are prepared to admit the tremendous difficulties of achieving it in practice in contemporary society. For instance, Father J. Edward Coffey, S.J., an American and former Professor of Sociology at the Gregorian University, in a conversation with the present writer, agreed that in the present state of society it is on the whole impossible to achieve an *absolute* family wage, but the principle is a moral one which should be defended. The family allowance system, he held, is merely a stopgap (though one which he approves) to assist the family pending the emergence of an organic social order which would organize the payment of an *absolute* family wage.

On the other hand, Father George Jarlot, S.J., a Frenchman, parts company with his colleague, Father Coffey. Like Father Valerie Fallon, S.J., in his *Principles of Social Economy* (1949), Father Jarlot distinguishes between an *absolute* family wage and a *relative* family wage in his *Compendium Ethicae Socialis*.

Father Jarlot's approach to the problem of family income is remarkably akin to that of the Australian Bishops, although he has never seen any of the Social Justice Statements which deal with the wage question. He is keenly alive to the difficulties and anomalies involved in paying a family wage both to single and married men, assuming it possible in practice in capitalist society. He teaches that a wage equivalent to the intrinsic value of work done is due in strict justice and would be a family wage, given a Christian social order. But, owing to the instability and injustice of capitalist society, it is not being realized. In the absence of a Christian corporative society, the only practical thing to do is to seek a just wage for the single individual worker and after his marriage build it up by family allowances into an adequate family income.

The same approach to the problem was taken for granted as obvious in modern society by Father Arthur Utz, O.P., Professor of Sociology at the Catholic University of Fribourg (Switzerland). In a discussion with the writer, he stressed the importance of distinguishing between ethics and economics in studying the social encyclicals. The Popes teach socioethical principles, not economics, and it can be confusing and misleading to give an economic meaning to a term in the encyclicals when it happens to be the same term in social ethics.

For instance, he indicated, the term "wage" does not necessarily have the same precise connotation or cover the same field in economics as in social ethics. The economic order is concerned with a productivity wage; the social order is concerned with a family wage. In economics, a just wage means payment for goods or services produced and is the right of the worker in commutative justice. In social ethics, a just wage is a broader concept involving both the worker and his family, and calling into operation both commutative and distributive justice. A just productivity wage for the worker is the responsibility of his employer; a just family wage is the responsibility of society. The family must receive in one way or another an adequate income. The Popes lay down the social principle, but not the economic method. How the principle is to be realized must be solved according to local standards, economic conditions, and political tradition.

It is perhaps not too much to say that the Catholic world has more or less abandoned hope of an *absolute* family wage, at least in contemporary capitalist society. Even Catholic sociomoralists who defend it as the only principle and hesitate to recognize, at least in social theory, the concept of a *relative* family wage, are all in favor of the family allowance system in practice. Certainly, the accelerating trend is toward a *relative* family wage or family income system in Europe, Scandinavia, Canada, Australia, and more recently in the Americas.

The Case for Family Allowances*

FRANCIS J. CORLEY, S.J.

At the Philadelphia National Catholic Family Life Conference in 1953, I proposed a system of family allowances for the United States. The proposal called for establishment within the Federal Security Agency of a bureau to administer a program which would give aid in support of larger-than-average families. Monthly payments of $12 for the third child, $10 for the fourth child and $8 for each succeeding child would be paid from general treasury funds.

The United States, the most highly industrialized country in the world, has been extremely slow in recognizing the problem of families with children. . . . Yet the need for some assistance for families will be apparent if we examine the economic position of children in modern industrial society. In an agricultural society children are far from total liabilities. At a quite early age they can begin to be economically productive, caring for small domestic animals, cultivating truck gardens, milking cows, aiding in harvest. But under an industrial wage system, especially when child labor is rigidly restricted, children become almost total economic liabilities. Alone among industrial nations of the world, the United States has not yet recognized the tremendous change which has been taking place and the greatly increased burden which has been placed on wage-earners with children.

In modern economies, operating under a wage system, there is no correlation between income and family need. The worker is paid for his time and effort according to his economic worth to his employer. Whether

---

* From "Why Federal Family Allowances," *Social Order*, June, 1954.

he is single or has a large family, his pay is the same as anyone else's for the same amount of work.

It is no blanket condemnation of the wage system to say that this puts the father of a large or even moderate-sized family at a serious disadvantage. If such families only had as much cash income as small family groups, they would be handicapped. Actually, however, we are confronted with the alarming fact that young, growing families with small children have as a group less income than others. Whereas families with no children under six years of age had a median income of $3,819 in 1950, those with three or more such young children had a median income of only $2,767.

This, as I have remarked before, is one of the "built-in" defects of our wage system. Actually, the "defect" of the wage system is the fact that it measures economic contribution, rather than need. . . .

The clear trend to family allowances throughout the world is based upon three human principles:

1. A man should be able to support his family at about the same level as others in his class. If, through no fault of his own, this is rendered impossible by the economic system, he and his family should not be penalized.

2. The most important and valuable contribution which man can make to society is people, for society is people. Society has an obligation to those who make the most valuable contribution which is at least commensurate with its obligation to those who contribute wealth, ideas, ideals.

3. The primary obligation for support of children must always remain with parents. Hence, family allowances should never be more than a partial contribution to the support of children — and anyone will admit that $8 monthly will never be more than part of a child's cost.

This, in briefest form, is the proposal I made and the reasons that urged it. The response was widespread and about equally divided between those who opposed and those who favored the measure.

One point which was frequently made by those who opposed the plan is that it involves another step in the direction of statism. A federal system of family allowances turns over to a governmental agency one more function, albeit indirectly and only partially, which traditionally has been the responsibility of individual families and, in cases of distress, private agencies of relief and assistance.

Obviously a federal family allowances system involves action by the state. It can hardly be called statism and is only a limited intervention of the state. At the present time a few of the family allowances systems in other countries are genuinely statist; that is, the state has taken over the entire responsibility for child support. However, only one such system exists in a nontotalitarian country, Sweden. . . .

The system of family allowances under discussion here makes no such sweeping change in traditional forms of family support. It urges, rather, that some part of the cost of child rearing be supported by society since society gains so immensely from the contribution of parents. But primary responsibility and total discretion in the care of children still remain with parents, within the limits of private and public welfare. . . .

There are further considerations which are pertinent when we are measuring the threat of "statism" involved in a federal system of family allowances.

One of these is that the system of family allowances I have proposed does not involve the complete assumption by the federal government of a new function. The aid given to families will relieve them of only part of the cost of child rearing, and in many instances the part would be comparatively small. This is a significant point; total responsibility for child care still rests upon parents, where is belongs. We want no state nurseries or total planning of child care by public agencies. What family allowances will do for low-income families the federal government already recognizes as an imperative need by allowing deductions for dependents from income in tax computations. Yet no one would think of this excellent and commonsense measure as a form of "statism."

On the contrary, income-tax deductions are a clear recognition of the first two principles mentioned at the beginning of this paper, namely that a man should be able to support his family at about the same level as others in his class and that society has an obligation to those who make its most valuable contribution.

Family allowances are simply an extension of the principle already recognized in income-tax deductions.

Moreover, the system I have proposed involves no population policy. In other countries family allowances have been established with a view to implementing policies adopted by the state. The schedule of grants suggested at the outset of this paper represents a choice made on the basis of four considerations: (1) the bulk of families with more than two children need some economic assistance, less in some rough proportion to increased total family income; (2) in the long run a universal system distributed without regard to need (without a means test), but with the possibility of recovery through income taxes, would be the more efficient and potentially economical system; (3) family allowances should be an aid to families in the care of children they desire, rather than an inducement to increase the population; (4) family allowances should be an aid to families but should not take over the entire economic responsibility for child care.

At this point, the question may be asked: "If family allowances are merely an extension of the deduction principle, why cannot the problem be met by increasing the amount which may be deducted for dependents?"

The reason is that in many instances the cash income of families is too small to benefit fully from deductions at the present level and would not be improved by increasing the deductible amount. Thus, if a man's income were $2,000, he would pay no income tax if he supported a wife and one child. But if he had three or six or ten children, he would be no better off. On the other hand, three or six or ten children would be very welcome possessions on March 15 to a man with $20,000 income. . . .

Family allowances will do for low-income families what deductions for dependents do for those better off. They will be an act of recognition on the part of society that raising children costs money — at whatever level of the income ladder a family may be stationed. They will be a subsidy, if you wish, but one which equalizes the economic burden of a tremendously important social service: building tomorrow's America. . . .

Growth of Profit Sharing*

B. L. METZGER

During the depression of the 1930's, interest in profit sharing was at a low ebb. However, in 1939, new interest was sparked by a penetrating report on profit sharing by the Vandenberg-Herring Subcommittee of the Committee on Finance of the United States Senate.

At that time there were only thirty-seven qualified deferred profit-sharing programs and a few hundred cash profit-sharing programs in operation. The Senate study documented the benefits certain companies were realizing with profit-sharing plans and concluded that profit sharing can be "eminently successful, when properly established, in creating

* From "Substantial Growth Attests Success of Profit Sharing," *Social Order,* November, 1963.

employer-employee relations that make for peace, equity, efficiency, and contentment." The Subcommittee went so far as to say: "We believe it [profit sharing] to be essential to the ultimate maintenance of the capitalistic system.". . .

Profit sharing is a very versatile concept. It can be designed in many ways to do many different tasks. Lodding Engineering Corporation started a cash profit-sharing plan in July, 1953, for its 100 employees with these stated objectives:

1. To share profits with employees.
2. To establish better relations.
3. To reduce turnover.
4. To stimulate initiative.
5. To strengthen loyalty.
6. To increase productivity.
7. To increase profits.
8. To provide severance and supplementary retirements benefits (in addition to a pension plan).
9. To identify each employee with the company.

In 1962, management rated numbers 1, 3, 6, and 7 unqualified successes. Numbers 2, 4, 5, and 9 were greatly improved and a start was made on number 8 by the initiation on January 1, 1961, of a 50 percent cash, 50 percent deferred plan for 40 percent of the employees (supervisory and clerical). Turnover became so negligible that it ceased to exist. Productivity maintained a 38–40 percent sustained increase. Net profits for the five years before 1955 averaged a little over 4 percent (of sales); from 1955 on, net profits (after payment of profit sharing) averaged over 9 percent. Since 1955, profit-sharing distributions averaged 22.5 percent of base pay per year, with a low of 17.6 percent in 1958 and a high of 27.03 percent in 1957.

Conditioned Air & Refrigeration Company in Fresno, California, thought that the mechanical contracting industry was "the most unlikely place for rational management to try to give away a part of its profits." It had nothing from which to give and was paying more in wages and fringes than it felt could be passed on to the public without a compensating improvement in service. Money was limited for capital outlay in tools and equipment; production and profits were falling off; competition was keen and good men hard to keep.

After abandoning a key-man incentive program (which was breaking down interdepartmental cooperation), the company adopted a broad coverage, deferred profit-sharing program in July, 1957. During the first four years of the plan, sales increased 230 percent, profits gradually rose percentagewise, employment was stabilized, production per man-hour went up each period as did the quality of work, company equipment received better care, constructive suggestions from employees often resulted in time-saving improvements, employees encouraged the installation of new machines and developed real zeal for the continued growth of the company. . . .

One common misconception about profit sharing is that it works only in small companies where workers can more easily see the relation between their greater efficiency and increased profit sharing. In fact, profit sharing has been practiced successfully for many years in some of America's largest companies: its largest bank (Bank of America, Inc.); largest soap company (Procter & Gamble Co.); largest wax manufacturer (S. C. Johnson & Son, Inc.); largest tobacco company (R. J. Reynolds Tobacco Co.); largest magazine publisher (Time, Inc.); largest mail-order house (Sears, Roebuck & Co.); largest photographic manufacturing company (Eastman Kodak Co.); and its largest investment banking firm (Merrill Lynch, Pierce, Fenner & Smith, Inc.). A list of other large companies with effective profit-sharing programs would include Standard Oil of California, American Tobacco Co., Dow Chemical Co., Farmers Insurance Group, Standard Oil of Ohio, Philip Morris, Prentice-Hall, Inc., McGraw-Edison Co., Bell & Howell, Ampex Corp., Quaker Oats Co., National Lead, J. C. Penney Co., Inc., Dominion Foundries & Steel Ltd., and American Motors Corp.

Another frequent feeling about profit sharing is that profit-sharing programs are unfair to stockholders — if labor gets more, stockholders get less. In an effort to measure the effects of profit-sharing programs on stockholder interests, the Profit Sharing Research Foundation in 1960 studied the financial records of the fourteen largest department-store chains and the sixteen largest food-store chains in the country (taken from *Fortune's* list of the fifty largest United States merchandising corporations). Seven out of the fourteen department-store chains and eleven out of the sixteen food-store chains had profit sharing. On every measure of importance to stockholders — ratios of net income to net worth, and net income to sales; in growth from a 1952 base of net worth, sales, earnings per common share, dividends, and market prices of stock — the profit-sharing group of firms did *appreciably* better over the seven-year period than the nonprofit-sharing group. Perhaps even more significant was the fact that the spread increased year by year. This was true for both department-store and food-store chains. In the profit-sharing companies, the nets were, of course, nets after profit sharing.

Although no universal conclusions can be drawn from these studies, and it would be an inaccuracy to attribute these gains exclusively to profit sharing, it would be contrary to evidence to claim that stockholders were penalized by these profit-sharing programs. The evidence (financial data plus management appraisals) supports the opposite conclusion: that the stockholders in the profit-sharing companies fared better than their counterparts in nonprofit-sharing companies and the profit-sharing programs contributed in a significant way to this superior performance. . . .

Employers discussing profit-sharing plans tend to stress frequently the intangible benefits of their programs. They claim that through profit sharing they can help employees realize that they are responsible, appreciated members of the corporate group.

The benefits of profit sharing from the employee's point of view can be substantial, particularly if the plan has been in existence for some time and the company has done well.

Zenith Radio Corporation, for example, started its deferred profit-sharing plan in April, 1950, and allocates its profit-sharing contributions among individual employees on the basis of earnings up to $6,000 (recently raised somewhat) with a substantial weighting for service. After eleven and three-fourths years of profit sharing, 1749 employees had credit balances in the trust ranging from $5,000 to $15,000; 1441 employees had balances ranging from $15,000 to $30,000; and 810 had balances in excess of $30,000. . . .

After fifteen years under the deferred profit-sharing program instituted by Motorola, Incorporated, in 1947, a $5,000-a-year employee who had contributed $200 a year to the trust had an account worth more than $21,000 — an average, with earnings and appreciation, of over $1,400 per year.

Since 1912, Eastman Kodak Company has distributed wage dividends to its employees. The amounts have varied considerably over the years. In 1953, for example, the wage dividend amounted to 10.7 percent of wages and salaries; in 1961, the total distribution amounted to slightly more than 16 percent. In 1961, the typical hourly employee received approximately the equivalent of seven or eight weeks' wages. In 1963, a record $53,600,000 was paid to about 47,500 Kodak employees in the United States or deposited for their benefit in the Eastman Kodak Employees' Savings and Investment Plan. Each eligible employee received or had deposited for his benefit in the plan $36.75 for each $1,000 earned in the five-year period 1958–1962. . . .

The Council of Profit Sharing Industries surveyed some 260 profit-sharing companies in late 1961 and found that the average profit share per participant among these companies for their latest year was $487, between 7–8 percent of salaries. This average, of course, varied from company to company.

Not all profit-sharing plans benefit employees as much as these programs, but these examples do serve to illustrate profit sharing's potentials. . . .

Union attitudes toward profit sharing historically have been hostile or indifferent. In the early days of business unionism, higher wages, better working conditions, and union security were chief labor goals. Workers wanted their gains in the pay envelope. Labor leaders were suspicious of profit-sharing programs because they felt managements were using profit sharing to avoid unionization and/or to avoid paying decent wages.

With accelerated union organization, the acceptance of collective bargaining as national policy, the increase in deferred profit-sharing plans relative to cash plans, and the increasing number of unionized employees participating under satisfactory profit-sharing programs, union attitudes toward profit sharing, at least in some circles, have been changing.

In the last few years, profit-sharing programs have been worked out at the Emerson Electric Company with the International Union of Electrical Workers, the American Tobacco Company with the Tobacco Workers, the Saramar Aluminum Company with the United Steelworkers, and at American Motors Corporation with the United Auto Workers. New profit-sharing programs have just been started at the Belle City Malleable Iron Company in Racine, Wisconsin, the Wells Aluminum Company in Indiana, and the Dumore Company in Racine, Wisconsin, covering UAW workers.

These are certainly not the first profit-sharing programs in unionized companies — 35 percent of the membership of the Council of Profit Sharing Industries are unionized profit-sharing companies (one of them, Standard Oil of California, has over thirty-five unions) — but these developments do signal a shift to active union interest in profit sharing on a broader scale than ever before.

Also, the unions involved played a more significant role in the development of the profit-sharing programs than was customary in the past. The role of unions in past profit-sharing practice has usually been minimal. In most cases, managements decided on the idea, worked out the program details, extended the programs to the unionized employees for their voluntary acceptance, and handled all aspects of administration. . . .

The American economy today is facing a number of very serious economic problems which are affecting the decisions of both management and labor. Foreign competition, persistently high unemployment, lagging economic growth, wage-price inflation, the breakdown of collective bargaining in key sectors of our economy, the rising costs of production and the resulting profit squeeze, and the uncertain impact of automation and its effects on job security are only a few of the problems which are calling for a reexamination of our current economic theories of wages and industrial relations.

Even in this clouded perspective, typical contracts are being negotiated with increases in basic wages and fringe benefits, but these are not geared in any automatic way to productivity gains or the firm's capacity to pay. Moreover, the increased benefits do not seem to solve in any essential way the disparity of interests between labor and management; nor do they seem to motivate workers in any appreciable degree to step up the productivity or profitability of the enterprise. Employees, by and large, however, are not being given access to earnings on investment. In most of these benefit programs, they are not being turned into stockholder employees. Neither is economic understanding of the profit system among workers being measurably furthered.

In this situation, both management and labor find themselves in difficult straits. With a competitive ceiling on prices and labor costs continually on the rise, management is caught in a profit squeeze; unions, seeking additional benefits and security for their members, tend to put the unionized firms at a competitive disadvantage — thus undermining the job security they are striving to protect.

In a March 20, 1962, editorial in the *American Banker*, Raoul D. Edwards proposed the following solution: "A new, bold approach to the problem of 'real noninflationary' wage increases is mandatory for the continued health of the American economy and for our continued ability to compete in world markets. . . . It seems to us that the tool is at hand — a tool which would permit the worker to share, and share on a 'real basis,' increases in productivity without penalizing the remainder of the economic system. That tool is profit sharing."

CHAPTER 5

THE INDUSTRIAL COMMUNITY

Rerum Novarum declares that the right of workers alone, or of groups of both workers and owners, to organize is a natural one. The same is said about the right to adopt that organizational structure which the workers consider most suitable to promote their legitimate occupational interests, and the right to act freely, without hindrance from anyone, and on their own initiative — within the associations — to achieve these ends.

Workers and employers should regulate their mutual relations under the inspiration of the principle of human solidarity and Christian brotherhood. This should be their principle because both competition understood in the sense of economic liberalism and class struggle taken in the Marxist context are contrary to the nature of man and the Christian conception of life.

Pope John XXIII in *Mater et Magistra*

Since the days when Pope Leo XIII defended the right of workers to organize, there has been both progress in trade unionism and decline. In most of the developed countries of the free world, trade unions have achieved not merely legal respectability but also considerable power. Wherever communism has spread, however, such free trade unions as previously existed have been abolished. They have been replaced by government-controlled organizations that regiment workers in the interest of the state.

Adverting to the growth of unions, Pope John wrote sympathetically in *Mater et Magistra* of their evolution from engines of class conflict to organs of collective bargaining. Though relevant to Western Europe, where unionism was largely socialist in its origins, the Pope's words had little meaning for the United States. From the very beginning, American unionism pursued justice for workers within the existing system of private enterprise. Over the protests of a socialist minority, it persisted in seeking change, not through revolution, but through free collective bargaining. Only when collective bargaining was seen to be inadequate, did American labor turn to government for necessary reforms. Even then, its purpose was not to destroy the private-enterprise system, but to improve it.

While the history of industrial relations in the United States has its black chapters, no important body of opinion favors repudiating the national commitment, now more than thirty years old, to free collective bargaining. There seems to be no democratic alternative to it. On the other hand, the concentration of power in the nation's basic industries and in the unions which represent their workers has given to many labor agreements an importance that is no longer merely private. In a number of cases, collective bargaining today is affected by a public interest to a degree never envisaged by the authors of the Wagner Act. The future is somewhat obscure, but the price of continued freedom for both industry and labor may well consist in some form of voluntary collaboration with government.

This is not as ominous as it sounds. Many of the most important economic decisions, those that have the greatest influence on the profitability of business and the earnings and security of workers, are now being made, as Pope John points out in *Mater et Magistra*, by public authorities. By cooperating with government, labor and industry gain a consultative voice in the decision-making process.

A number of issues — the fast pace of technological change, the civil-rights revolution, the imbalance in our international payments, the continuing pressures of the Cold War — are pushing employers and unions in the same direction. As a purely private endeavor, collective bargaining cannot resolve them.

The Church and Labor*

MOST REV. PATRICK A. O'BOYLE

Three or four years ago, a new theological seminary for the training of Catholic priests in the State of Michigan was formally dedicated by His Eminence, Edward Cardinal Mooney, the Archbishop of Detroit.

---

* From "The Church and Labor," *Catholic Mind*, February, 1956.

The Cardinal said something on that occasion which richly deserves re-peating. "Our students of today come, like those of us of a former generation," he stated, "from the homes of people who, in overwhelming proportion, labor in workshop or office or on the land. They look for-ward to a pastoral ministry among that same kind of people." Therefore, he continued, "They need not only to know, in the abstract, the principles of social justice, but also to feel, out of their own experience, that sym-pathy with those who work which befits ministers of a Divine Savior who for thirty years lived and worked in the bosom of a workingman's family in a remote village of Galilee."

If the seminarians to whom the Cardinal was speaking follow his advice and live up to his expectations, they will be perpetuating a long-standing tradition of which the Church, in my opinion, can be justly proud. Traditionally the clergy of the United States, by and large, have always shown a friendly interest in the labor movement, which helps to account for the fact that our Catholic workingmen have always been extremely well represented in the ranks of organized labor and have probably produced more than their proportionate share of outstanding labor leaders.

Will Herberg, a distinguished Jewish scholar, refers to this fact more than once in his book, *Protestant, Catholic, Jew,* which is deservedly being hailed as an important contribution to the relatively new field of religious sociology. "In the labor movement . . ." he says, "though no exact figures are available, there can be little doubt that Catholics make up, and have long made up, a considerably greater proportion than they do in the population as a whole. . . . The religious affiliation of labor leaders would seem to be consonant with this fact."

Mr. Herberg attributes this in part to the heavy concentration of Catho-lics in urban and industrial areas, but he hastens to add that "perhaps the notably friendly attitude of the Church in America to labor organi-zation is also a factor." For my own part, I would be inclined to eliminate the word "perhaps" and to say, instead, that the friendly attitude of the Church in America to the cause of trade unionism is the principal explanation of what would seem to be the disproportionate percentage of Catholics in the American labor movement. I trust that this is not wishful thinking on my part; but, whether it is or not, the fact re-mains that the Catholic Church in the United States has always had implicit confidence in the essential aims and aspirations of the American labor movement and has consistently urged her own members, so many of whom are working people, to take an active interest in union affairs as one very important means of practicing the virtues of social justice and social charity.

Mr. Herberg sympathetically corroborates this statement when he says in another context that "the Catholic Church has remained, by and large, prolabor and has shown a deep concern for retaining the allegiance of its working people." We shall have occasion to explain later on precisely in what sense the Church is "prolabor" and in what sense she is not. Meanwhile it is important to emphasize that the Church has had no ulterior motives in the field of organized labor. That is to say, if the Church has encouraged her members to take an active interest in union affairs, she has not done so for the purpose of "capturing" the labor movement or of bringing it under clerical or ecclesiastical control. On the contrary, as I have already indicated, her only motive has been to promote the cause of justice and charity by encouraging her members to practice these virtues at every possible opportunity in cooperation with all other men of good will.

The farsighted policy of the late Cardinal Gibbons of Baltimore has been decisive in this respect. In his famous memorial to the Holy See in defense of the Knights of Labor, the beloved Archbishop of Baltimore, speaking on behalf of the majority of his fellow Bishops in the United States, forcefully expressed his confidence in the integrity and the judgment of the working people of this country and in their ability to conduct the affairs of their unions according to sound moral principles without benefit of direct ecclesiastical supervision. . . .

The credit for this happy state of affairs — this wholesome spirit of cooperation between religion and labor in the United States — belongs to labor as much as it does to the Church. If the Church has supported the cause of organized labor, organized labor, in turn, has supported the cause of religion, or to put it negatively, has never looked upon itself as a substitute for religion or an enemy of the Church. In this respect, as in many others, American unions differ radically from the Marxist unions of certain other countries, which, even today to some extent, are propagandists for a doctrinaire and completely outmoded philosophy of rationalism and anticlericalism. . . .

The Catholic Church could not and would not support a labor movement which did not respect a scale of values that puts God, family, and country before unionism. Furthermore — if I may return to Mr. Herberg's statement that the Church in the United States is prolabor —

it is perfectly obvious that the Church cannot and will not support any labor movement, including our own, uncritically and without reservations. The Church is admittedly in favor of the organization of workers into unions for their own economic and moral betterment. But she is not prolabor in the sense of rationalizing or condoning or winking at labor's defects, nor is she prolabor in the sense of being antimanagement or anti-anything else. This, of course, is a truism, but it ought to be mentioned, if only in passing, in order to clear away some of the confusion which too often surrounds the discussion of the subject of religion-and-labor in the public prints.

If I may put it another way, the Church believes that unions are desirable and necessary, not only for the protection and advancement of the worker's interests, but, even more important, for the development of a sound social order. The ultimate purpose of unions, in other words, is to serve the general welfare in cooperation with the other organized economic groups in our economy and to do so with malice toward none and with justice and charity toward all.

This, I take it, is the prevailing concept of unionism within the contemporary American labor movement. . . .

The American Labor Movement*

WILLIAM J. SMITH, S.J.

The American labor movement is the largest and most complex free labor organization in the world. Reflected in its 16-million-member collectivity of citizens and aliens are all the traits and traditions, the personalities and the philosophies, the converging racial groups and their conflicting environments which go to make up the melting pot that is America. The economic, political, and social activities, on the national plane and at the local level, are guided by 600,000 men and women exercising the responsibilities of office. They represent 68,000 local unions, each of which is affiliated to one of 139 national unions in their respective industrial fields.

From trends the movement has taken in recent years some keen observers discern three types of unionism. They speak of economic union-

* From "The American Labor Movement," *Catholic Mind*, November–December, 1957.

ism, political unionism, and a third brand which for the want of an uglier name they label "business" unionism.

The term "economic unionist" is applied to the leader who sees in collective bargaining, i.e., the union-management contract, the primary, the most effective, and the most important means for achieving trade union aims and objectives.

The type termed "political unionist" accepts collective bargaining as a primary function of the trade union, but places greater stress upon political action and government assistance, at least as the main supplementary prop for the accomplishment of overall aims.

The distinction between the economic unionist and the political unionist is not a clear-cut one. In their practical application, the two theories overlap. Among the more important union officials it is a question of emphasis rather than of conflict. George Meany and Walter Reuther, the two recognized top leaders, for instance, subscribe to both economic and political unionism. It should be emphasized that both are motivated by and tenaciously cling to a good concept of trade union idealism.

The third class, sponsors of the so-called "business unionism," openly admit they are not interested in social reform or trade union philosophy. Trade unionism, with the opportunity to capitalize on it for personal gain, is to them merely a "business." The title "business unionist" is attached to such individuals as a term of opprobrium.

The philosophy of the business unionist has been aptly expressed by Jimmy Hoffa, a power in the Teamsters Union, when he says: "I'm not interested in changing the world. Strength today lies in [economic] power and cash. There are two ways to engage in politics. One is to make speeches and the other to spend dough. We spend lots of dough." . . .

Actually what we have had in America for some years has been a dual labor movement — one of legitimate labor activity, constituting about 95 percent of the movement, led and inspired by relatively good and honest men; the other five percent a conglomeration of unscrupulous exploiters of the needs of the working people trading upon the democratic nature of the trade union organization. . . .

Substantially, organized labor in the United States is, in my judgment, socially sound, politically correct, ethically earnest, and economically necessary. I will go so far as to say that I would not want to live in a country, certainly not one the size of the United States of America, where no free labor movement was in existence. In spite of the glaring weaknesses of the workers' organizations revealed by the McClellan Committee, I am convinced that what we have at present is preferable to what the nation would be under an economic dictatorship free to carry on its relentless pursuit of profits without let or hindrance from the limited but organized power of a free labor movement.

Time prevents me from recounting the numberless, unprecedented accomplishments of the American labor unions in the past two decades. I say in the past two decades for the simple reason that for fifty years previous to the Roosevelt Administration the unorganized workers of America were the victims of a sustained, calculated suppression. The small percentage of truly free organized workers were constantly harassed by antiunion employers. What relatively little organized strength the workers were able to develop was emasculated by collusive and corruptive influences habitually exerted by a hostile management. Pre-Wagner Act days in America are a black page in our industrial history.

As a matter of fact, much of the maladjustment which today exists in employer-employee relations can be traced to a common source in the far dim past of American industrial experience. . . .

The simple fact is that in America, as in every capitalistic nation, the original scriptwriters of economic liberalism forgot an essential factor of social order. Nowhere was there written into the script a proper and legitimate role whereby the workers of a nation could play a proper part in the social, economic, and political life of their country.

To put it a bit more graphically, in the United States they left the child at someone else's doorstep. The wee one grew up to be a nature boy. Two decades ago he came back to the old homestead demanding his share of the inheritance. He brought with him a mixed brood. Almost overnight, unprepared for the responsibility, knowing no other role for fifty years but that of a guerrilla fighter, he and his tribe suddenly found themselves possessed of power — tremendous power — political, economic, and social. The scandals of today can be summed up in one, trite, age-old sentence, "Power corrupts," or as Brutus put it, "The abuse of greatness is when it disjoins remorse from power."

Good there has been and good there is, nevertheless, in the American trade union movement — sound and old-fashioned good; enlightened and progressive good. From the earliest struggles for the eight-hour day down to its present plans for a four-day week in the future, it has fought for economic justice. The modern union-management contract is a synthesis of correct conditions of employment due the dignity of the worker as a human being. No organization in the nation has worked so hard and so consistently to eliminate unfair discrimination because of a man's race, creed, or color as has the CIO. Politically, socially, and economically, the influence of the trade unions is leaving its imprint on American life.

There is more than a little truth in the contention of Henry Ford II when he says: "The primitive and relatively unstable capitalism of the past has given way to a consumer-dominated, self-regulating system that broadly serves the interests of the great mass of our people." By the same token, it can truly be said that without the constant prodding of the trade unions, and their constructive contributions to industrial and social progress in America, the advent of this better system would not have come or at least it would not have come on schedule.

That necessary spur to the economy can never come from a weak labor movement. The trade unions have to become strong. They have to generate economic, political, and social power. They have a right to it. In the nature of things, the use of power brings with it the danger of the abuse of it. Neither labor nor industry is an exception to the rule. . . .

Challenge to the Catholic Business Man*

LAURENCE J. McGINLEY, S.J.

Today the free world looks to America to feed its desperately hungry peoples, to rehabilitate its broken machines, to supply "know-how," material, and arms to preserve its freedom. Looking toward America for this assistance, the eyes of the free world focus on the leaders of American business. In the past these men organized miracles of production. They are expected to organize new miracles of production in the future. To them, and to you, who are training yourselves to be leaders of American business, it is not permitted to be mediocre.

If you are to surpass mediocrity, if you are to live up to the expectations of a tortured world, you will need two precious and essential endowments: skills and vision. You will need skills in accounting, statistics, market analysis. And you will need a realistic vision rooted in deep faith in God, who sets the total purpose of peoples, machines, "know-how," matériel, and arms. In forwarding reconstruction of the social

---

* From "The Challenge to the Catholic Business Man," *Catholic Mind*, March 1951.

order, the Church has constantly been faced with this problem: there are too many people who have the skills of management but not the vision; too many people who have the social ideal but not the skills. You must aspire to both.

To surpass mediocrity in your role as Christian business leaders, you must first of all be intelligent and well prepared *business* men. Management is not just a more serious way of exchanging marbles or of bartering butter for wheat. It is a complex set of skills for developing teamwork, streamlining distribution, providing employment and producing incomes for all participants and products for all buyers. Management is a profession "servicing" owner, worker, consumer. Like many other specialized functions, it has grown far beyond the understanding of the average citizen. Ordinary people simply do not know how a business should be organized so that it may realize both legitimate profits and essential social ideals. They leave this task, therefore, to professional business men, just as they leave care of their health to the medical profession, protection of their civil rights to the legal profession, and a large part of their mind's education to other professional groups with other special skills. . . .

But you are also to be *Catholic* business men. This is where the vision comes in. Unlike so many others, you will not acquire the skills and then proceed to fashion a vision with them alone. This would truly be an earthbound, material vision — just like the skills themselves. You already have a vision, beyond the skills, capable of inspiring you beyond mediocrity.

To be a Catholic business man means so much more than just being a business man who is a Catholic. There may not be a Catholic system of cost accounting or a Christian system of retailing, but there is a genuinely Christlike way of being a business man. For you, setting a price or negotiating a wage is much more than applied economics. It is applied morality, as well. The first is relatively easy. The second is admittedly difficult. In their successful combination is your challenge to be more than mediocre. Skills and a vision! This is your goal as Catholic business leaders: to master the science of management and then employ it in the fulfillment of the social ideal of your Catholic faith.

I would like to comment on three of the basic convictions of that faith. The first is the conviction of God's purpose: that all the resources of the earth exist ultimately for all the peoples of the earth; that God wishes these resources — the fertile fields and willing waterfalls, precious ores, and mysterious energies stored away by nature — to serve all his children for His glory as their Creator and their full personal development as His creatures.

Here surely, in making these resources useful and available to all peoples, is a challenge to the productive and distributive genius which marks management that is skilled and genuinely alert. In facing this challenge, management — the executive, the owner, the supervisor, the "coordinator" — must see beyond private advantage alone, beyond good quarterly reports, comfortable reserves, and inventories geared to the latest directive from Washington. Here is where management becomes truly a profession and not a mediocre role for mediocre men. It can become so only if it is inspired by the first element in your faith as Catholic business men — a conviction about the real purpose of the riches of the earth.

A second challenge confronts the Catholic business man, based on the conviction of his responsibility for the welfare of his employees. Where industry has long been established and a vast number of men have access to the goods of the earth only through employment on the property and under the direction of others, the Christian social ideal is most concerned about the worker, be he janitor or be he vice president in charge of sales, but especially if he be janitor.

Bringing the resources of the earth within each man's reach takes on a new phrasing and meaning here. How to organize a business enterprise so that the family living wage can always be paid: how to organize so that the employee can develop his own human dignity and contribute his special genius to our business life through his labor organizations: these challenges are a vital part of the Christian social program. Employee rights present great problems to business men, but in recent years splendid progress has been made toward solving them. What business men have done so often under compulsion in the past they must now continue to do freely, spurred on by this second conviction of responsibility for employee welfare rooted in the vision of Christian faith.

A final challenge confronts the Catholic business man in his conviction that business competition must be free but ordered — and ordered from within. It is a task of the manager, as we have seen, to place the resources of the world at men's disposal through employment of workers on the one hand and through sale of products on the other. Surely it cannot be that this serious task is to be fulfilled in a blood-stained arena wherein men are utterly free to thrust and parry for profits alone, umpired only by that invisible policeman called "self-interest."

No, all social life — its economic phase particularly — must be regulated by an order from within as well as by legal sanctions from without. The satisfaction of human needs is not something which can be bandied about by inflationary price changes, business recessions, and other economic "trends" for which no one seems to take responsibility. Free competition must be ordered competition. How can it be better ordered than under the leadership of management itself, by that genius for organization which has accomplished so many productive marvels before? How order it better than by recognizing the responsibilities of group to group, by more profoundly realizing the natural unity which already exists between employer, worker, and consumer? The intimate nature of an organization which will channel competition along the lines of the total common good has been discussed by scholars in all lands. Its achievement in practice will be brought about by business men with a Christian vision, men who are capable in the skills of management and faithful to the convictions of their vision. Here, surely, is a goal surpassing mediocrity.

These three important convictions of your Catholic faith — God's purpose, responsibility to employees, and ordered competition — are sometimes referred to as unreal. To practice them would not pay, it is objected, and the risk would be prohibitive.

To this we must reply again: "This is not the hour for mediocrity." The Christian social ideal admittedly cannot be realized by following certain old-line doctrines still masquerading as "sound economics." It cannot be realized by those who clamor for protection under the aegis of free enterprise, but who understand by that the petty concept of private gain to be reached at all costs, free from any of those risks that the true enterpriser assumes for the sake of his fellowmen. The Christian social ideal will be realized only by those who are driven by a sense of serious and sacred stewardship to bring to the service of all men the rich resources which modern management and technology make at least physically possible. It will be realized by men possessed of vision as well as skills, men who will hold the challenge and all its risks well worthwhile when accepted in a spirit of faith in the purposes and providence of God.

Ethics and Antitrust Laws*

THEODORE L. THAU

The Business Ethics Advisory Council of the United States Department of Commerce has gone to business firms and said: "Here we have issued a call to action. We ask you to take all steps you can to raise the level of ethical performance in your company. Whatever it may be today, raise it. We're not accusing you of being unethical. We're saying: Do better."

In a number of lines of business the response has been as follows: "We would like to very much, but our industry is highly competitive. If we take the lead, we're liable to find that our competitors will cut us to ribbons. If there is to be any raising of the standard or performance of ethics in our industry, it will have to be done not on a company-by-company basis but on an industry-by-industry basis."

Fine, the Council said. Then let's go to the industries. And the Council talked to leaders and association executives. It told them of the plight of the individual business firms. The response was: "We would like to do this very much, but we don't dare do anything in the way of establishing industry codes with enforcement teeth in them. And without enforcement teeth they are meaningless in our industry."

To them enforcement teeth meant the power of the association to expel a member for breach of the industry code of ethics. Why were they afraid to adopt a code with teeth?

Their answer was: "The firm that we throw out of the industry can sue any one of us who took part in the expulsion action, charging us with a conspiracy to restrain trade. Damages can be sought under the Sherman Antitrust Act. We might win, but it might take several years and cost a lot of money and time. We'd much rather spend those years working at our own businesses."

We talked to officials of the Justice Department and the Federal Trade Commission. We felt sure there could be nothing to such statements; that this fear was groundless. But we found that the FTC and the Antitrust Division do take the position that when a trade

---

* From "The Business of Government and the Government of Business," in *The Concept of Business Ethics*, edited by Daniel N. DeLucca, Council of Business Ethics, St. Joseph's College, Philadelphia, Pennsylvania.

association expels a member for unethical acts or seeks to impose sanctions on a firm that is not a member of the association, there can very well be violations of the laws they are committed to enforce.

The officials also said that what may be unethical to the members of an industry may be the lifeblood of competition to newcomers in the industry. In other words, the code of ethics may seem to be a code of ethics but is actually a device to restrain trade. They recognize that this means in a sense that under our laws people have a right to compete unethically until the day comes when the unethical act has been banned by positive law. . . .

This is a very perplexing problem. There is a lot to be said for the views of the FTC and the Antitrust Division. Experiences of the NRA days indicate there may be some basis for their concern. I submit that we do have a very serious problem here if these business men are really finding it difficult to raise ethical standards on a company basis and the industries to which they belong are having difficulty raising industrywide standards because of laws restricting combinations or groups seeking to police the ethical field.

Examination of Conscience for Labor and Management*

RICHARD McKEON, S.J.

Employers

Moral Aspects. Am I fully aware that the moral law applies to human actions in the marketplace and industry?

Is the policy of my company guided by a Christian moral code?

Am I conscious that my status as employer presents opportunity to fulfill to a high degree the great commandment of love of neighbor?

Do I recognize the dignity of the individual worker as a child of God, redeemed by Jesus Christ, as a person with an immortal soul and eternal destiny?

Do I know that for every right of management there is a corresponding duty? Have I a clear knowledge of my rights as an employer? Am I aware

---

* From "Examination of Conscience for Labor and Management," Le Moyne College, Industrial Relations Association, 1955.

that many rights, formerly exclusive, are now moderated by union and government action?

Do I seriously study the social doctrine of the Church? Am I aware that certain economic systems are opposed to that doctrine?

Does my company practice discrimination on racial, religious, or nationalistic grounds?

Economic Policy. Do I strive to achieve a fair balance between the aims of workers, owners, and consumers?

Do I hold that human relations are more important than technical relations?

Do I know that materialistic (laissez faire, liberalistic) capitalism as well as materialistic, atheistic Communism has been condemned by the Church?

Do I strive for the reformation of the private enterprise system?

Do I plan intelligently, as far as possible, to insure stable employment? To eliminate seasonal ups-and-downs?

Do I understand the concept of the common good?

Do I offer the consumer a quality product at a reasonable price?

Unions. Do I accept the natural, God-given right of workers to organize? Do I firmly believe in the principle of collective bargaining?

Have I developed a cooperative attitude toward responsible unions?

Am I proud of the labor relations within my plant? Have I carefully placed the right man to handle them? Are my foremen well trained, informed on company policy, with sufficient responsibility and authority? Is there an efficient grievance procedure?

Do I ever strive to interfere in the internal affairs of the union? To make use of "stooges"?

Do I bargain in good faith and faithfully observe the agreement?

Workers. Do my workers enjoy just wages? Good working conditions? Am I familiar with the question of family allowances?

Does my company have a sound pension system? Insurance programs? Other fringe benefits? Do I discriminate against older applicants for work?

Do I encourage the formation of credit unions?

Do my workers have pride in their job and product? A real sense of participation in the company?

Do I avoid all trace of paternalism?

Varia. Am I a member of a progressive, fair-minded management association?

Is my personal and family life an inspiration to my employees?

Workers

Dignity of Work. Do I constantly call to mind my dignity as a child of God and my destiny of eternal life in heaven?

Do I know that through my work, however humble, I can honor, love, and serve my God and my neighbor?

D I reflect on how Christ the Carpenter bestowed dignity on all work?

Do I appreciate what the Church has done for the workingman?

Am I interested in the principles of private property?

Do I understand the danger of Communism to the worker? the nation? the Church?

Education. Do I strive to improve my skill?

Have I tried to gain more knowledge of industrial relations? by reading? by adult education?

Do I understand the true nature of unions and collective bargaining?

Do I have a sense of participation in my company? Is it my fault that I do not understand its general policies?

Duties at Work. Do I always do an honest day's work? Am I absent from work without due cause? Frequently or seldom? Is alcohol the reason? How much of my work is rejected?

Am I guilty of featherbedding? Stretching-out the work? Am I doing this because of subservience to the union or on my own responsibility? Do I realize that this is a waste of manpower?

Unionism. Do I realize the importance of promoting public confidence in labor unions?

Do I attend my union meetings regularly? Do I participate without fear in the discussions? Do I always vote for the best officials?

When I have a just grievance, do I present it through proper channels?

Is my union free from subversive elements? from racketeers?

Is my political vote based on conviction and not merely union pressure?

Management. Do I have respect for my foreman and higher management? If not, what is wrong?

Do I appreciate the efforts of management and owners to have an efficient and successful company?

Do I respect the property of the company entrusted to me?

Am I proud of my company and its products?

Do I sincerely appreciate all the fringe benefits which my company affords?

Varia. Do I appreciate the benefits of the Social Security Act?

Do I discriminate among my fellow-workers because of color, race, or creed?

Am I familiar with the question of family allowances?

Am I familiar with the principle of subsidiarity in the social doctrine of the Church? With the idea of Christian industry councils?

Am I convinced that a worker who can sincerely give answers to these questions is making his most important contribution to industrial peace and prosperity?

Labor Leaders

Moral Aspects. Do I recognize that the actions of labor unions fall under the moral law? Am I convinced that industrial relations cannot be divorced from morality? Do I see that religion, not the state, will reform industrial society? Do I affirm that the Church has the right to speak on problems of the social order?

Do I recognize the dignity of all men as children of God, by true love of neighbor?

Do I discriminate on racial, religious, or nationalistic grounds? Am I honest and above reproach from all parties concerned? Have I made certain that welfare and other funds are safely protected from fraud and scandal? Would I act in collusion with an employer to check legitimate union gains? Do I realize that opposition to unionism is largely due to corrupt leaders — men who betray their fellow workers?

Rights and Duties. Have I a clear knowledge of the rights of labor? Do I recognize that the right to organize is a God-given, natural right, not from the state? Do I know that every right has a corresponding duty?

Am I conscious of the duty of promoting greater public confidence in unions? Am I willing to make sacrifices in my field of action? Do I strive to solve difficulties before they become hot issues?

Do I insist that workers give an honest day's work for an honest day's pay? Do I check to see that they live up to the contract? Do I try to break down the outmoded attitude of antagonism of workers toward their employers?

Union Members. Do I possess the high respect of members of my union? Do I know that my acts reflect on the members I represent?

Am I proud of the relations between my union and the plant? Have I made certain that my union members have a fair knowledge of the contract?

Do I strive to have grievances settled fairly and quickly? Do I make union meetings worthwhile to attend? Do I seek to advance within the union by flattery, by selfish cliques?

Is my zeal for true unionism still strong? Do I see in my work an apostolate for social justice? Do I endeavor through personal conviction and example to sell the benefits of unionism to the unorganized?

Do I know that unions are the prime target of Communism? Have I been guilty of disloyalty by joining or unwittingly giving help to subversive movements?

Private Enterprise and Management. Have I a moderate knowledge of the American enterprise system? Am I alert to the dangers to that system inherent in socialism and Communism?

Where do I stand in regard to economy in government and to restriction of government activity in conflict with private enterprise? Am I alert to problems, like automation, which affect employment? Do I advocate programs of labor-management cooperation to reduce costs and increase production? Am I familiar with the general policies of the firm?

Do I advocate programs of ownership of stock by unions and union members? Have I developed a cooperative attitude toward fair-minded management? Am I still a devoted, energetic representative or have I fallen into a lazy, bureaucratic state of mind?

Labor Arbitration*

LEO C. BROWN, S.J.

Despite the prevalence of labor arbitration, its function remains widely misunderstood. Arbitrators regularly are explaining to friends that they do not settle strikes. Arbitration has been adopted precisely to avoid strikes and threats of strikes. In the past ten years labor arbitration has become so common that the possibility of a work stoppage during the life of an agreement normally does not occur to either party. The matter is routinely referred to the arbitrator, a date for the hearing is set, the hearing is informal but businesslike, the award is received with good grace by loser as well as winner and, what is more important, is promptly given effect.

The arbitration process in the United States is completely the creature

---

* From "Labor Arbitration," *Social Order*, February, 1957.

of the particular union and management who resort to it. They freely enter the arbitration pact. They jointly select the arbitrator or determine the process by which he is to be selected. They determine the scope of his authority and, if they choose, the kind of evidence which he will consider and the criteria he is to apply in reaching his decision. Many of these points and others may be set out in a formal stipulation, but often the agreement to arbitrate is oral and not infrequently many details are matters of tacit understanding or are left to the arbitrator's judgment. . . .

While arbitration hearings are rather informal, they are nonetheless orderly. At the outset of the hearing the parties usually agree upon a statement of the issue to be submitted to the arbitrator. This "submission agreement" is important because it defines the arbitrator's jurisdiction by specifying the issues under dispute. Thus the arbitrator is commissioned to decide the questions proposed to him and no others. Commonly such a stipulation covers other details, such as an agreement between the union and the company to share the expense of the proceedings, including the arbitrator's fee. The union, which normally is the moving party, presents its case first. The spokesmen proceed without interruption from the other side, except in those instances where questions are needed to clarify some point that is being made. The right of cross-examination is recognized.

Unlike court proceedings, in an arbitration few objections are raised about the admissibility of evidence. In jury trials, such legal objections have the purpose of preventing a litigant from misleading the jury by introduction of improper or nonprobative matter. The arbitrator, however, is both judge and jury and is normally assumed to be as well qualified to judge the relevance of evidence as spokesmen of either party. Moreover, in courtroom proceedings attorneys frequently object in the hope of making a record upon which an appeal from the trial court may be based. In an arbitration such a record is useless because the arbitrator's decision is final.

Finally, unlike litigations before the courts, a hearing before an arbitrator is not a proceeding in an adversary forum. In the normal civil suit the parties may be at odds only once in a lifetime. After the suit they may be under no compulsion of dealing again with each other. The verdict is the prime objective and, under such circumstances, lawyers' tactics do not have to be weighed in the light of their possible detrimental effect on future relationships. But the parties in a labor dispute are an employer and his employees who, when the hearing is over, must continue to work together in harmony and good will. Excessive technical objections by either side or offensive tactics in cross-examination might severely damage future relationships. . . .

People who have limited experience with labor arbitration frequently ask whether results would not be better if labor courts, operating under procedures determined by statute, were substituted for the wholly voluntary and largely informal processes of private arbitration. Such a question fails to recognize that arbitration is successful largely because it is the creation of the parties, devised by them to meet their own peculiar, well-defined, and clearly-recognized needs. Its informality, relative economy, and freedom from technical rules are among the qualities which make it attractive. Because it grows out of a pact between the parties, the use of such a procedure, over which the parties retain so much control, is a very short step removed from settlement by the parties themselves. . . .

Most puzzling to continental European students of labor relations (who have been visiting the United States in considerable number in recent years) is the lack of readily-available machinery for enforcing arbitrators' awards. Apart from the states with especially-designed arbitration statutes there are only the broad provisions of the common law. However, enforcement procedures at common law are slow, somewhat cumbersome, and uncertain. The success of arbitration, however, has not been appreciably hampered by lack of enforcement machinery. Experienced arbitrators can recall few if any instances in which a party refused to give effect to an adverse award. . . .

Arbitration of disputes about the content of agreements, in contrast to disputes about their meaning, is the exception rather than the rule. There are indications, however, that even in these matters labor and management are becoming less reluctant to submit their differences to an impartial third person. Each succeeding year adds to our experience of the arbitration process and to our number of experienced labor arbitrators. We are discovering more and more that arbitrators' awards fall within "the range of expectation" of the parties. Experienced arbitrators do not impose intolerable burdens nor introduce sweeping changes. As a result, the parties are tending to place greater confidence in arbitrators with whom they have had considerable experience.

Furthermore, there is limited but increasing evidence that labor and management are also calling upon arbitrators to act as private mediators during contract negotiations. In such circumstances, of course, the person invited to aid the negotiators does not function as an arbitrator, since he has no power to make an award. He lends the benefit of his experience to the negotiators in their search for mutually satisfactory solutions of their common problems. Precisely because the arbitrator has the confidence of both parties and is invited by them specifically to make recommendations, his authority and influence are great. Here we have a procedure which produces results substantially similar to arbitration without some of its limitations. Both labor and management have shown an unwillingness to give third parties the unreviewable right to determine the content of their labor contracts. This fact makes it probable that the limited authority of the private mediator will be increasingly resorted to by negotiators endeavoring to forestall a particularly damaging strike.

This preventive mediation is one of the most promising of recent innovations in industrial relations and its use has been endorsed by the Federal Mediation and Conciliation Service. Increased experimentation with it should be encouraged by all who are interested in promoting industrial peace.

A Functional Society*

JOHN F. CRONIN, S.S.

Pope Pius XI considered that the proper function of government had been badly perverted under the influence of liberalism. First, the theory of laissez faire caused the state to abdicate its function of protecting exploited groups and seeking the general welfare. The reaction to this extreme, and the fact that pluralism in society had broken down, then led the state to overburden itself with excessive powers. Government should be sovereign in a pluralistic society. It should have final decision on matters affecting the common good, but it should encourage diffusion of power in areas better handled by less comprehensive societies. Society exists to strengthen and help its constituent members. This is the famed principle of subsidiarity expounded in *Quadragesimo Anno*.

In this connection, the question of the proper role of the state has been seriously discussed in our nation for many years. Under the New Deal, we reacted against the laissez-faire attitude previously in the ascendancy. World War II accentuated the trend toward centralization.

---

* From "The Message of Quadragesimo Anno Today," *Social Order*, January, 1956. Also in *Catholic Mind*, November, 1956.

Currently there is a reaction against excessive concentration of power in the federal government, in favor of more state-local activity. But much more can be done in the direction of pluralism, especially in encouraging effective activity by subsidiary groups.

Certainly this appears to be one of the key ideas in the celebrated and much debated section, often called the heart of the encyclical, on vocational organization. In describing this type of economic society, Pope Pius XI uses the term *"ordines"* in quotation marks. German and French translators use the terms *Berufstände* and *organisations professionnelles*. So far as can be determined, the reference is to a type of social structure not common under our legal system but well known in countries influenced by German law. It refers to an organization, private in nature, but possessing legally enforceable powers in governing the profession or group concerned. Such a group would be the exclusive representative of the occupation in question, affecting all persons in the occupation. The closest parallels generally known here would be the medieval guilds, our medical and bar associations, and possibly a group such as the National Association of Security Dealers.

The main purposes of such a type of social organization would be: (1) to build a framework which would facilitate the practice of social justice; (2) to restore pluralism into society, thus achieving a structural barrier against either individualism or statism and (3) to replace a class-struggle, overly competitive mentality with a cooperative approach to common problems. The Pope considers this form of organization just as natural to man as the formation of cities or towns to meet man's social and political needs. By contrast, he considers atomistic individualism in industry and the class struggle between workers and management as foreign growths harmfully introduced into the body economic. The Pope is realistic enough to see the value of proper competition, and the inevitability of some clash of interest between capital and labor. But he rejects an economic order that emphasizes exclusively the divisive elements in the economy, to the detriment of cooperation and order.

Social order, rightly conceived, calls for organized cooperation within industries and occupations, as well as cooperation among these groups. Such cooperation would be directed toward the common good of the country. Undoubtedly these groups would have considerable powers of self-regulation, thus freeing government from the excessive detail burdening it today. They would not replace organizations, such as labor unions or employers' associations, dedicated to exclusive interests of a particular class. They might absorb and expand such fledgling groups as exist today to promote common interests of an industry.

The reception given to this concept here has been mixed. On the one hand, many non-Catholic thinkers have either welcomed it or developed similar ideas independently. On the other hand, some have rejected it out of hand as implying fascism or regimentation. Many of these latter difficulties may have been caused in part by overeagerness on the part of American Catholic thinkers to work out a detailed blueprint for such a pluralistic society. This was further complicated by the introduction of economic or political preconceptions not contained in the encyclical. . . .

Instead of presenting detailed blueprints, often foreign to our type of political and economic organization, we would have been wiser to have singled out the main ideas of economic pluralism and to have explained how these could be adopted with minimum changes in our basic economic system. Progress is more often evolutionary than revolutionary. If we can make progress in: (1) joint organization of labor and management to meet common problems; (2) transfer of many government regulatory functions to these groups, with safeguards for the common good; and (3) emphasis on cooperation rather than class struggle, then we could go far toward the ideal social order. By emphasizing, publicizing, and encouraging developments in this direction, we could make substantial progress. What the final result will be, in detail, we do not know, nor do we have any right to pretend to know. . . .

CHAPTER 6

THE FARM SECTOR

> *It is our opinion that farmers themselves as the interested parties ought to take the initiative and play an active role in promoting their own economic advancement, social progress, and cultural betterment. They can readily perceive and appreciate the fundamental nobility of their work. It is carried on in the majestic cathedral of nature. It constantly deals with plants and animals, whose life is inexhaustible in its modes of expression, inflexible in its laws, rich in allusions to God, the Creator and Provider. And finally, it produces not only the variety of food needed to nourish the human family but also an increasing supply of raw materials for manufacturing.*
>
> Pope John XXIII in *Mater et Magistra*

In discussing the contemporary exodus from rural regions to urban centers, which has created new slums all over the world, Pope John recognized that some shifting of this kind is normal and inevitable. "As an economy develops and flourishes," he wrote in *Mater et Magistra*, "the labor force engaged in agriculture decreases."

This process has been under way for a long time in the United States, and it will almost certainly continue.

From a purely economic viewpoint, this is all to the good. The fewer the workers needed to satisfy the nation's needs for food and fiber, the more who will be available for jobs in industry and commerce. The shift from farms to cities represents an efficient use of manpower.

What is economically efficient, however, may not always be socially desirable. Farming is a way of life as well as a business, and for this reason Americans have traditionally had a special regard for it. The sturdy, independent farm operator has always been regarded as a bulwark of democracy, the possessor of all those virtues that men associate with a sound society. While most of us, like Pope John, recognize that

121

a decline in farm population, and even in the number of farms, is inevitable and, in the circumstances, even desirable, some farm experts warn against a blind, fatalistic assent to change. They tell us that the combination of technological forces and human acquisitiveness can, if not controlled, destroy agriculture as a way of life. In that event, the moral repercussions on our society would be serious and far-reaching.

Technological progress in agriculture has raised another great ethical and cultural issue — the issue of abundance. Though the number of farms and farmers has been falling for years, we are still able to produce much more food than we can use ourselves or sell profitably to others. In order to save farmers from the economic effects of their efficiency, and to guarantee them a measure of justice, the government has been striving since the early 1930's to maintain farm prices at parity with other prices. To do this, it has been obliged to manage the supply side of the supply-demand equation. In other words, it has had to restrict production to prevent the piling up of price-depressing surpluses.

In a world where nobody was hungry, that policy would be morally acceptable as well as sound economically. The question is, can a restrictionist policy be justified today? Though the United States, at considerable cost to taxpayers, has given away to needy nations — or sold for local currencies — tons and tons of foodstuffs, not all Americans are persuaded that we are doing as much as we can and should do. Abundance, alas, has its problems no less than scarcity. As the articles that follow show, the great debate over farm policy rages unabated.

The Farmers' Share of the National Income*

JAMES E. KENNEY

The farmers' share of the national income is naturally related to the share of the national income which arises from farming. As an economic activity, farming is the application of labor and capital to land. The farmer, acting as a farmer, uses tools, equipment, raw materials, and miscellaneous supplies purchased from other industries. Exercising his skill and relying upon his knowledge, applying human, animal, or mechanical power, the farmer synthesizes the chemicals of the soil, air, water, and

---

* From "The Farmers' Share of the National Income," *Review of Social Economy*, March, 1962.

sunlight to create the products of agriculture, which we generally classify as food and fiber.

After making the necessary deductions for the value of inputs used in farming, we arrive at what may be termed the *net wealth increment* which originates in the agricultural industry. This represents a net contribution to the total income of the nation. In other words, as a result of their *farming operations*, farmers add quantities of cotton, tobacco, corn, soybeans, vegetables, beef, and other agricultural commodities to the so-called "goods heap."

Once the farmer has brought a net wealth increment into existence, he is then able to acquire a share of the output of other industries. It is this share which is the primary concern of our analysis.

In order to obtain a statistical notion of the magnitude of the farmers' share, we start with what must obviously be the largest single item in *gross* farm income, namely, what the farmer gets for the sale of his products — "cash receipts from farm marketings." To this total are added payments made by the government under its various agricultural programs, as well as estimates of the value of farm products consumed on the farm, the rental value of farm dwellings, and any net change in the value of inventory.

Next, specific costs of agricultural production are deducted: purchases of seed and fertilizer, repairs to equipment, depreciation, etc. What remains constitutes *net income* from the whole agricultural operation.

If we define a farmer as "a person who operates a farm," it is necessary to make further subtractions from net income: wages to hired workers, rent, interest. This gives *net income of farm operators*. Since, however, this item still includes an estimate of the net change in inventory, we subtract the latter in order to arrive finally at *realized net income* of farm operators. In 1960, American farm operators had a realized net income of $11.9 billion. With this amount, they could exercise claims against the output of the nonagricultural sector.

However, this $11.9 billion total does not represent the entire sum of farmers' claims against the output of the rest of the economy. In recent years, there has been a significant rise in the income of farm people from nonfarm sources. According to the 1961 *Economic Report of the President*, the farm sector earned in 1960 a record $6.9 billion for work done off the farm. This is more than half as much as the net income from farming alone in the same year. . . .

Hence, it would appear that the American farmer today, as a single individual, is actually the recipient of two shares of the national income — one for his purely agricultural operation, and the other as a full-time or part-time wage earner in manufacturing, trade, construction, or some other economic activity.

This raises an interesting point: since the farmers' share of the national income is not coextensive with the national income going to farming, should not the two be treated separately in analyzing the farmers' welfare? Presumably, income earned by the farmer from nonfarm sources is used to acquire goods and services for farm consumption, and hence would tend to affect favorably the level of living in rural areas. Thus, it is possible for farmers to receive a smaller and smaller income from farming, without experiencing a corresponding retrogression in their level of living.

As a recipient of income, how does the farmer compare to other groups in the national economy? By all the usual criteria of dollar returns, he is clearly low man on the totem pole. This is true, even when nonfarm income is included. For example: throughout the period from 1934 to 1958, the per capita income of farm people was, rather consistently, about half the per capita income of nonfarm people.

In 1958, the median income of persons with income stood at $2,666 for urban and rural nonfarm persons, as compared to a median of $1,087 for rural farm persons. Between 1945 and 1958, this median income figure for nonfarm persons rose by $1,134, while during the same period median farm income advanced only $420.

Data supplied by the Department of Commerce for the period 1946 to 1960 indicate that the average annual earnings per full-time employee have consistently been lowest in farming. In 1960, the average for all industries was $4,705, while in farming it was $1,555. Even in the second lowest category, that of services, employees' average annual earnings were more than twice as large as those in farming.

In 1959, 30 percent of farm operator families had family personal income before taxes of $4,000 a year or less; whereas only 7 percent of nonfarm families had incomes of $4,000 or less for that year. . . .

In 1940, the farm population received 6.5 percent of the national income. In 1960, the share of the farm population stood at 3.3 percent.

The net income of farm operators from farming declined by 34 percent from the peak in 1948 through 1956, falling from $17.7 billion to $11.6 billion.

In view of all we have heard recently about the importance of gearing income increases to productivity changes, it is enlightening to note that during this period of decline in farm income the farm sector established new records in output and productivity. The farm output index rose from 97 in 1944 to 127 in 1960. The index of production per man-hour on the farm advanced from 81 in 1944 to 191 in 1959. In 1944, with a total farm employment of 10.2 million, the agricultural sector supported 13.84 persons per farm worker. In 1959, with total farm employment reduced to 7.4 million, there were 23.69 Americans and foreigners supported per farm worker.

Taking 1947 as a base year, since output was then most nearly equal for the farm and nonfarm sectors, a comparison of the indexes of real output shows that during the period from 1909 to 1959, the output of farm workers increased about 3.5 times, while the output of nonfarm workers increased 2.6 times.

It seems reasonable to conclude, therefore, that the declining share of national income going to farmers is not explainable solely in terms of a lessening productivity or output. It should also be pointed out that per capital farm income would have been considerably smaller if there had not occurred a substantial exodus of population from rural areas. The economic attrition resulting from falling farm income also shows up in the number of farms. The nation now has fewer than 4 million farms. This is a reduction of 23 percent from 1954 to 1959.

With the available statistical information as background, is it possible to determine whether or not the American farmer is receiving an adequate income? Indications are that the farm sector is not keeping pace with the growing well-being of the nonfarm sector. Is this as it should be? After a close look at all the tables and charts, can we say that the farmer is not getting a *fair* share of the national income? . . .

One of the most widely-held theses in farm income analysis is that the farmers' share is inadequate — hence, unfair — because it does not enable him to live as well as his city cousin. In the *American Economic Review* for March, 1956, Professor John D. Black of Harvard has stated it this way:

> Of course the overwhelming reason that the 86.5 per cent of the people of this country who do not live on farms should want to help those who do is that the people who live on farms are part of this country and should live as well and happily as the rest of us. Our analysis has demonstrated that, considered as one group, they are not doing this, even after the publicly released statistics are needfully supplemented.

Mater et Magistra also stresses this as a fundamental question meriting special consideration:

> . . . what to do in order that the standard of living of the rural-farm population may approximate as closely as possible that of city dwellers who draw their income from industry and the services . . . (N. 125).

This thought is expressed again in a somewhat different form later on in the encyclical:

> It is true that farm products are destined above all to satisfy the primary needs of man; hence, their price should be within the reach of all consumers. Still, this fact cannot be used as an argument for compelling a whole class of citizens to live in a permanent state of socioeconomic inferiority by depriving them of the purchasing power that a decent standard of living requires. For this would be diametrically opposed to the common good (N. 140).

Inadequacy of the farmer's income to support a level of material prosperity comparable to that of the nonfarmer carries with it strong overtones of social injustice. However, there is a related thesis which relies more heavily on basic economic considerations. This thesis stresses the interdependence of the various productive sectors of the economy, the chain reaction set up by explosive changes in a particular sector, and the aggregate gains to be derived from maintaining an overall balance.

Mater et Magistra states that "the economic systems of nations ought to be developed gradually and a balance maintained among all sectors of production (n. 128). The encyclical also indicates what tools are useful in achieving this objective:

> Systems of social insurance and social security can contribute effectively to the redistribution of national income according to standards of justice and equity. These systems can therefore be looked on as instruments for restoring balance between standards of living among different categories of the population (N. 136).

Professor Black, in his paper at the 1955 Annual Meeting of the American Economic Association, opined that the nature of the interdependence between the farm and nonfarm sectors needs to be stated more definitely. Even if it has not been analyzed fully, the existence of this interdependence has never escaped the attention of agricultural economists. In the usual treatment, emphasis is laid upon the gain to the whole community, in the form of lower prices for farm products, resulting from the considerable improvement in agricultural productivity. There is also a stated social gain from the increased output of nonagricultural goods produced by the labor and other resources released from the agricultural sector. Furthermore, the concept of mutual benefit relates agriculture's demand for manufactured goods to the economic welfare of the nonfarm sector, particularly workers in factories.

Mater et Magistra, after calling for special help to agriculture, enabling it to keep up with new methods and techniques, continues:

> In this way, the agricultural economy comes to absorb a larger amount of industrial goods and to demand a higher quality of services. In turn, it offers to the other two sectors and to the whole community products which best meet, in quality and quantity, the needs of the consumer. In this way, it contributes to the stability of the purchasing power of money — a very helpful factor in the orderly development of the entire economic system (N. 129).

From the domain of business cycle analysis comes the view that the degree of cyclical swing for the whole economy is strongly influenced by what happens in agriculture. A depressed agriculture acts as a drag on the business sector; a prosperous agriculture supplies an economic stimulant. . . .

Low or falling farm income is thus no longer exclusively a farm problem, but rather a national problem, requiring the attention of the entire country.

The case for strengthening farm income (or, at least, not permitting it to fall further) also goes directly to the question of preserving social values. Farming, particularly that done on the family farm, is a fundamental American institution. The farmer is an almost heroic figure in American culture. He represents the virtues which comprise the American ideal — self-reliance, hard work, initiative, neighborliness, and so on. As Pope John expresses it, farming is "a work characterized by its own moral dimension. For it demands of the farmer a capacity for orientation and adaptation, patience in the face of an uncertain future, a sense of responsibility toward the demands of the task at hand, a spirit of perseverance and initiative" (N. 145).

In this context, the argument for greater financial returns to agriculture takes on the hue and form of social philosophy. Low or falling farm income threatens the extinction of a way of life which should be preserved for the good of the whole nation. . . .

If a reliable analysis of farm income reveals that it is inadequate in a substantial degree, or that the farm sector is trailing the nonfarm sector by too wide a margin, we are drawn inevitably into an investigation of the possible methods or techniques to be adopted in improving the farm income situation. Here *Mater et Magistra* will be a godsend for those economists who have so far hesitated to adopt a position vis-a-vis the legislative program of the federal government as it pertains to agriculture.

In examining the Papal recommendations for the relief of the distressed areas of farming, the arch-conservative will be dismayed to discover that the ideas advanced in *Mater et Magistra* are clearly realistic, progressive, and even liberal. Evidently Pope John does not fear that we will be on the road to communism if we use the legislative arm of the government to redress economic imbalance and to promote the welfare of special groups.

In the program outlined in *Mater et Magistra*, the government plays a key role. Government policy, in the Pope's view, should cover questions of taxation, credit, social insurance, price protection, the fostering of processing industries, and the adjustment of farm managerial structures.

In levying taxes in rural areas, government agencies are advised to consider the uncertainties and uneven flow of farm income. A special credit policy should be evolved for farmers. Since agricultural investments do not yield a high rate of return, and the farmer has difficulty obtaining capital, credit institutions should be set up to provide the farmer with capital at a suitable rate of interest.

The Papal view is that two forms of insurance are essential in agriculture: one to cover farm products, the other to cover the farm labor force and their families. There is no *specific* mention of price supports, surplus removal, or acreage allotments. The general recommendation is that "farm prices should be protected with the help of some of the many devices which economic experts have discovered" (N. 137). It is revealing to note the explicit suggestion that price protection be carried out primarily by the interested parties, under governmental supervision.

Mater et Magistra also advocates action to help farm families supplement their income without leaving a rural environment. This can be done by establishing in rural areas both food-processing industries and enterprises connected with other economic sectors and professional activities.

I would only belabor the obvious if I pointed out how closely the Pope's prescriptions for the ills of farming parallel the agricultural program adopted here in the United States since the first AAA.

One passage in *Mater et Magistra* is particularly intriguing in view of frequent and often bitter criticisms of the pressure tactics employed by farm organizations when new farm legislation is pending in Congress:

> It is also essential that they [the farmers] form a flourishing system of cooperatives and professional organizations. They ought likewise to take an effective interest in public affairs that concern not only administrative agencies, but also political movements. It is Our opinion that farmers themselves as the interested parties ought to take the initiative and play an active role in promoting their own economic advancement, social progress, and cultural betterment (NN. 143, 144).

Besides coming out strongly in favor of farm lobbies, Pope John also advocates government action to improve essential public services in rural areas: good roads, education, health facilities, recreation, and so on. Action along this line will make rural life more attractive.

The foregoing prescriptions are doubly useful: first, they should help to blow away the lingering wisps of laissez-faire smoke still obstructing the vision of even the best economists when they look at our present farm policy; second, they should serve to mark out the areas of agricultural economics which now need much more extended professional treatment. For example: is the farmer getting a fair return on his capital investment? how does the return on farm capital compare to that in nonfarm use?

I would conclude by offering this one suggestion: whatever professional studies of the farmers' share of the national income may be pursued in the future, those who address themselves to the problem of analyzing the farmers' economic status, and those who are more concerned with related policy matters, should consciously and conscientiously regard the end or objective proposed in the encyclical:

> . . . that farm workers in every community may enjoy both an adequate share of economic blessings and a decent life (N. 148).

Drift From the Land*

FRANK ORAZEM

The farm population in the United States continues to shrink. In the ten years between 1950 and 1960 it fell from 30.5 million to about 20 million. This is at a rate of about one million persons per year. Announcements of these facts by the Bureau of Census usually bring forth expressions of alarm from various sources that family farming is in danger.

---

* From "Drift From the Land," *Social Order*, April, 1961.

There are localized areas where an increase in other types of farms has been taking place. This, however, is not true for most of commercial agriculture. Factual evidence indicates that the family farm is not necessarily in danger. In general, it is in a relatively strong position. The 1959 census indicates that so-called corporation farms make up only a small fraction of the total number of farms.

It is true that operators on many farms are getting low returns for the time they spend in farming and for the capital they have invested in land, buildings, and machinery. But there also are farms that continue to provide good incomes even with relatively low prices. Nevertheless, few people will dispute that returns on resources in agriculture, by and large, are lower than those in other industries. The pressure for long-run adjustments is mounting from forces in and outside of agriculture.

The process of change is painful for many individual operators; however, adjustments in the organization of many farms are inevitable. Actually, the adjustments that are taking place in agriculture are not new. Agriculture, like the rest of the economy, has been adjusting to changing needs and conditions continuously, and this more rapidly in the past thirty years. As a result, rural standards of living have improved.

The pushes and pulls that influence some people to leave the farm do not stem from agriculture alone. They also stem from the state of our national economy, of which agriculture is a part. This economy is not stable. It is in a continuous state of flux. Thus, some adjustments can always be expected and cannot be eliminated in a dynamic economy. For the most part, people who leave the farm do so because they think opportunities are better elsewhere. They will continue to leave so long as attractive employment opportunities exist in the rest of the economy.

While rural exodus seems large, this does not by any means constitute a mass-movement. People who have deep roots in farming will not give up. Neither will persons whose farming operations, ability to adjust to changing needs, experience, skills or age make farming still the best alternative for them. For most families the decision to leave or to change occupation is and has been entirely their own. Such a decision does not mean that agriculture or family farming is a sinking ship. What it does mean is that total manpower of those directly engaged in farming is declining and that individual farms are getting larger.

The adjustments that are taking place within agriculture concerning the number of people on farms and the size of farms are largely the result of three types of forces.

One factor goes back to the original settlement of the United States, when farms of the same size were established on soils differing in productivity. The Preemption and Homestead Acts generally established the quarter-section farm (160 acres), which has long been the most typical farm size in many states. Farms of 160 acres were a good size for the farming techniques and capital of 100 years ago. They remained a "good size" so long as horses and mules furnished most of the power for farming operations; in some areas, the 160-acre farm still continues to provide adequate family incomes. The change, then, in the number of farms and sizes has not been uniform. There are differences in adjustments not only between regions but also between states and even counties within states.

Generally, the number of farms has declined most in soil areas where yields have been lowest. In these areas, too, most of the farms established were of the 160-acre size, though in many cases a smaller proportion of the land could be cropped and yields per acre were lower than in other areas. It is obvious that a farm with relatively poor soil will not produce as much income as the same size farm with a more productive soil. A farm located in the Great Plains might have to be four or five times as large to produce the same income as a farm located in the Corn Belt. A trend correcting these differences has been under way since the 1920's.

It is true that for many families income is not the ultimate nor the unique goal. Satisfaction obtained from rural living may substitute for money income. However, the price to be paid — in the form of low income — for remaining on farms has increased in recent years. In addition, today's higher standard of living increases desires for purchased goods. By increasing both their output for sale and their purchases of production supplies, farm families have developed a dependence on the market system. More cash is needed to satisfy an ever increasing list of wants. Thus, for the small farmer to remain in agriculture and be content with the nonmonetary returns of living on a farm, he must now make greater sacrifices in income than in the past.

The second force causing the drift from the land is that of new technology, which lowers costs for larger farming operations and permits one family to operate more acres. This factor encourages farm operators with sufficient capital to increase their acreage. Machinery increases total costs; but if the costs are spread over enough acres, there is a lower cost per acre and per unit of output. So the lower costs help increase net income per acre and thus provide a larger total income for family living. In this process, too, some farms disappear as separate units and some people are squeezed out of farming. This process is not unique for the farming industry; it can be found in other businesses and even in whole industries. It is not pleasant for the people adversely affected but it is part of the price of progress.

In addition to the "pushing" force there is also a "pulling" force. This force is that of general economic growth and growth in nonfarm employment opportunities. Aside from temporary setbacks, the economy is constantly pressing forward. This forward press and growth are reflected in the size of the nation's productive plant and in the quality of goods and the amount of services produced.

Our American standard of living continues to increase not only in terms of incomes but also in the amount and the variety of things a family can buy. Many of the goods that were considered luxuries in the recent past are now considered more or less essentials on every family's list. Developments in agriculture contributed to this progress. By tremendous increases in productivity and efficiency, agriculture has freed labor to produce other products and services the American consumer wants; at the same time the American farmer still continues to produce food at relatively low cost.

Many farm families realize that they could improve their lot by moving to a nonfarm job. This is particularly true for families who are unable, because of shortage of capital, to enlarge their farming operations. Employment opportunities and relatively higher wage rates in nonfarm industries provide an incentive for these families to change occupations.

These types of adjustments are made more easily in some areas than in others. Some communities have not lost population as a result of adjustments in farm size and number of people on farms. These are areas where the rate of industrial growth has been large enough to absorb the number of persons shifting from farm to off-farm employment. This type of adjustment is the least painful. People can continue to live in the same community. The relatively rapid rate of industrialization in much of the South, for example, in the postwar years has already allowed for some shifts of this type.

Not all agricultural areas, however, can match the need for employment with economic growth in local industries and services. The opportunities depend on local markets for finished products, water and power supplies, local tax laws, transportation, skills of available workers, quality of local government and other factors considered for a good job climate. If these conditions favor sufficiently rapid growth in local industries, shifts from farm to nonfarm employment can be made quite readily. In other areas, the shift can come only through more extensive movements of people to jobs. This type of readjustment usually is more painful.

Of course, there is no inherent merit in having an increasing population, nor is there necessarily an inherent disadvantage in a decreasing population. But in some areas the sparse rural population is already at a point where it is too small to support certain institutions, unless there is a change in the organization of these institutions and a change in the manner of services rendered.

Agriculture is faced with definite problems. Evidence indicates that agriculture is not sharing fully in the fruits of the growing economy. If it is to regain its share, certain adjustments are needed. Some of them are hard to encompass. Putting off adjustments will make them still harder to face as time goes on.

The Migratory Worker*

MSGR. GEORGE G. HIGGINS

The American community rejects the idea that the power and authority of government should be used in such a manner as to perpetuate a farm labor system that is based on poverty and destitution both at home and abroad.

Yet, at the present time that is the kind of farm labor system we have in the United States. The proof of this thesis lies in the answer to two basic questions:

1. Where would agricultural employers find domestic workers willing to migrate from harvest to harvest at substandard wages, working and living conditions, if there were not poverty and unemployment in the home areas of our migratory work force?
2. Where would agricultural employers who employ foreign labor obtain their hired hands if poverty and unemployment were not widespread in the countries from which these workers originate?

The answer to these questions is simple. If this pool of underprivileged workers were not available, American growers would have to compete on the open market for their labor. Like industrial employers, they would have to plan their production schedules in accordance with the labor

---

* From a lecture for the Mott Adult Education Program, Flint, Michigan, January 21, 1965, *Catholic Mind*, May, 1965.

market situation. They would have to offer wages and working conditions that would appeal to domestic workers, that were covered by such protective legislation as minimum wage, unemployment insurance, and workmen's compensation. In short, they would be forced to raise employment standards in agriculture.

However, because there is poverty at home and abroad, the American grower does not have to worry about such things. Because his workers are not protected by most social and labor legislation, he can ignore taxes for unemployment insurance, insurance rates for workmen's compensation, industrial child labor laws, and laws which guarantee workers the right to organize into unions. Most important, because there is no floor on wages for agricultural workers, he can recruit workers at wages far below the level necessary to maintain human dignity.

As a result, American farm workers — especially migrant workers — are among the least privileged of any major occupational group in the nation. Anyone who has seen the conditions under which most of these workers live knows that it is not necessary to go abroad to observe human beings living in abject poverty.

The question that must be decided on all levels of government, but especially on the federal level, is — "Shall we make it a matter of public policy to perpetuate these conditions, or shall we attempt now to eliminate this social blight from the American scene?"

There is no way that this problem can be rationalized out of existence. The basic causes of the farm labor situation — low wages and underemployment due to labor surpluses in some of our rural areas — must be eliminated once and for all. It should be public policy to adopt those measures which will achieve this goal. . . .

Up to the present time, our lawmakers have compromised on the issue of farm labor. Not only have our institutions failed to adopt policies that would assure an adequate supply of farm labor at decent standards of employment, but they have also been used to procure foreign labor in a manner which in many cases has had an adverse effect on the employment conditions, wages, and working conditions of domestic farm workers. Moreover, government at all levels has seen fit to deprive agricultural labor of most of the benefits of the great social and labor legislation enacted during the past thirty years.

In other words, it has been public policy for too long a time to perpetuate the substandard labor conditions that exist on American farms.

If we are to change this policy, one of the most important steps that must be taken is to extend the legal minimum wage to agriculture.

At the present time, the American farm labor force is a casual, unstructured entity. Farm employers have little personal interest in the performance of their employees. During peak seasons they will hire anyone, whether he be an efficient or inefficient worker, on a piece-rate basis. The fact that there is a pool of underprivileged and/or socially maladjusted workers available for employment on this basis tends to hold down wages for all farm workers regardless of their skill and efficiency.

As long as this rural labor surplus exists, there is little incentive for farm employers to attempt to increase the efficiency of their employees. As a result, farm workers are literally considered to be, by many who employ them, a commodity to be bought at the lowest possible price.

The extension of a minimum wage to agriculture, by setting a "price" below which labor cannot be bought, would eventually eliminate this anachronistic view of the value of human labor. If the minimum were set at seventy-five cents an hour, it would result in a substantial raise in wages to many farm workers who now receive less than that, and this raise would, in turn, exert an upward pressure on the wages of those farm workers who now receive more than seventy-five cents an hour. Does anybody seriously question the need for such action?

The gap between farm wages and industrial wages is growing wider every year. In 1947 the ratio between farm wages and wages in manufacturing was 44 percent. Twelve years later, in 1959, despite constant rises in the cost of living, farm wages were equal to only 36 percent of those earned by workers in manufacturing.

The extension of a minimum wage to agriculture would help to close this ever-widening gap. It is true, of course, that some farm workers would be displaced if the minimum wage were extended to agriculture. Farmers would be forced to seek ways of using labor more efficiently. They would no longer be willing to hire all who wanted to work during peak seasons; rather they would hire only those who were good workers. Moreover, a minimum wage, by increasing mechanization, would decrease the size of the farm labor force.

This would not necessarily be a bad development. Oversupply and the casual nature of farm labor employment have always been the bane of those who labor for hire on American farms. Minimum wage legislation, if it had the effect of helping to create a structured rather than a casual farm labor force, would be fulfilling its primary purpose. . . .

Would minimum wage legislation boost food prices for consumers? In my opinion, this question has no bearing whatsoever on whether or not the minimum wage should be extended to agriculture. As the late James P. Mitchell said when Secretary of Labor:

> In this country we do not choose to keep down our bills, including our food bills, at the cost of overworking and underpaying human beings. We choose to pay the price necessary to support an adequate wage.

I am in complete agreement with this statement. It is doubtful, however, that the extension of minimum wage legislation to agriculture would have a significant effect on consumer prices. In 1957 farmers received forty cents of every consumer dollar spent for food. Of the receipts, farmers paid 9.6 percent in wages. That is, less than 4 percent of consumers' food expenses went for farm labor. If the farm wage level should rise, even if farmers were able to pass the increase straight along, the consumer would scarcely feel its effect upon his budget. If wage costs rose 25 percent, for example, retail prices would be pushed up a mere one percent.

One of the chief arguments used by opponents of minimum wage legislation is that such legislation would have an adverse effect on the small farmer. The key to this problem is to discover who are the chief employers of farm labor. The following information, released by the Department of Commerce a few years ago, is to the point:

1. Fifty-three percent of the farms in the United States do not hire any labor at all.

2. Farm families provide most of the labor on 9 out of 10 of the nation's farms.

3. On almost 2 million farms with a cash expenditure of less than $2,000 for hired labor, 50 percent or more of the labor is performed by the farm operator and the members of his immediate family.

4. Only 242,000 farms have a cash expenditure of $2,000 or more for hired labor. These farms account for only five percent of the total number of farms in the United States.

A bill which would limit coverage to those farms which use 2,224 or more man-days of hired farm labor per year would have no effect whatsoever on small, family farms. . . . In these days of industrialized agriculture, there is no legitimate reason why those who labor for hire on the nation's large agricultural enterprises should not receive the protection of minimum wage legislation.

The exploitation of children in agriculture is another ugly facet of the farm labor situation. Child labor has all but disappeared in industry, but it is still very much in evidence on some of our industrialized farms.

The Bureau of the Census estimates that in 1957, 457,000 children between the ages of 10 and 15 years were employed in agriculture. This figure does not refer to the children of small farm operators who are not paid for work they do on a family farm. Rather, it refers to those children who work for pay on our larger commercial farms.

The same arguments that were used against the passage of child labor legislation for industry 50 years ago are still being used today against the extension of child labor legislation to agriculture. We are told that it is good for children to work, that child labor prevents juvenile delinquency, and that the parents of child laborers could not get along without the extra income the children bring home. These arguments are no more valid today than they were then.

Agriculture in the United States is a "big business." The exploitation of children by agriculture is harmful not only to the children who are employed on American farms, but to adult workers as well. The presence of thousands of child workers in our fields exerts a downward pressure on the already rock-bottom wages earned by adult workers. If we are to improve wages in agriculture, we must not only extend minimum wage protection to farm workers, but we must also eliminate the widespread use of child labor on farms.

The reasons for eliminating child labor in agriculture, however, are not solely economic. The effect of this employment on the children themselves is equally — if not more — important.

In a 1958–1959 survey made by the Labor Department, of approximately 1,700 migrant children under 16 years of age who were found to be illegally employed during school hours and who furnished information on the last school grade attended, 66 percent were in grades below normal for their ages. A comparison of the attendance of these children by age indicates that educational attainment is proportionally lower as the age increases. Thus 80 percent of the migrant children 15 years of age were in grades below normal for their ages compared with 40 percent of the eight-year olds. . . .

No matter how it is viewed, the child labor situation in agriculture is not a pretty one. Steps must be taken immediately to eliminate this blight from the American scene. The Congress should eliminate the exemption from the child labor provisions of the Fair Labor Standards Act which now applies to work in agriculture. It should afford children in agriculture the same protection that is afforded children in industry. It would also help raise wages for adult farm workers by removing from employment approximately 450,000 children under 16 years of age. . . .

In March, 1959, I was asked by the Secretary of Labor to serve on a committee to review the Department's experience in administering Public Law 78 and to suggest recommendations to meet some of the difficult problems arising from the Mexican importation program. The consultants chosen were men of different background, experience, and point of view. . . . Their report, while acknowledging some favorable aspects of the foreign labor importation program, makes it clear that the program has hurt our American citizens who labor in the fields to earn their daily bread. For example, despite the efforts of the Department of Labor to require employers to hire qualified United States workers, the consultants found indications that domestic farm workers were losing out to foreign labor. So strong are the preferences of some growers for a captive labor force that in certain areas almost all of the seasonal work in certain activities is performed by foreign workers. Even those domestic workers who are employed find the duration of their jobs shortened because the availability of Mexicans, particularly at peak, has compressed the work season. This plus technological changes reduced the number of days of farm work obtained by the average farm laborer from 156 in 1947 to 128 in 1958.

Another area that disturbed the consultants was the manner in which the farm wage structure was affected by bringing in Mexican workers. Agriculture has been historically a low wage industry. Farm wage rates for the country as a whole averaged 80 cents per hour in 1959 as compared to $2.22 in manufacturing industries. Even the laundry industry, one of the lowest paying nonfarm activities, offers $1.17 per hour. Not only is the gap between farm and nonfarm wage rates very large, but, even more significantly, it is getting wider. In view of this, the effect of any program sponsored by the United States Government which further depresses the farm wage structure must be viewed with great apprehension.

The consultant's report concluded that the Mexican importation program has had such an effect. . . .

In 1964, the Congress — acting, however belatedly, on the recommendations made by the Department of Labor's study committee away back in 1959 — terminated Public Law 78. As soon as this happened, some growers sought to meet their labor needs by taking advantage of the more inclusive immigration law — Public Law 414. To prevent the will of the Congress from being thus flouted, the Department of Labor immediately scheduled a number of public hearings to determine just what wage and employment standards should be established to discourage the importation of foreign workers to take jobs which domestic workers would probably accept if certain minimum standards were observed.

To United States employers who claim that foreign workers are absolutely necessary because they do work which United States workers won't do ("stoop labor" in vegetable, sugar beet, cotton, and citrus crops), the Secretary of Labor, W. Willard Wirtz, made a direct reply.

"A good deal of this work is unquestionably hard and unpleasant," Mr. Wirtz said, "but that is only part of the story. The rest of it is that the wage rates which have been paid for these jobs have been less than the rates paid for other kinds of work which are just as hard and just as objectionable. And the working conditions maintained by some of the growers have been so bad that church and civic groups and labor organizations have protested bitterly."

Nailing down the problem further, Mr. Wirtz said the importation of hundred of thousands of foreign workers, paid often as low as 60 cents an hour, has been going on while about four million United States men and women are unemployed. In light of these facts, investigations have revealed that United States workers would be ready to do this work under decent conditions and for wages comparable to those which have been generally established for other hard and unpleasant jobs.

He seeks now to carry out an "orderly transition" to the use of United States workers in those areas where reliance has been previously placed on foreign workers: Texas, Florida, Arizona, New Mexico, and 23 other states, North and South. . . .

To implement this new policy, Secretary Wirtz will press an active domestic recruitment program in this sector of the economy. He urges cooperation among growers, organized labor, and government employment services. His main objective is not so much to regulate the importation of labor as to reduce, and even eliminate, the large-scale use of foreign labor. . . .

I have dwelt at some length on the economic position of the farm worker. However, I am not unmindful of the tenuous financial status of the small farmer. I am convinced that the interest of the great bulk of family farmers is adversely affected as they try to compete with large commercial operators who, with Mexican labor at their disposal, do not have to bargain for labor in the marketplace. To the extent that much of the income of the family farmer represents a return for his own labor, depressed wages levels are a major factor in depressed total farm income.

Finally, as far as the consuming public is concerned, there is legitimate concern over the cost of living. But who among us wants to enjoy food and fiber grown at the expense of exploited souls? As a matter of fact, increases in farm labor costs would have only a slight effect on the price of the market basket.

There is no doubt in my mind that the pitiful status of our bypassed farm workers has been further depressed by bringing in, year after year, hundreds of thousands of foreign laborers.

I have purposely confined these remarks to certain legislative and administrative proposals which, at best, would result in no more than a partial solution to the problem of migratory labor. We cannot hope to solve this problem once and for all by legislative action. We need to reorganize the farm labor market, but this will never be done until agricultural workers are organized into bargaining associations of their own free choice.

The Agricultural Revolution*

JAMES L. VIZZARD, S.J.

The overwhelming fact of American agriculture today is the agricultural revolution. After having stagnated technologically for countless centuries, agriculture is now undergoing a revolution of a scope and depth comparable to the Industrial Revolution of the eighteenth and nineteenth centuries.

This agricultural phenomenon began in the United States with the widespread substitution of the gasoline engine for horse and mule power during and after World War I, and continued with the development and the now almost universal availability of electrical power. It was greatly accelerated by the rapid application to agricultural production of improved farming and conservation practices, the scientific breeding and feeding of livestock, the development of highly productive and disease-resistant crop varieties, and the introduction of much more effective insecticides, pesticides, and fertilizers.

The most obvious result of the agricultural revolution has been a spectacular increase in productivity per acre and an even more spectacular increase in output per man-hour of farm work. In 1963, one hour of

---

* From "The Agricultural Revolution," *America*, December 12, 1964.

farm labor produced five times as much food and other crops as it did in 1919–1921. In the same period, crop production per acre increased by 75 percent, and output per breeding animal by 92 percent. In the decade of the 1950's, productivity of the American farm worker increased by 5.4 percent a year, while in nonagricultural industry the increase was only 2.1 percent a year. Today, one farm worker produces food, fiber, and other farm commodities for himself and 28 others. There is every reason to believe that these trends will continue into the indefinite future. It is equally certain that eventually the phenomenon will become worldwide.

In the United States, this peaceful revolution has already led to the first era of true agricultural abundance ever achieved by any major nation. It enables our consumers to obtain a high-quality and varied diet for a good deal less than what a poorer diet costs even in other technologically advanced countries. In 1963, food costs represented only 18.8 percent of the average United States family's income after taxes. By contrast, consumers in the United Kingdom spent 29.5 percent of their income for food; in France, 30.6 percent; in Italy, 34.7 percent; in Japan, 46.9 percent; and in Russia, 53 percent. In the less developed areas of the world, virtually all personal income is spent on food.

By releasing many millions of persons from the necessity of tilling the soil, the agricultural revolution has enabled the rest of our economy and society to grow to its present developed status. If farmers today produced at the productivity level of 1910, in order to feed our population, which now approaches 200 million, we would need to have kept about 20 million more persons in our farm labor force and would have that many fewer for manufacturing, trades, services, professions, and the arts.

It is evident, then, that the agricultural revolution has already made important and beneficent contributions to the welfare of our country. But what has it meant to those most directly involved in it — to farmers and rural communities? Has it been an unmixed blessing? The answer, unfortunately, is no.

Instead of being the chief beneficiary, the farmer has been the chief victim of this revolution. . . . He and his government have found no adequate answer to the three chief problems that result from the agricultural revolution: (1) the seemingly uncontrollable tendency of production to outrun effective demand; (2) an inexorable cost-price squeeze, which leads to bankruptcy; and (3) the accelerated exodus from farms and rural communities to cities, often with disastrous results to both. Let us consider each of these problems in order.

It is obvious that we have not yet learned how to control the exuberant flood of products flowing from our farms and ranches. The production pipeline that supplies consumers with food and fiber, and that once flowed with grudging slowness, now pours out abundance that threatens to swamp us. Markets and concepts geared to scarcity must now be revised to cope with abundance. For the first time in the history of the world, a nation's concern is focused not on shortages but on surpluses.

Nor is this a passing phenomenon. Great as is our present productivity, if effective demand existed, our farms, simply by applying more intensively and more widely the already available knowledge and techniques, could easily double production. Moreover, science and technology show no signs of a slowdown in the discovery and development of new means of increasing productivity. We are not at the end but rather still at the beginning of the agricultural revolution.

Almost everyone recognizes that such abundance and the productivity that makes it possible are a blessing of unprecedented proportions. It makes it at least theoretically possible to guarantee that no American citizen need go hungry. Even more, it makes it possible for our nation to provide urgently needed foods to the countless millions of the world's peoples who previously have never said any prayer with more desperate urgency than "Give us this day our daily bread."

But for the farmer who produces this abundance, things have not been so favorable. Operating within the one major part of our economy still characterized by free competition, in which the law of supply and demand still holds considerable sway, the farmer finds that as the volume of production goes up, the price he receives in the marketplace goes down. In the process of becoming ever more efficient and productive, the farmer is in danger of bankruptcy.

Other industries that have increased productivity have found ways to control both production and prices. When signs appear that the market can absorb no more steel or autos at a predetermined price, United States Steel shuts down its furnaces and General Motors its production lines. They create their surpluses not in products but in idle plants and unemployed workers.

Farmers, however, are too many and have been too lacking in organization to be able to act thus. Moreover, their productive plant cannot be shut down overnight. They cannot stop pigs from fattening or corn from growing. And even if the individual farmer should respond to oversupply and low prices by cutting back his operations where possible, too many other farmers at the same time will be expanding production to the utmost to make up in volume what they cannot secure through adequate prices.

This kind of problem, of course, did not exist when productivity was low, demand was generally high, and farmers found a profitable outlet for whatever they could produce. But in this new age of abundance, the inability of farmers to limit supply and in some degree to control prices has become a major national crisis.

Most people would agree that, if it were possible, control of supply and prices would best be left in the hands of the farmers themselves. All experience indicates, however, that except for relatively minor and geographically limited crops, farmers have not been able to organize so as to achieve this end. To be sure, one of the most encouraging developments of recent years has been the growth of the cooperative bargaining approach, by which farmers unite to contract with processors for specific volumes of products at mutually agreed-upon prices. Should this movement reach sufficient size and power, it could well solve one of the farmer's most pressing problems. It is not yet clear, however, whether this approach will be able to provide an adequate answer, in the near future, to the productivity and price problems of the agricultural revolution.

If farmer-sponsored and farmer-controlled efforts do not succeed, the size and nature of the problem demand and justify government intervention. For three decades and more, a great variety of farm programs have been proposed, and some adopted, by which the government was committed to help farmers control overproduction and achieve satisfactory prices and income. Most of the programs have been based on voluntary cooperation of the individual farmer. Each farmer could choose to come in or stay out. Various kinds of government supports and subsidies have encouraged him to participate, but if he judged he could do better on his own, he was free not to participate.

Repeated and varied experiences, however, prove that voluntary programs simply have not worked with much success. Witness the billions of dollars of taxpayers' money that the government spent in vain efforts to harness runaway productivity. Farmers acting individually in their own interest have frustrated every effort at control.

From an ethical standpoint, moreover, it is becoming increasingly clear that if farmers are to receive the government assistance and support that they need and deserve, in justice they must be willing to accept such limitations and controls as are necessary. Important though farmers are, their needs are not the only ones that government must consider. It is doubtful that the common good, which is the central concern of the state, allows farmers, or any other group, to make unreasonable and unlimited demands on the public treasury. Taxpayers have no right to begrudge such expenditures as may be necessary to solve the critical problems of disadvantaged groups, but they surely have a right to expect that such expenditures should ultimately lead to a solution.

It should be evident to all, by now, that voluntary controls are expensive and inefficient. To retain them in the face of accelerating productivity-increases is both an imposition on taxpayers and an invitation to disaster. Without yielding to an inferiority complex, farmers must recognize that they now represent a small and decreasing proportion of the United States population. Their importance in the economy is not diminished, but their power at the polls and in Congress is a thing of the past. Unless nonfarm voters can soon see that their tax money is being spent for a constructive solution to the farm problem, inevitably and not without justice they will rebel and put an end to the whole attempt.

A word should perhaps be said here about the opinion held by some that controls themselves are morally wrong, a violation of the purported God-given law of supply and demand. One can only answer that if they are so, every manufacturer who limits production and administers prices, every profession that limits the entrance of new candidates, every union that negotiates for wages not freely granted by the "market," in other words every other major segment of our economy stands indicted of violating this presumed law. Even the most ardent advocates of free enterprise admit in practice, if not also in theory, that cutthroat competition is and should be dead.

It is generally agreed, as previously observed, that, where possible, controls should be voluntary. But as is proved by innumerable laws at every level of government, where voluntary controls are inadequate, mandatory controls must be imposed. This world is no Utopia where every individual citizen on his own initiative and responsibility modifies his personal aims and actions to conform to the requirements of the common good. One of the most basic purposes of a civil society is to impose and enforce precisely such limitations on the individual in the interest of the general welfare. The no-control school of thought can find no support either in theory or in practice.

The second major problem that follows in the wake of the agricultural revolution is the cost-price squeeze that has ruined and continues to ruin so many farmers. In the simpler days of agriculture, almost any farmer with an adequate piece of land could at least get by on hard work and frugality. Even though his production was small and the prices he received were low, his expenses and his need for cash were low, too, and he could be sure of eating well on homegrown food.

In today's agriculture, however, the farmer is entirely caught up in the market and money economy. He has to buy his factors of production at inflated prices and, as previously indicated, must sell his products in the largely unregulated free market. In effect, he buys at retail and sells at wholesale.

As a result, the farmer finds his costs constantly increasing while the prices he receives for his products fail to keep pace. This cost-price squeeze can perhaps be best illustrated by comparing the year 1947, the historical high point in farm income, with 1963. Between these two years, while realized gross farm income *increased* from (in round numbers) $34 billion to $41 billion, realized *net* income *decreased* from $17 billion to $12 billion. This discrepancy is explained by the increase of production expenses from $17 billion to $29 billion.

This vast and crucial increase in production expenses is the price that farmers must pay for modern, efficient farming. Almost all the increase goes for products that did not exist before the agricultural revolution. Each year, for instance, the farmer has been spending an average of $3.1 billion on new tractors and other motor vehicles, machinery, and equipment; $3.3 billion for fuel, lubricants, and maintenance of machinery and motor vehicles; and $1.6 billion for fertilizer and lime. Moreover, each year he purchases products containing enough rubber to put tires on six million automobiles, uses enough electricity to supply the annual needs of Baltimore, Chicago, Boston, Detroit, Houston, and Washington, D. C.

Concealed in overall figures on declining farm income is the fact that in 1963 farm people received $1,480 of personal annual income per capita, of which $510 was from nonfarm sources; whereas per capita annual personal income of nonfarm people was $2,515 from all sources. Again, the average hourly return for farm work was $1.01, while, by contrast, one hour's work in a factory averaged $2.46.

Almost any statistical index illustrates the deteriorating position of the farmer. For instance, the average worker's family paid 15 percent more but farmers received 15 percent less in 1963 for the same kinds and quantities of foods purchased in the years 1947–1949. Items in this "market basket" include bakery products, of which the farm value of all ingredients declined 12 percent from 1947–1949 to 1963 and the retail cost increased 42 percent. The farm value of a fixed quantity of dairy products dropped 5 percent in this period, while the retail price of these products increased 18 percent.

These data are cold and abstract, but to farm families the cost-price squeeze is something very real and personal. For hundreds of thousands of them it means decreased income, increased debts, and a constant precarious battle against bankruptcy. Indeed, since 1945, two and a half million farmers have lost that battle and their farms have disappeared.

This last statistic indicates why the third major problem created by the agricultural revolution has been an accelerated exodus from farms and rural communities. It is true that surplus farm population has always migrated to the city, but in recent decades the trickle has turned into a flood. The United States farm population has decreased from 24 million in 1945 to 13 million in 1963, and this, of course, was during a period when the total United States population was growing by tens of millions.

Most, but by no means all, of the farm people who have left the land have been from smaller farms, particularly in the deep South. In 1959, some two and a quarter million of these smaller farms were still operating with total annual sales of less than $5,000 (net income, of course, averaged a great deal less than that). But each year before and since 1959, hundreds of thousands of these farmers fell victims to the agricultural revolution, pulled up such roots as they had, and, with their families, headed for the cities to look for work.

This exodus, forced by stark economic hardship and often accompanied by racial pressures, has only rarely led to improved conditions for those who moved. Most of them, in fact, only fled from a rural slum to an even more distressing urban slum. Whether white or colored, their assimilation into the urban environment has been slowed by their poverty and lack of education and their total lack of preparation for urban living. . . .

Meanwhile the rural communities that the cityward migrants have abandoned, poor and deteriorating as they already were, disintegrate still further. Without enough business to be economically viable, they gradually turn into ghost towns. The side roads of major parts of rural America already present a sorry spectacle of abandoned homes, ruined barns, and decaying towns.

This process, however, is not inevitable or irreversible. There still are economically valuable resources in most of these distressed areas, which, if mobilized, if given new directions and incentives, can revitalize local economies.

The chief of these resources, of course, is the people themselves. Given better education, job training, and local opportunity, they will easily recognize that they can do far better for themselves as well as for their communities in at-home jobs than by fleeing to heartless and jobless city slums. It is precisely to achieve these constructive purposes that the Area Development Program and the Rural Areas Development Program have been undertaken in recent years. If these programs work as planned, one can look forward to a reversal or at least a significant slowing down of the rural exodus, a new and more vigorous life for rural communities and an easing of the already overwhelming problems of city slums.

But it is not only the small, inefficient subsistence farms that are disappearing. Many a farm that only a few years ago was considered adequate and even substantial is now succumbing to the pressure of the cost-price squeeze. Perhaps because of inadequate capital and credit, or perhaps because of limited education or managerial ability, the farmer just can't make it. He gets tired of the struggle and sells out.

When the farmer finally sells out, the land rarely goes out of use. Rather, it is incorporated into another larger and probably more efficient operation. Thus, despite the loss of two and a half million farmers in 20 years, agricultural production, as we have seen, has continued to increase. In the meantime, though, farms become larger and fewer. In a generation, the average size of farms in this country has increased from 150 acres to well over 250 acres. It is not easy to see how far this trend will continue, but it seems clear that it will go on indefinitely unless checked by conscious and effective national policy.

CHAPTER 7

THE STATE AND SOCIALIZATION

Socialization is, at one and the same time, an effect and a cause of the growing intervention of the state in areas which, since they touch the deepest concerns of the human person, are not without considerable importance nor devoid of danger. Among these are care of health, instruction and education of the young, control of professional careers, methods of care and rehabilitation of those physically or mentally handicapped in any way. Socialization, however, is also the fruit and expression of a natural tendency almost irrepressible in human beings — the tendency to unite for the purpose of obtaining objectives that each ambitions but which are beyond the capacity of individuals.

Pope John XXIII in *Mater et Magistra*

Unless there is some radical, revolutionary change in the human nature that God made, men will continue to gather together and form civil societies, and they will at the same time make arrangements for governing those societies. They will also organize themselves in more limited ways to achieve a wide variety of objectives — economic, cultural, recreational — that they cannot accomplish acting individually. This is the way men have always acted, voluntarily restricting freedom in some directions in order to guarantee and enlarge it in others. It is the way they are acting today. If they behaved differently, they would be doing violence to their natures. For although God creates men individually and gives to each a personal destiny, He so fashions them that they cannot fulfill themselves as individuals except by association and cooperation with others. Man is a social and political animal, not a hermit or anarchist.

The only reason for discussing the state and socialization today — the reason Pope John wrote about them in *Mater et Magistra* — is that the individual and social urges in human nature tend since the Fall to generate tensions, both in individuals and in society, that oblige men to reconsider from time to time the arrangements under which they live. So it was in the nineteenth century, when overemphasis on the individualistic side of human nature led to serious abuses and widespread injustice. So it is today, when some fear that the social aspect of human nature has been so exaggerated that personal freedom and individual development are jeopardized.

If one compares organizations today — both public and private — with those that existed a hundred years ago, and then goes on to estimate their respective influence on the lives of individuals and families, it will be obvious that organizations now are much bigger and more numerous than they were then and touch people in many more ways.

A more intensive study will show that this development is only partly a reaction to the excessive individualism of the past century. To an even greater extent it is a response to changing circumstances, to what Pope John calls "the growing interdependence of men in society." It reflects the shift from a dominantly rural, agricultural society to the highly industrialized urban culture of today. It is an adjustment to the modern revolution in transportation and communications. It is an answer to the challenges of higher living standards at home and enormously expanded responsibilities abroad.

The point is, have the reaction to the nineteenth century and the adjustment to circumstances gone too far? Is the individual in danger today, as the social fabric was a century ago?

Although he was aware of the risks and problems, Pope John, speaking in broad, general terms, did not think so. In this age of technology and organization, man can, if he acts prudently, remain master of himself and lord of all visible creation.

Social Security and Social Insurance*

LOUIS F. BUCKLEY

One of the major contributions of the encyclical *Mater et Magistra* is its acceptance of the role of social insurance as a means of extending social progress.

---

* From "Social Security and Social Insurance," *Catholic Mind*, December, 1962.

Since Pope John XXIII introduced *Mater et Magistra* with a review of *Rerum Novarum* by Leo XIII and *Quadragesimo Anno* by Pius XI, let us briefly consider these two great encyclicals from the viewpoint of social insurance. Unlike *Mater et Magistra*, no specific reference was made to social insurance or social security in *Rerum Novarum* or *Quadragesimo Anno*. However they included principles and norms for proper state action which were interpreted by leading Catholic scholars, such as Monsignor John A. Ryan, Bishop Francis Haas, and Monsignor John O'Grady, as a basis for endorsing programs of social insurance.

Supplementary statements by Popes preceding Pope John XXIII made specific and favorable comments on social insurance. For example, Pope Pius XI, in the encyclical *On Atheistic Communism* (*Divini Redemptoris*), recognized the importance of social insurance when he stated that social justice cannot be said to have been satisfied so long as workingmen "cannot make suitable provision through public or private insurance for old age, for periods of illness and unemployment." Pope Pius XII, in his 1945 address to Italian workers, gave social insurance as an illustration of proper state action.

In the United States, the conclusion was reached in "The Bishops' Program of Social Reconstruction," issued in 1919, that "the state should make comprehensive provision for insurance against illness, invalidity, unemployment and old age." It is noteworthy that this pronouncement was issued 13 years before the American labor movement endorsed social insurance and 16 years prior to the enactment of the Social Security Act itself. A second bishops' statement, entitled "The Church and the Social Order" and issued in 1940, emphasized the need for social insurance. . . .

In the encyclical *Mater et Magistra*, Pope John XXIII gives priority to the "development of systems for social insurance and the introduction of social security systems" in listing the contemporary trends in the social field which gave rise to the need for the issuance of a new encyclical.

The emphasis placed by Pope John on the importance of the trend toward expanding social insurance and the introduction of social security systems is very appropriate. During the past twenty years, the number of countries with old-age, invalidity, and survivor insurance and workmen's compensation almost doubled; those with sickness and maternity insurance more than doubled; those with unemployment insurance increased 40 percent, and those with family allowance programs increased from seven to 60 countries.

An understanding of the scope of the term social security and social insurance as used by Pope John may be obtained from a letter sent by Amleto Cardinal Cicognani, Vatican Secretary of State, to the Canadian Social Week in 1961 on behalf of Pope John. This letter stated:

> It is impossible to create an atmosphere of serenity in the organization of production, unless the uneasiness of workingmen, arising from the uncertainty of their future, can be eliminated or reduced as far as possible. This can be done by setting up effective systems of social insurance or social security capable of protecting them in those events which either impair their working ability, increase their responsibilities, or force them into involuntary idleness.

The scope includes not only social insurance systems, such as old age, invalidity and survivor insurance, sickness and maternity insurance, unemployment insurance and workmen's compensation, but extends also to programs such as family allowances.

The objectives and nature of a social security program were stated by Domenico Cardinal Tardini in 1959, when he was Vatican Secretary of State, in a letter to Spain's Catholic Social Week. The papal spokesman said: "Social security, properly understood and honestly functioning, must tend to decrease progressively cases which today are the objects of relief and charity." A good social security program, he continued, "must grow in such a way that it ceaselessly embraces more subjects, more cases, more needs. We must seek a social security system which is not strictly defensive, but one that strives to improve situations that can be improved."

In discussing the influence of changed conditions on the concept of private property, Pope John makes the following observations in *Mater et Magistra*: "It is also quite clear that today the number of persons is increasing who, because of recent advances in insurance programs and various systems of social security, are able to look to the future with tranquillity. This sort of tranquillity once was rooted in the ownership of property." The Pope recognizes in this statement the significant contribution made by insurance and social security programs in giving economic protection to individuals and families when contingencies strike, contingencies such as unemployment, old age, sickness, accident, or death of the breadwinner of the family.

Pope John, in his discussion of demands of justice with regard to productive institutions, stresses that the state should make special provision for the craftsmen and members of cooperatives in regard to social security and insurance.

Emphasis is placed by Pope John on the necessity of extending insurance or social security benefits to cover farmers and their families. He states:

> Because, as experience shows, the income of individual farmers is, on the average, less than that of workers in industry and the services, it does not seem to be fully in accord with the norms of social justice and equity to provide farmers with insurance or social security benefits that are inferior to those of other classes of citizens. For those insurance plans or provisions that are established generally should not differ markedly one from the other, whatever be the economic sector wherein the citizens work, or from which they derive their income.

The reference to the injustice and inequity involved with respect to farmers is very pertinent to our social insurance programs. Farm workers are generally excluded from coverage under our unemployment insurance, workmen's compensation, temporary-disability insurance programs and, to some extent, under old-age, survivors and disability insurance. This is especially serious in that the unemployment and accident rates among farm workers are relatively high. . . .

Pope John devotes a paragraph to another aspect of social insurance in the following words: "Moreover, since social security and insurance can help appreciably in distributing national income among the citizens according to justice and equity, these systems can be regarded as means whereby imbalances among various classes of citizens are reduced." Emphasis has not been placed in the United States on using the social insurance system as a device to equalize the distribution of income as proposed by Pope John. Our social insurance systems were adopted and based on the private insurance principle of paying benefits that bear a direct or close relationship to the contributions paid. The whole costs were, and still are, paid by beneficiaries and/or the employers, and no contribution was or is made from the general revenue. . . .

Readers who may consider some of Pope John's observations on social insurance to be radical in terms of American standards should realize that social insurance programs are much more extensive in other countries. Sixty countries, including Canada, also have family allowance programs. It should also be recognized that redistribution of income, as suggested by Pope John, is accomplished through governmental subsidy of the social insurance systems in many countries. . . .

The major current issue in social insurance in the United States is the question of whether or not the problem of financing health and medical care for the aged should be met through the established social insurance system as is done in many countries.

Health insurance, on a much broader scale than is being considered today, received serious consideration in the United States following the adoption of the British Health Insurance Act of 1911. Throughout the two decades following the issuance of "The Bishops' Program of Social Reconstruction," which emphasied that the state should make comprehensive provisions for insurance against illness, Monsignor John A. Ryan was an outstanding exponent of health insurance. In 1939, Edward Cardinal Mooney, in an introduction to the twentieth-anniversary edition of the bishops' program, commented on the failure to realize all its proposals, and pointed out that "the social insurance provided in the Social Security Act is by no means perfect. To say nothing of other defects, it fails to provide for workers' insurance against sickness." Father R. A. McGowan, director of the Department of Social Action of the National Catholic Welfare Conference, stated in 1940: "From 1919 until the passage of the Social Security Act, the National Catholic Welfare Conference continued to advocate the social insurance program, and now we are advocating the extension of the act to health insurance."

In 1947, when health insurance was before Congress, Reverend Alphonse Schwitalla, S.J., president of the Catholic Hospital Association, opposed it because there are "too many personal, inalienable rights of citizens that are bound up intimately with health." He had no objection to the means test as a basis for rendering health service under public assistance. Father McGowan favored the health-insurance approach. He maintained that a means test would detract from the dignity of human personality, and that any system which would provide for a pauper's oath for health purposes would not be in accordance with good, sound Catholic thinking.

In 1949, a joint statement was issued by the Bureau of Health and Hospitals, the National Catholic Welfare Conference, the National Conference of Catholic Charities, and the Catholic Hospital Association. It was entitled: "A Voluntary Approach to a National Health Program." This document opposed the health-insurance proposal of President Truman and proposed "a program of service by voluntary associations and private initiative backed by government financial support." They considered such a program to be more in keeping with the principle of subsidiarity. . . .

We noted above that Amleto Cardinal Cicognani, in his letter on behalf of Pope John, specifically included illness as a contingency to be protected against through social insurance, and that Cardinal Tardini emphasized that a good social security program must grow by embracing more needs and by decreasing relief and charity cases.

It is pertinent to note that Pope John raises the issue of the serious nature and possible dangers involved as the result of the intervention of public authorities in matters which pertain to the more intimate aspects of personal life, such as the care of health. He concluded, however, that such intervention makes possible the satisfaction of many personal rights, and answers in the negative the question as to whether this will result in men ceasing to be personally responsible. Similarly, Pope John stated the principle of subsidiarity in the encyclical, although he does not specifically refer to it in his discussion of social insurance as he does with respect to public property.

The principle of subsidiarity is used by some Catholics as a basis for maintaining that health services should be financed through voluntary insurance organizations rather than social insurance. Other Catholics differ from that group, especially with respect to social insurance proposals which are restricted to individuals over 65 years of age and to limited health services. They maintain that the aged are too high-cost, high-risk, and low-income customers to rely on the voluntary approach to resolve their health service financing problems. Furthermore, they point out that a limited social insurance program to finance medical care would be supplemented by voluntary health insurance, especially with respect to younger workers, by individual and family resources and by public-assistance programs. They believe that each of these approaches has an important part to play in meeting the problem of financing an adequate level of high-quality health care.

Pope John XXIII told laymen in an audience on June 1, 1962, that Roman Catholics were committed to striving to translate the social teachings of their Church into the laws of their countries. He said they were responsible for inserting the social doctrine of the Church into "the reality of modern life" and for making it "penetrate into social legislation for the benefit of the entirety of mankind." The Pope made it clear that he was referring to his encyclical *Mater et Magistra* as a fundamental document for increased Catholic social and political action.

In order to carry out this advice of the Pope, it is essential that we become well acquainted with the basic teachings of the encyclical and all the facts involved in applying them to specific legislative proposals. It must be recognized that there are sometimes differences of opinion in the application of teachings to specific legislation.

In formulating our view on legislation, it is important that we take a careful look at the record on the crucial questions of fact. We must avoid partisan emotion and attempts to discredit a program through the use of a label. In some quarters, for example, the term "socialization" is used as a scare word when applied to legislation. "Socialization," Pope John reminds us in his encyclical, "is the fruit of a natural tendency — to unite for the purpose of obtaining objectives which each ambitions but which are beyond the capacity of individuals." It should be recognized that the private insurance approach to meet problems such as health care is also a form of "socialization." . . .

The Opponents of Social Security*

JOSEPH M. BECKER, S.J.

In my experience, the people who oppose a governmental program of social security are to be found in one of two groups.

They are both neatly portrayed in a story I picked up while working last summer in Wisconsin. The Groves bill, to provide a system of unemployment compensation in Wisconsin, was before the State legislature. (This was several years before the national act of 1935.) Hearings had been set for consideration of the bill. Its proponents managed to secure a number of influential people, including a lone employer, to speak in its behalf. After those favoring the bill had presented their case, the chairman of the hearings committee called for those who wished to speak in opposition. Two men got to their feet and started for the platform to have the honor of opening the attack. Those two men were: (1) the lone Communist representative in the Wisconsin legislature, and (2) the president of the Wisconsin Manufacturers' Association at that time.

The Communist, being somewhat closer, and a younger man, got there first. He assailed unemployment compensation as a protecting wall around the rotten and already tottering institution of capitalism, which would only make its eventual liquidation more difficult. The representative of the manufacturers' association drily acknowledged his "comrade in arms," but said that his organization opposed compulsory unemployment compensation for exactly the opposite reason, namely, that it

---

* From "Who Are Opposed to Social Security?" *America*, May 15, 1948.

represented a threat to capitalism, the system under which this country had grown great.

To the one man, the capitalist spirit and system were too inherently evil to be cured by any such palliative as unemployment compensation; to the other, the system was too good to be spoiled by a device which he considered so inconsistent with individual initiative as the proposed measure.

I am not concerned with the amount of rightness and wrongness in each position, but simply with trying to make the two positions clear. Practically any case of opposition to social security will be found to be rooted in one or other of these two fundamental positions. Although that is a simple fact, it is a very useful one, and one not universally perceived. To repeat: a man will be predominantly critical of social security, either because he thinks the present economic system reasonably satisfactory and he does not want to run the risk of spoiling it; or because he thinks the present system is intolerable and he does not want to run the risk of prolonging it.

It goes without saying that the opposition can exist in varying degrees. One person may oppose without qualification all forms of social security: unemployment compensation, old age and survivors insurance, public assistance (to the indigent, aged, children, the blind), health insurance, children's allowances, educational grants. Another may oppose only some of the programs. Thus, the United States Chamber of Commerce approved President Truman's recommendation to extend the coverage of old age and survivors insurance, but disapproved of his recommendation for a program of health insurance. A third person may always cast a favorable vote for any given concrete social-security proposal, and yet always speak against it in the abstract, never missing an occasion to belittle it. But in whatever way the phenomenon of opposition manifests itself, it has its roots in one of the two fundamental positions described above.

Both of these basic groups can claim representatives in almost every state of life. I have come across priests, for example, in both groups. Labor is rarely represented these days in either group, it is true; but, earlier, the American Federation of Labor belonged to the group which feared that social security would harm the existing order. Management, of course, is found in large numbers in this latter group.

The peopde who fear the harm that social security may bring to the existing order do so because they admire the accomplishments of capi-

talism, and because (the crucial point) they attribute those accomplishments to a particular attribute of capitalism: its individualism. The freedom which capitalism accords the able individual to "get ahead in the
world" is the invisible hand which has guided the Western world to
its present enviable position — as compared, say, with the East. . . .

This group is inclined to agree with the thesis of Carl Snyder's *Capital
the Creator*, and with the similar though milder praise contained in the
first part of Schumpeter's newest book, *Capitalism, Socialism and Democracy*. It also finds Hayek's *Road to Serfdom* highly agreeable reading.
General Motors is currently sponsoring a new book called *Mainspring*,
which argues that progress was regrettably retarded when the authoritarian
Christian culture won out in Europe over the unregulated Saracenic culture of Mohammed. Catholics may feel that the example is unfortunate
(and wonder why the public-relations man sent it to a priest), but
if they belong to this group they will agree that the general point is
well taken: freedom from regulation *is* the mainspring of progress. This
is the group that published, or read approvingly, the large ads that appeared recently, like the following one, which was published in the New
Year's edition of the New York *Times*:

THE CLIMATE OF FREEDOM

America has more passenger cars than the rest of the world put together —
far more bathtubs, and many more radios. It's that way with clothes or
food or almost any comfort, convenience or necessity you can mention.

Other countries have as much metal and enough manpower. There are
no atom secrets in a four-door sedan. Modern bathtubs are hardly confi-
dential. And the mysteries of the light bulb are old hat.

What other countries *don't have* is "The Climate of Freedom," the
economic and political freedom of enterprise that lets a man or a company
pick its own destiny and labor towards it.

A man of this group, liking what our economy has achieved over the
last century or so ("If the lot of the medieval European worker was
like these, then give me modern industry," wrote a missionary from
China last month), and agreeing that the "climate of freedom" was
necessary for that achievement, will tend to react unfavorably to anything as regulatory as compulsory social security. He dislikes social
security precisely because it interferes with the economic system as it has
traditionally operated.

In passing, note two subtypes of this group: the man who knows
something of economics and social security, and the man who does not.
The first is aware how in the modern complicated and interrelated

economy thousands of competent, industrious individuals can be reduced to destitution through no fault of their own. The opposition of this subtype is often only partial, and is always regretful — that it is thus necessary for a few to suffer for the greater common good. The second subtype, the ignoramus, thinks any well man who cannot support himself and family must be personally at fault, and needs only the touch of the whip of necessity to improve his state.

To the opposite group, which dislikes social security precisely because it is a logical part of the present system and may prolong it, belongs the Communist. Who else? Well, the Amish of Pennsylvania would probably be in the group, if they knew about social security. But let us confine ourselves to active, vocal folk — and, since my space is running short, to Catholics. I would put in this group the Chester-Belloc school of Distributists, and the leaders of the *Catholic Worker* movement. Belloc, in his new edition of *The Servile State*, remarks:

> Neither has it seemed worth while to emphasize the points on which advance towards the Servile State has been made since the first publication [of this book]: they are obvious to all: the rapid growth of monopoly on the one hand and the *new measures for providing proletarian security* and sufficiency on the other. . . . (Italics added)

On the tenth anniversary of the Social Security Act, Dorothy Day wrote in the *Catholic Worker:* "We believe that social-security legislation, now hailed as a great victory for the poor and for the worker, is a great defeat for Christianity."

Not all these Catholics would — some would — offer active opposition to a concrete proposal for social security. Dorothy Day in the same article added: "Of course, Pope Pius XI said that when a crisis came about, in unemployment, fire, flood, earthquake, the state had to enter in and help." Still, they merit inclusion in the ranks of the opposition insofar as their influence generally works in its disfavor. They speak of it seldom, but when they do they disparage it. . . .

This group would be unimpressed by the "Climate-of-Freedom" advertisement. They would argue against its first paragraph that a purely materialistic standard of progress cannot measure the spiritual price paid for that progress; and against its last paragraph that actually only a few can pick their own destiny.

It is clear that although these Catholics share the radicalism of the Communist, they differ from him in nearly every other way. They reject not only his materialism (they are willing to accept a lower standard of living in exchange for a kind of work that facilitates union with God) but also his reliance on the state. They speak in accents curiously similar to the capitalist's about the value of individual opportunity and responsibility. What they deny, of course, is that the mass of men under capitalism have an opportunity to be such creative and responsible individuals.

It does not matter that I have been speaking of "capitalism" throughout this article without defining the term. No definition was needed. What is under discussion is the concrete economic system in which we have lived these past one hundred years. To the one group this existing arrangement is the best of systems, and owes that superiority to a principle which is incompatible with social security. To the other group, it is the worst of systems, which ought not to be saved from the disintegrating influence of its own principles by introducing what appears to them to be the extraneous institution of social security. . . .

The Welfare State*

HONORABLE EUGENE J. McCARTHY

It is difficult to remain objective and nonpartisan in a discussion of the "Welfare State." Its meaning is very flexible. For William F. Buckley, Jr., writing in the *Commonweal* some months ago, it is identical with "the state" and, in his opinion, both must go. In John T. Flynn's best-selling political travel guide, it is "the road along which this country is traveling to its destruction." For Clarence Manion, in the Heritage Foundation edition of his *Key to Peace*, under the more threatening name of "statism," it means nearly all things bad, including the French Revolution and the British Government at the time of the American Revolution. . . .

On the other hand, Father Wilfrid Parsons, S.J., writing in *America* in December, 1949, pointed out that "Catholic professors of the Social Sciences have long calmly spoken of 'the welfare state' in an approving manner as describing the plan of the Encyclicals." The same term has respectable standing among non-Catholic students and teachers of the Social Sciences. When the Constitutional Convention finished its work at Philadelphia approximately one hundred and sixty years ago, the words

---

* From "The Welfare State," *Commonweal*, November 7, 1952. Also in *Catholic Mind*, November, 1953.

"welfare" and "state" were both acceptable. The authors of the Constitution did not hesitate to declare in the preamble of that document that "to promote the general welfare" was one of the principal functions of the state.

Their political philosophy was sound. It was based upon acceptance of the idea that the state, or government, has a positive responsibility for the welfare of its citizens. It was based upon the realization that government does have a responsibility, not only to protect and police its citizens, but also to assist them in securing those things that are necessary for their physical well-being, and necessary also as a condition to intellectual and spiritual growth. . . .

The problem of the "welfare state" raises many questions. The question of whether or not the state has a right to interfere in the economic and social order is not one of them. This right is clearly established by philosophy and by historical experience. If one is going to argue about the "welfare state," it is necessary that he have in mind either an existing state, one that has existed in history, or a specific proposal or plan for such a state. There is a great difference between the "welfare state" program in Soviet Russia today and the "welfare state" program in the United States. There is a great difference between the "welfare state" program proposed by Karl Marx and that proposed by Pope Pius XII. Let us begin with the papal proposals as a point of departure for an examination of the welfare program existing in the United States.

Pope Pius XII lists the following as the fundamental prerequisites of social justice: "1) a wage that will cover the living expenses of the family and, as such, will make it possible for parents to fulfill their natural duty to rear children who will be healthfully nourished and well clothed; 2) a dwelling worthy of human beings; 3) the possibility of securing for children sufficient instruction and a becoming education; 4) foreseeing and forestalling times of stress, and sickness and old age."

If we agree that Pope Pius has here defined a minimum program of social justice, it follows that legislation designed to provide fair and just treatment of workingmen, to insure minimum wages, and to protect farmers against loss of income through crop failure and depressed farm prices is certainly defensible. It follows, too, that a case can be made for programs to provide a measure of security against the uncertainties of unemployment, of disabling accidents, of sickness and old age, and that legislation to assist families in acquiring adequate housing and adequate education for the children is in order. Yet the specific program and proposals to accomplish these purposes are the very ones which, day in and day out, in the press and in public speeches, are labeled as dangerously "collectivist," "Socialist," or even "Communist," as comprising the "welfare state."

There are three fair questions regarding the welfare program in the United States:

1. Has it gone far enough or has it gone too far?
2. Have the means and methods used been the best?
3. Is our program set in a pattern which will eventually lead to totalitarianism?

Examined by the standard of the proposals of Pope Pius XII, the program in the United States appears to be within limits. Our minimum wage law is certainly modest. Agriculture remains a high-risk, low-income occupation. The housing needs of the nation are not yet satisfied, and the special needs of the middle-income families have not received legislative recognition. The social security program has been improved and broadened, but there remain great gaps in it, too.

We have not really approached the goal of "forestalling times of sickness" as set forth by Pope Pius XII, or the goal of "insuring our workers against accident and ill-health," as defined by General Eisenhower in his Boise, Idaho, speech. Leaders of both major political parties have recognized the need for a program to assist the people of the United States in meeting costs resulting from unusual and catastrophic sickness or disabling accidents. It is becoming increasingly clear that the present unemployment compensation program is inadequate to meet the demands made upon it by the extreme shifts of industry which occurred during the war and postwar period, and which are likely to continue in the rapidly changing economy of the United States. There is daily demand for increased government aid to education at both the national and state level.

The serious question about the "welfare state program" in the United States is that of means and methods. Whereas it is true to say that, theoretically, government should do for its citizens only what they cannot do for themselves, in the practical situation it may be sometimes necessary to do for them what they should and could do for themselves but do not do either individually or through corporate efforts below the level of government action. In any governmental program, the principle of subsidiarity should be observed, insofar as it is possible or practicable.

Individuals and families should first be assisted. Nongovernmental agencies and organizations, such as cooperatives, should be permitted, aided, and encouraged in their efforts to meet social problems. Those agencies of government which are closest to the problem and closest to the people should, in accordance with their strength and authority, assume responsibility. Eventually, of course, the federal government must accept some responsibility.

As a matter of fact, this principle of subsidiarity has been surprisingly well observed in the division of authority in the welfare program of the United States. Only two of the numerous programs generally included in the "welfare state" are administered by the federal government alone: The Social Security Act and the Fair Labor Standards Act. Of these two, the second is limited to interstate commercial activities, which, under the Constitution, fall within federal jurisdiction. The Old-Age Assistance program is a joint federal-state project, with the states in turn passing some responsibilities on to local governing units. The Public Housing Act requires participation of state and local governments. The farm program is, of course, principally a federal activity, but it too requires participation of state and local governments, as well as the participation of farmers and farm organizations. Aid to education has been reserved for the most part to state and local governments. . . . The unemployment insurance and workingmen's compensation programs remain principally matters of state law and state administration.

It is clear from this cursory examination of the "welfare state" that our private lives are not subject to the "bureaucratic control" of the federal government, as is so often charged. The "control" is distributed among the various government units, local, state, and federal.

Critics of the "welfare state" will usually grant that the state does have some right to interfere in economic and social life. They may even admit that a general program such as that outlined by Pope Pius XII is defensible and concede that the program in the United States has not gone too far. Ordinarily, however, they will make a final stand on the argument that once a "welfare" program has begun, it inevitably continues by some inner dynamic until all human activities have been subjected to state control. This predicted progression is ordinarily defined as "creeping socialism."

There is nothing inevitable about government change so long as responsible citizens control their own government. England and Australia have "socialized" themselves beyond the limits set by the New Deal and Fair Deal. In each of these countries political, economic, and social conditions are very different from those prevailing in the United States. In each case, the process, if it can be called that, has stopped short, a long distance from complete socialization. In both countries, the program has been moderated, and in some respects reversed. It is encouraging to note, too, that in other European countries, socialization or an inordinate extension of the welfare program has run into difficulties when it reached into the cultural fields of education and of religion. In those countries where political action remains free, the area of the mind and of the spirit has been successfully defended.

In conclusion, let me point out what I believe to be a reasonable attitude toward the "welfare state." If, by the term, we mean to define a state which undertakes to control every action of its citizens, a state which enters into every phase of life, unduly restricting freedom, not only at the economic level, but also at the level of the intellect and of the spirit, seeking to determine personality so as to fit each person into the totalitarian pattern, that "welfare state" is to be condemned.

If, however, we use the term "welfare state" with somewhat more regard for its established and traditional meaning, it is a good and usable term. It then describes a state which is seeking to meet its institutional responsibilities in assisting its citizens in their efforts to secure those things which are necessary to the good life, to the happiness of man. It then describes a state which is seeking to accomplish what Dr. Heinrich Rommen defines as the basic purpose of government: namely, "that of bringing about peaceful change in accordance with the demands of distributive justice."

The government, that is, the state, which seeks to establish a political order "in accordance with the demands of distributive justice" may well be called a "welfare state." It is the kind of state to which we have been committed from the beginning of our national existence and, beyond that, from the very beginnings of Western civilization.

Economic Aspect of the Welfare State*

HENRY SOMERVILLE

. . . So far I have spoken only of state provision of social services: family allowances, pensions, housing, medical care, and the like. It is

---

* From "What Is the Welfare State?" *Messenger*, November, 1952. Also in *Catholic Mind*, November, 1953.

these social services that the ordinary reader identifies with the welfare state. Professor Maurice Tremblay, in an article in the June, 1951, *Industrial Relations*, deals with a different question, equally important and less generally understood. The Liberal State (as he calls the laissez-faire state) was subject to long periods of unemployment. The economic system followed a course of booms and depressions, called the trade cycle. This is a fact of which everyone is aware. Economists now generally hold the theory that the cycle is inevitable in an economy which has the profit-making motive as its prime mover. The theory is not easy to explain in a few words nor is it yet absolutely proved. Still less proved is the efficacy of the state measures taken to correct the faults of the private-enterprise system.

The argument is that depressions follow underinvestment, and underinvestment results from profit falling below the rate of interest. The cost of investment becomes high because of the demand for liquid capital (money) necessary to finance investments when trade is active. The falling-off of investments starts unemployment, which has a cumulative effect. The unemployed curtail their demand for goods and thus lessen employment for others. The process of decline goes on, causing more and more unemployment. If the government economizes in order to reduce taxes because the taxpayers are short of money, its economics reduce the income of some of its citizens, and thus reduce trade and employment.

The new theory is that, when trade shows signs of decline, the government should spend more and not less, and it should borrow from the banks in order to spend. Bank borrowing increases the supply of money and stimulates trade. Government expenditures are not dominated by considerations of profit and loss, and expenditures are cumulative in their effects, for what one pays out another receives. Government spending, when it is financed by credit creation and not by taxation, increases trade and encourages private investment.

While the new theory calls for government action to increase expenditures when there are signs of recession from full employment, it calls for government restraint when capital and labor are being fully utilized, for then the danger is not depression but inflation. Thus the government should hold back public works when there is full employment and push them forward when there are signs of slackening trade. Professor Tremblay says: "The principle which is the basis of the economic policy of the welfare state consists in making public investments fluctuate exactly opposite to private investments, and to finance capital expenditures in such a way as not to go against these, at a time when investment opportunities are exhausted, at least for a certain period."

The aim of the state is said to be to stabilize the economy at a level of full employment. I think that any state, whether it professed to be a welfare state or not, would want to do this if it could. Whether any state can achieve this aim without unending inflation can be proved only by experience. The welfare states are making the attempt. Not only Britain with its Labor governments, but the United States and Canada are now being directed in the light of the new theory. It is not my purpose to discuss this theory or the economic policies based upon it, but it is mentioned here as an illustration of the new responsibilities that the present-day state is taking upon itself. . . .

The Morality of Organization*

J. A. RAFTIS, C.S.B.

In the vastly complex structure of our civilization, the problem that organization presents is a tremendous one. Pope John faces it in the beginning of Part II of *Mater et Magistra*. The principal source of the problem is an incorrect conscience arising from the heresy of nineteenth-century liberalism, or individualism. The liberalist had no true place for a positive morality of organization, and thus this natural exigency of human life was condemned by liberalism, as other natural exigencies have been condemned by negative moralities down through history — sex and marriage, economic activity and property, power and political institutions.

The efforts of *Rerum Novarum* and *Quadragesimo Anno* to establish a morality of association and organic structure are the best examples of the Church's efforts to overcome this liberalist heresy. Today very many people are confused by this dilemma of the liberal in an organized world — the "conflict of values," as it is called. We see this in the studies of "togetherness," of the "organization man," bureaucracy, etc.

The problem is present in another way. Organizations often began without a proper moral inspiration. Capital organization was dominated

* From "Clergy and Laity Lag Behind Pope John's Thought and Action," *Social Order*, December, 1962.

by individualism; banking and credit organization often tended to financial dictatorship; technological development subordinated man to the machine, assembly line, and automatic process; political organization was vitiated by nationalism and socialism; labor organization came under power control. One by one each of these excesses had to be curbed in one way or another: the antitrust and anticartel laws; the control of finance from the 1930's; limitations on labor power from the 1940's; reaction against welfare government in the 1950's; an increasing criticism of "inevitable automation" over the past decade.

If we have grown suspicious of various species of organization in the development of the modern world, it is not surprising that we have slight commitment to the generic principle of organization itself. . . .

However, even though Pope John cautions us against the abuses that can and do attend organization, he asks that we accept the principle itself as necessary for social justice today. How and why can he demand such a revolutionary moral conviction from us? The proximate answer is quite simple. As Pope John declares, organization has become the dynamic principle of modern life, and in itself this is a natural tendency of man. But the more fundamental reasons for this conviction are not so simple. In payment for a greater freedom and a greater control over matter, man must assume more responsibility today for the determinism in his life. Industrial society is the free choice of man as no other society has been. The fact that we take this choice for granted does not make it any the less fundamental. But by taking it for granted we have overlooked some important consequences: our failure to develop an adequate philosophy of matter, a sense of social laws, and a responsible concern for necessary planning.

The great catalyst of change in our society is natural science, and the focus of scientific change is man's control over matter. Scientific decisions do not change the intrinsic nature of matter itself — its deterministic element — but these many scientific advances in our society cannot fail to have a deterministic effect on human life. But it is naïve to suppose that this means a loss of freedom. History tells us how geological strata, natural resources, climate, etc. determined where a given people lived, how they dressed, their mode of travel, and what they had to eat. Science interposes itself between us and the elements, shifts the determination of matter from the land to the laboratory and from the farm to the factory and back again. But the basic drives of science are still for the material needs — as expressed in the standard of living, guaranteed wages, full employment — of the same elemental unit of the human species. The basic drive of science to conquer need is as impersonal as the things of nature that it handles. It is, therefore, more efficient, more successful, when applied as widely as possible — be it by automation, mass production, or mass marketing.

Pope John's approach to the problem of how to harness science to the service of genuine human needs is to anticipate the consequences of science. To do this we need to study the philosophy and psychology of man's use of material things in an industrial society. We are all aware of the power of the scientists to develop our natural resources, plan our cities, and organize our housing and recreation. But if we fail to use the data they make available, and don't sufficiently advert to the social laws in our plans to control matter, we shall, by this omission, sin against freedom.

We shall only begin to measure the consequences of scientific action, and be able to take steps to assume a proper responsibility, when we are sufficiently mature to accept the reality of social laws and planning. We can avoid much concern for this problem by simply facing up to the facts of the situation in the manner of Pope John:

> For socialization is not to be considered as a product of natural forces working in a deterministic way. It is, on the contrary, as We have observed, a creation of men who are free agents intended by nature to work in a responsible manner. This is so even though they are obliged to recognize and, as it were, obey the laws of economic development and social progress. Nor can they entirely escape from all the pressures of their environment (N. 63).

This notion of laws is by now an elementary consideration of the social sciences, just as the norms of the new economic morality indicated by Pope John — standard of living, full employment, planned production, etc. — are ordinary considerations in economic policy. But our general thinking is much too far behind the work of the natural scientist and the social scientist. This is true unfortunately of those in Catholic philosophy and theology. They have not yet incorporated the realities of the natural and social sciences into their thinking, and so tend to stress only the prudential act and free will, and, consequently, miss the real scope of social decisions in modern society.

We see some of the results of this in the panic among some Catholic philosophers, moral theologians, and canon lawyers over the use of the word *socialization* in the recent encyclical. This term really involves a notion about as revolutionary as the necessity of having a surveyor for a housing development. Unless these important spokesmen of Catholic thought are willing to adjust their antennas, they are in danger of missing the meaning of the social aspirations of modern man as completely as some schools of Catholic thought missed the democratic aspirations of European man in the nineteenth century.

Does this recognition of a certain degree of determinism, of social laws, and of necessities for planning imply a loss of liberty in our total situation — a blind submission to the industrial order, as it were? By no means! These steps imply rather a maturity of outlook in our civilization and bring freedom in line with maturity. For this is not so much an accretion of new controls as a challenge to the narrower limits, the narrower laws, by which our society has lived. We might say that the doctrine of *Mater et Magistra* frees us from these narrow laws and from a too close dependence on certain traditional temporal institutions.

First, with respect to laws, the main contribution of the social encyclicals to Western society has been to modify so-called laws — by now a built-in yen that we seem to have for automatic solutions to an involved area of human relations. The more fundamental theological and philosophical perspectives taken in these encyclicals make it possible to give due merit to the element of honest aspiration in the modern world and at the same time to recognize where excess has entered in. The doctrines that have dominated the minds of our age came from those naïve scientific laws of the eighteenth and early nineteenth centuries — the classical economic law of diminishing returns, the iron law of wages, the Malthusian law of population, the social theory of market competition, survival of the fittest, nationalism, economic imperialism. Over against such doctrines were the Marxist law of surplus value and the more general socialist laws of absolute human equality.

These various theories were first given the status of "natural law" from the eighteenth century, then of "scientific law" from the nineteenth century, and finally, in the twentieth century, an enshrinement in political ideology.

The Church has always opposed this narrowness of modern man — his tendency to depend upon inexorable scientific progress and to set organization against the individual. In *Mater et Magistra*, the Pope recognizes that the potential of science and the organizational possibilities of man free him from a direct dependence upon science and industry. Rather science and industry can, by organization, be put more directly at the service of human needs. Industrial society, more than many other societies of the past, requires a spiritual challenge. Otherwise, the powerful material orientation of this society will become the religion of secularism — a condition that Will Herberg already finds challenging the churches in America. Organization can put modern life at the service of the natural law — the person, the family, the common good. Indeed, organization is the instrument whereby those twin norms of Catholic social doctrine — the person and the common good — can be implemented and give vitality to our society:

> As the interlocking organizations of modern society develop, right order will be realized more and more through a renewed balance between a demand for autonomous and active collaboration on the part of all — individuals and groups — and timely co-ordination and encouragement of private enterprise by government.
> So long as socialization is kept within these limits of the moral order, it will not of its nature seriously restrict individuals or overburden them. Instead, it offers hope of promoting in them the expression and development of their personal characteristics. It results, too, in an organic reconstruction of society, which Our predecessor Pius XI, in *Quadragesimo Anno*, put forward and defended as the indispensable prerequisite for satisfying abundantly the demands of social justice (NN. 66, 67).

Let us recall here that organization is not only an acceptable but a desirable principle, for organizations are the instruments of free development today. Free action is not restricted to the individual alone, nor is social development to be predicated solely on state action. Perhaps the greatest danger today lies in political conformity. We have tended more and more to be "tuned-in" only to political ideologies. . . .

Mater et Magistra can help us get out of this unfortunate drift, for in this papal doctrine we find defined the scope for healthy government activity. At the same time, and perhaps more important, this encyclical makes clear how socialism is not only not an acceptable moral alternative but is a failure as a system of government. Socialism arose in the nineteenth century as an extreme antidote to individualism. The organizational abilities of twentieth-century man render both systems obsolete. In the words of Pope John, social development has shifted away from these extremes to intermediate bodies:

> Moreover, We consider it necessary that the intermediate groups and numerous social enterprises through which socialization tends to express itself should enjoy an effective autonomy. They should, in addition, pursue their own special interests in true harmony without damage to the common good. It is no less necessary that such groups manifest the nature and

aspect of a true community. They will do this only if their individual members are always treated as persons and encouraged to take an active part in the community's affairs (N. 65).

Throughout the remainder of Part II, Pope John illustrates his principle of intermediate vitality. In considering a growing economy to which scientific progress is being applied, he says that all economic agents must adjust to this advance. He finds in every case that the economic unit is able to adjust in turn to the persons involved in the new ways and that this adjustment is made easiest on the local level through the criterion of community, and on the national and international levels through the notion of common growth and common participation in growth. The state has an essential function to perform in all this, but the state is not the principle of organization.

It is increasingly clear that the basic demands of morality in modern industrial society point to new hope and new freedom for the whole human community. The moral pivot of this new freedom, Pope John stresses, is the elemental right of every human being to subsistence — and to better subsistence if possible. The second dictate of this morality is that a generally higher level of material well-being is possible today through science, and therefore, everyone has a right to the fruits of science — as basic as the right to breathe.

This is an exciting new frontier of human endeavor that holds out unprecedented gains for mankind: gains that would abolish the roots of class war in society, of colonial wars, of nationalist wars; gains that would be as moving and fundamental as the history of the victory over slavery and famine. The most serious liability regarding the future of the industrial world is a lack of faith in the great vistas Divine Providence is giving us.

A selfish pessimism still shrouds our thinking. In Part III, Pope John urges us to respond optimistically to the challenge of Providence, to face our moral obligation to use science to overcome want, etc. To implement these improvements, Pope John insists upon the necessity of organized attacks on social evils and stresses the need of collective efforts to capitalize humanly on the forward sweep of science. . . .

CHAPTER 8

INTERNATIONAL COMMON GOOD

> We appealed in Mater et Magistra to economically de-
> veloped nations to come to the aid of those which are in
> process of development.
>
> We are greatly consoled to see how widely and favorably
> that appeal has been received. We are confident that in the
> future it will contribute even more to the end that the poorer
> countries, in as short a time as possible, will arrive at that
> degree of economic development which will enable every
> citizen to live in conditions more in keeping with human
> dignity.
>
> It can never be sufficiently repeated that this cooperation
> should be effected with the greatest respect for the liberty of
> the developing countries; for these must realize that they
> are primarily responsible for, and are the principal artisans
> of, the promotion of their own economic development and
> social progress.
>
> Pope John XXIII in *Pacem in Terris*

Pope Pius XII may appropriately be called "The Pope of the International Common Good."

In his 1940 Christmas Eve address, he set down as one of the "indispensable prerequisites" for a new world order "the triumph over
those germs of conflict which consist in excessive disparities between
nations in the field of world economy." Accordingly, he exhorted governments to "progressive action . . . to arrive at some orderly arrangement that would give to every state the means of securing for its citizens
of all classes proper standards of living."

In his Christmas message the following year, the Pope insisted that
"within the limits of a new order founded on moral principles there
is no place for that cold and calculating egoism which tends to hoard

the economic resources and materials destined for the use of all to such an extent that nations less favored by nature are not permitted access to them."

As he neared the end of his pontificate, Pius XII was still intent on developing these ideas, emphasizing over and over again that nations, though independent and sovereign, are at the same time members of a world community. As a Christian "sees the pressure of events giving rise to a more and more strictly defined world community," he told a group of Catholic scholars on April 25, 1957, "he knows that this divinely willed unification should result in a union of hearts and minds in a single faith and love."

Despite the Cold War, which has vastly complicated the task of organizing the international community, much progress has been made toward the goal of justice for all peoples. The international institutions established twenty years ago — especially the Bank for Reconstruction and Development, the Monetary Fund, and the General Agreement on Tariffs and Trade (GATT) — have notably contributed to world economic development and a large expansion of trade. Many countries have liberalized their immigration policies and have cooperated in resettling millions of refugees from war and oppression. Western Europe and, more recently, Latin America have adopted regional economic plans that supplement the inadequacies of the individual participating countries. In various constructive ways, the United Nations has assisted the developing countries and dramatized the increasing interdependence of all peoples, developed as well as underdeveloped, in a world that has suddenly become a large neighborhood.

What distresses many today — as it distressed Pope John — is the slowness with which individuals and nations are moving toward a just world order firmly and juridically established. Despite many heartening achievements, the gulf between rich and poor nations grows daily larger, and the spirit of nationalism, with all its pride and selfishness, sometimes seems as vigorous and entrenched as ever. The concept of the international economic good has still not become one of those dynamic ideas that capture imaginations and spur men on to rise above themselves. For this failure, as Pope John intimates in Mater et Magistra, those who are members of Christ's Mystical Body are more blameworthy than the rest.

Population and Resources*

LINUS GROND, O.F.M.

In the third part of his encyclical, *Mater et Magistra*, Pope John XXIII dedicates some fifteen paragraphs to the problems of world population and subsistence. . . .

The rather brief treatment of the subject has, without doubt, caused some disappointment here and there. However, one might take into account that it is not the task of the Pope, and therefore cannot be the scope of an encyclical letter, to give a scientific explanation of the many complicated problems connected with the subject, problems which are demographic, economic, sociological, financial, technical, and organizational in character. The consciousness of these problems, however, constitutes the background of the normative and socioethical thesis which the Pope underlines in this encyclical. . . .

We shall try to pick out the most important points of the encyclical.

1. Concerning the central problem of the increase in world population, the encyclical points out that, in the opinion of some people, the rapid increase of population compared to economic development will soon cause a lack of balance between the population and its subsistence. It is, therefore, argued that an active policy of birth control is an urgent necessity. Those who oppose this opinion do so on the grounds that the relevant data available are so doubtful and so subject to change that they cannot be used to prove anything with certainty. Furthermore, the encyclical states that the relationship between the birth rate and the means of subsistence is such that there are no serious difficulties at present, nor will there be any in the near future. The data which the encyclical considers to be doubtful or subject to change are, in the mind of the Pope, those which deal with the possibility of increasing production. The reason for believing this is that it is very difficult to prove that the expert investigations of the UN Population Department on the future development of world populations are not correct.

These figures largely depend on two suppositions: that present-day trends will continue to develop in the same way in the future, and

---

* From "Mater et Magistra and the Population Problem," *Pax Romana Journal*, No. 1, 1962. Also in *Catholic Mind*, May, 1963.

that outside influences which have a bearing on the problem will also remain constant. According to this hypothesis, the world population will develop as follows:

World Population in 1980, in Millions, as Forecast in Three Different Years

Hypothetical			
Maximum	3636	3990	4280
Average	3277	3628	4220
Minimum	2976	3295	3850

The three forecasts certainly differ considerably, but they are not doubtful or contradictory in the sense indicated in the encyclical. On the contrary, the figures for world population are increasing with each new forecast because of improved methods of calculation and the increasing reliability of demographic information in a number of areas, especially in the newly developing countries.

Moreover, in actual fact, the observed increase in world population has grown more rapidly than was forecast, even though one takes the maximum hypothetical figures. Therefore, there is no convincing argument to prove with certainty that the latest population studies go too far in their conclusions, which are that the world population will be about 4.22 billion by 1980 and 6.2 billion by the end of the century.

Notwithstanding the enormous increase in population, the encyclical is optimistic about the possibilities of developing food production to a point where a catastrophe can be avoided. The Pope comes to this conclusion as a result of his often repeated confidence in human ability to develop scientific techniques which will probe more into the potential of the physical world. Thus mankind will benefit from the almost inexhaustible resources which God created and put at man's disposal. It is this confidence which the Pope uses in opposition to the dubious and often contradictory arguments put up by some people to support their pessimistic views on the world's future. These are the people who advocate a policy of restricting population.

Indeed, the human race has a full right to share in the optimism of the encyclical. There is a close connection between the divine commandment "Be fertile, multiply and fill the earth" and the words following immediately afterward "and dominate the earth" (Gn 1:28). The first implies a mission to become a world population, and the second means that man must solve the problem of population and its means of support. For many centuries man has failed to obey these commandments. Human beings did not become a world population, nor did they dominate the earth and the forces of nature; on the contrary, they were dominated by them. World population developed in the slow tempo dictated by the forces of nature, which were not understood and not brought under control.

However, since the period of the great discoveries, man has found out more and more how he can dominate the world and its forces. One can say without doubt that the constant increase in population since 1650 is closely connected with this phenomenon. If one studies the reports on the almost limitless possibilities for increasing world production, on the enormous food resources offered by the oceans of the world, on the techniques for improving the calory content in food, one becomes convinced that the exploitation of the world offers immense possibilities for improving the living conditions of human beings — indeed, of far more human beings than are actually living in the world today.

2. The Pope is very well aware that all this does not alter the fact that there are parts of the world where very serious discrepancies exist between the population and the resources available. The encyclical states:

> We appreciate the fact that in certain underdeveloped areas and states serious problems and difficulties of this nature can and do present themselves. These problems frequently result from a defective economic and social organization which does not provide means of subsistence in a measure proportionate to the rate of population increase, and also from the fact that a sense of solidarity among peoples is not operative to a sufficient degree (N. 190).

The encyclical here takes us to the very heart of the problem that faces the newly developing countries. In the first place, it states that in these countries there is much misery and poverty, and that the standard of living, instead of getting better, is constantly falling.

It cannot be stressed too often that the impoverishment of two-thirds of the world's population is proceeding at a cumulative rate. The poor countries are growing poorer per head of population — not only relatively but absolutely — and the rich countries are continually growing richer. This happens in spite of the millions of dollars invested in projects for financial and technical assistance. In the opinion of the Pope, the foregoing proves that the socioeconomic policies of the wealthy countries are responsible for this situation, which is steadily deteriorating. On this point, the Pope stresses the fact that technical assistance has thus far been insufficient and wrongly directed. The encyclical is very convincing in its elaboration of these two points.

On the question of man's domination of the forces of nature, the Pope says that modern science and technical developments, as well as economic wealth, have been debased, so as to become instruments of death and destruction, and, in consequence, they are being used contrary to God's will. This is brought about by the lack of cooperation between nations. There is not enough mutual confidence; states and peoples are afraid of each other. Because armaments are being continually increased, enormous human energies and natural resources are being dissipated, to the detriment of society instead of for its benefit. The root cause of this is the refusal to believe in a transcendental, absolute and universal moral order. As a result, any conception of international justice has been falsified by completely subjective and contradictory interpretations.

What the Pope has written, as authentic interpreter of moral obligations, can be accepted as being contained in a number of conceptions, such as democracy, self-determination, peace, and liberty. If these ideals are deprived of their foundations and are debased into political slogans, they then give a false air of justice to acts which are nothing more than grievous sins against God and mankind.

3. We must consider, against this background, the condemnation of various methods to limit the procreation of human life. In effect the Pope's argument is this: because of the misdeeds of governments, the forces of nature have been used to harm and destroy man rather than benefit him. As a result, the steadily growing needs of an increasing world population are not being gratified. Consequently, many people seek to escape from this impasse by advocating a new sin — planned birth control. Although it does not say so explicitly, we believe that two distinct theses are implied in the text of the encyclical.

In opposing those who have recourse to methods which are an offense to the dignity of man, the Pope says:

> . . . the solution is to be found only in socio-economic progress achieved in a moral atmosphere befitting the dignity of mankind and the immense value of a single human life. . . . The transmission of human life is effected by a personal and conscious act. . . .

For this reason it is stated that man must continue to be the subject of his personal and conscious acts. This is denied by those who want to make man the object of various plans and projects to regulate his numbers.

First, we have the neo-Malthusian population experts who, whether for

egoistic or altruistic reasons, would reduce the numbers of the population, especially in the newly developing countries, because of insufficient subsistence. In doing this, they consider human beings as objects
in their calculations. This may be unconscious, but it is nevertheless an
offense against human dignity because it denies man his right to act
as a conscious person. The neo-Malthusian experts pretend to be cham-
pions of deliberate parenthood, but the measures propagated and introduced by various authorities are bound to offend against the principle of
conscious and personal parenthood. These are the very methods advocated
by the neo-Malthusians.

In the second place, it is clear that a proper conception of human
dignity is undermined by the policy which most Communist leaders seem
to favor. They claim that the process of liberating the proletariat from
capitalist dictatorship is being accelerated by the growing strength of
the Communist countries and their increased production, and therefore
by an ever increasing number of producers. This is the so-called active-
population policy pursued in the majority of Communist countries. Once
again man is reduced to the level of an object for planning, and he is
denied his right to regulate his procreation in accordance with his own
conscious and personal responsibility.

This personal responsibility, so clearly underlined by the encyclical,
was also stressed by the last Lambeth Congress of the Anglican bishops.
The relevant statement by the conference emphasized that no power in
the world has the authority to interfere with the rights of parents to
retain absolute freedom in their personal and conscious decisions about
parenthood.

In considering what means may be employed to regulate conscious
parenthood, the encyclical condemns "all expedients that offend against
the moral order established by God and do violence to the very origin
of human life," and it points out once again that "since the transmission
of human life is effected by a personal and conscious act, it is therefore
subject to the laws of God, which are sacred, inviolable and immutable."
By stating this once more, the Church repeats her teaching about the
unlawfulness of contraceptive techniques which prevent the act of procreation from being fully completed.

Efforts to find a solution to the serious difficulties of many people
must be inspired by "a renewed scientific and technical effort on the
part of man to deepen and extend his mastery over nature." This might
include an improved knowledge of the fertile and infertile periods, with

the possibility of identifying these periods with ever greater accuracy. . . .

It is to be hoped that the stand taken by the encyclical may be reinforced by the highest Church authorities, and may be taken up at all levels of the ecclesiastical hierarchy. Complicated problems are revealed, on the one hand, by the demographic evolution of the population of the world and, on the other, by the socioeconomic development and radical structural changes of the newly developing countries. Faced with these problems, the Church cannot allow her principles and directives for the well-being of nations to hang in midair. Her knowledge of social realities must be realistic and based on facts which have been carefully analyzed on a scientific basis.

The Right to Migrate*

REV. JEREMIAH NEWMAN

Both by word and deed the Church has sought to arouse the conscience of Catholics and of the nations of the world to a sense of responsibility in dealing with the problems which migration creates. In 1951, at the special request of the Pope, the International Catholic Migration Commission was formed. With headquarters at Geneva, it serves as an agency for the coordination, information, and representation of the Catholic effort to meet migration problems. Its two Congresses, held at Barcelona and Breda, have contributed much toward the drawing up of a Catholic migration policy.

The Holy See itself has also been active and has issued a number of important statements on principles in recent years. In August, 1952, it issued *Exsul Familia,* an Apostolic Constitution on the spiritual care of emigrants. This has been followed up by many addresses, chiefly by Pope Pius XII, dealing with emigration questions . . .

From these addresses it is possible to derive a body of principles which represent what might be called the Catholic approach to migration problems. It can scarcely be said that a complete policy has as yet been formulated. The subject is a new and developing one, the principles being fashioned as concrete problems arise. Nevertheless, it will be profitable for us to survey the Catholic approach to emigration and the principles by which practical efforts should be guided.

---

* From "The Right to Migrate," *Christus Rex.* Also in *Catholic Mind,* May–June, 1957.

The Catholic attitude to migration was well summed up in a short paper to the International Catholic Migration Congress at Breda (1954) by Monsignor Rodhain of the French *Secours Catholique*. The first thing, says Monsignor Rodhain, which must be remembered, is that the earth was given by God to all men to enable them to lead a life that will lead to Him. Therefore, for any group to arbitrarily close the frontiers of its territories to others is unequivocally inhuman and unjust.

Secondly, it must be remembered that the countries of the world consist of organized communities and nations. In the measure in which this is true, a migrant has no right to impose himself on a country without accepting its just laws and striving to integrate himself into the community which he finds there. These are considerations which flow clearly and immediately from the twin orders of charity and justice. In addition, there are the orders of providence and of redemption. Taking a short view of things one could regard the phenomenon of migration as merely the consequence of economic, political, and social disorders. But there is an important sense in which these factors themselves are subordinate to a higher purpose — "Increase and multiply and fill the earth" (Gn 1:28). And who will say that migration has no significance from the point of view of the order of redemption and the growth and vigor of the Mystical Body of Christ?

The standards by which migration may be adjudged successful from the Catholic viewpoint are threefold.

First of all, the preservation of religious integrity. It was with this that *Exsul Familia* was especially concerned. It involves the special preparation of the migrant before leaving his country of origin, so that the new pattern of life in the country to which he is going may not prove injurious if not fatal to his religious practice. It is important to realize the tremendous psychological effects of being uprooted from one's native *milieu* and of finding oneself cast adrift in new surroundings. The terrible anonymity of industrial city life, for example, can be a chilling experience for a migrant from a country village.

Secondly, the integrity of the family must be safeguarded. There are special dangers attendant on the migration system under which the breadwinner goes abroad and is separated from wife and family for indefinite periods. It must be the constant object of Catholic migration activities to seek to bring about the reunion of such families.

Thirdly, there is the preservation of cultural integrity. Migration studies have conclusively proved that human dignity suffers very considerably by the feeling of losing cultural traditions. Language, culture, and traditions are part of a man's personality and he should not be required to strip himself of them, at least immediately, when he migrates from his mother country to another. It is true that the ideal is that he should integrate himself into his new *milieu* eventually, but the process should be gradual and discriminating and of such a nature as will allow, in so far as is possible, the coexistence of varied cultural patterns.

At the concrete level the Catholic attitude may be expressed as follows:

As regards emigration: (1) No country has the right to place obstacles to those of its citizens who, for serious reasons, may wish to leave it and live elsewhere; (2) If emigration is a necessity for large numbers of its citizens, a country should help them to emigrate and to settle down in their new home.

As regards immigration: (1) Underdeveloped countries should open their doors to all serious applications on the part of immigrants; (2) they should also help them to settle down after their arrival.

It is the Church's policy to try to bring about more human legal arrangements in regard to migration, especially immigration, to draw the attention of Catholics, especially in the immigration countries, to their duties in the matter of receiving and aiding immigrants, to call the immigrants' attention to their duty of striving to integrate themselves into their new country and to aid them in doing so and thus avoid becoming *déracinés*. . . .

Duties to Developing Countries*

LEON H. JANSSEN, S.J.

It will be fruitful to begin any analysis of the moral obligation to aid underdeveloped countries with what will seem an egregious digression into nineteenth-century social history, an examination of the moral mood of the Industrial Revolution.

Relations between employer and employee were settled by contract, commonly an oral one. According to the moral lights of the time, the arrangement was considered eminently fair: a voluntary arrangement had been made whose stipulations were protected by law. All the requirements of justice, then, were fulfilled to the letter. To be sure, the

* From "Duties to Underdeveloped Countries," *Social Order*, May, 1958.

working class lived in misery, despite the valiant efforts of Christian charity to alleviate extreme necessity. For this situation employers as a class felt no particular responsibility. Their conviction that they were doing all that could be expected of them in living up to their side of a contract was an expression of the extremely individualistic outlook of the past century. The distress of the working class, they would concede, was unfortunate, even pitiable, but it was as irremediable as earthquakes and floods and other so-called acts of God. The workings of the economic system were deemed as fixed as the law of gravity.

Such an attitude strikes us today as morally monstrous. We know that there are obligations antecedent to any law or any contract. We realize that contracts, no matter how solemnly concluded, can cloak shameless exploitation when they merely ratify the overwhelming power of one of the parties to the bargain. We know that, in addition to obligations toward individuals arising out of contracts, there are duties in justice to the community as a whole. We now see, in short, that social justice supplements commutative justice and by its claims makes every member of the community responsible for the well-being of every other member.

This change in industrial relations, this new cognizance (however vaguely expressed) of social justice, was the fruit of a conviction that something should and could be done to give every member of the community the opportunity to lead a fully human life. Such a belief implied, of course, a new understanding of the supposedly fixed mechanism of economic processes. It demanded also a fresh appreciation of fundamental human rights and a recognition that free conventions are not the only source of obligations covering these rights. Inspired by such convictions, men took steps to give these human rights legal protection. The implications of social justice were institutionalized in social legislation. . . .

The awareness of relationships of justice governing the international community is today as primitive as was the moral mood of the nineteenth-century view of industrial relations.

Statesmen, when they admit a duty to aid the economic growth of underdeveloped countries, are wont to concede at best the existence of obligations arising out of contracts — legal agreements which, when concluded among sovereign powers, are called treaties. Such agreements do certainly give rise to obligations but they neither exhaust nor do they originate such obligations; at bottom, these are founded on international social justice. . . .

There *is* an international community, however imperfectly organized.

The solidarity of this community is the basis of obligations of international social justice. This solidarity is the consequence of the common origin and the common destiny of all men, whatever be their race or nationality or fortune. . . .

True, compared with the consciousness of membership in a national community, the sense of belonging to an international community is disappointingly feeble. As a result, the realization of obligations of international social justice is retarded and reluctant. Like the property-owning class of the last century, we have been aware of the poverty of the masses of the underdeveloped countries. We have felt that such misery was unfortunate, even pitiable, but we have believed that such situations are inevitable and, anyhow, beyond our responsibility. To be sure, missionaries have expended themselves valiantly to relieve extreme need, and funds have been raised by popular subscription on the occasion of a catastrophe in a distant land. Yet, the rich nations, as such, felt no obligation to undertake measures which would prevent poverty in the underdeveloped countries. . . .

Will I be reminded at this point that realism shapes the direction of a nation's foreign policy, that the improved industrial relations of earlier generations were the result, not of a changed ethical attitude, but of the powerful pressures of the trade unions, that the actual motives for aiding the underdeveloped countries are not moral but economic and political? We need them as customers and as producers of raw materials, I will be told, and it is better for business if they are prosperous, productive, and politically stable. Moreover, we must keep them, whatever the cost, from the maws of an all-devouring Soviet imperialism. These and not some irrelevant moral principles, it is insisted in some quarters, are the real motives for whatever aid is extended to the underdeveloped countries.

Such arguments neither surprise nor shock me. The property-owning class of the nineteenth century was first compelled to change its economic practices and in the process changed its moral attitudes. Once this new attitude had become generalized, it became a strong force in establishing everywhere more equitable relations between employers and employees. Pragmatic considerations are undoubtedly the primary factor today in aid to underdeveloped countries. And yet simultaneously a growing change in the common moral attitude on the topic can be observed. . . .

The very term "underdeveloped countries" supposes that these nations should be more fully developed. Is this so? A crude sort of objection challenges this assumption, pointing out that the people of these areas of the world have endured this condition for centuries and insisting that they are happier as they are.

Whether it suits our prejudices or not, growth is a law of life, one imposed by nature herself. True, minimum standards will vary, depending on local circumstances. As long as Asia and Africa lived in their traditional isolation, this minimum standard was a stationary and perhaps even an endurable one. Contact with other nations through the media of contemporary communications has produced an impassioned refusal to be content any longer with any such meager standards. Generalized illiteracy becomes as unacceptable (and as impossible) within the narrowing limits of the international community as individual illiteracy is in a civilized national community. Much more is this true with regard to widespread poverty, the lack of technical knowledge, and endemic ill health.

Rapidly increasing populations make economic growth in the underdeveloped countries imperative.

The static societies of the past are impossible to prolong, even were one prompted to make the attempt. Indeed, the Western conception of the primitive but happy savage is a romantic delusion. The same patronizing view was held of the industrial worker in the nineteenth century. Let him stay where he is, it was said; not knowing any bettter, he is content; by giving him more, you will create new wants and leave him unhappier than before. Such an attitude can be maintained only by closing one's eye to the massive poverty, disease, ignorance, and even starvation rampant in the underdeveloped countries. . . . Economic progress is not, to be sure, a guarantee of personal happiness but the misery that is identified with economic stagnation clearly brings unhappiness.

How serious is the moral obligation to help underdeveloped countries?

A quantitative answer to this type of question will not be expected. Principles of priority are, to be sure, available to aid our analysis of the question; these are the familiar principles of *caritas ordinata*, ordered charity. That these principles are drawn from the category of charity does not weaken their relevance (though admittedly the distinction between charity and justice has been so stressed as to leave the impression that charity is to be invoked only when no obligation in justice is demonstrable). The fact is that social justice and social charity each supposes the other, both having a common origin in the solidarity of all mankind. The principles of specifications are the same, then, for social justice as for social charity.

These principles can be summed up in three words: (1) need, (2) relationship, and (3) possibility.

1. The first principle of specification declares: *The greater the need, the greater the obligation.* The less a man can help himself in his distress, the greater is my obligation to aid him.

How great is the need of the underdeveloped countries and to what extent can they help themselves?

The actual material poverty of the underdeveloped countries is palpable. Two out of three humans, Boyd Orr has stated, go to bed hungry every night; very few of these unfortunate people are found in countries of economic growth. Living at best on a mere subsistence level, the people of these lands have no reserves in times of frequent crop failures. Most of them are, in short, in extreme necessity. "Extreme necessity" is a technical term in moral philosophy for a situation imparting in another a grave obligation, even at the cost of substantial sacrifices, to aid the person in need. This poverty, it may be added, is becoming more intolerable as the underdeveloped countries become increasingly aware of the enormous differences in the standard of living of the rich and the poor nations. Their poverty is both absolute and relative. The evidence, then, would seem to indicate a grave obligation to aid them.

But cannot the underdeveloped countries help themselves? Why, in the first place, are they poor? Ultimately because their productivity is low, a fact with many explanations, the primary one being the low per capita equipment of their workers. Or as the economist Ragnar Nurkse puts it: they are poor because their productivity is low and their productivity is low because they are poor.

How break through this vicious circle? As history proves, it can be done. England did so without outside help; indeed, at that time there was no other nation capable of aiding her. The price England paid for her present prosperity was the misery of her workers during the Industrial Revolution. Russia's relative success was comparatively simpler: her "take-off into self-sustained growth," to employ Professor W. W. Rostow's phrase, was prepared by foreign loans under the last Czars. Even so, the Soviets have persistently imposed restrictions on consumption, a policy that has caused periods of starvation when millions died. The spurring of economic growth in these two countries, it should be noted, differed only in method. In England the Iron Law of Wages was the mechanism; in the Soviet Union it has been the iron absolutism of state policy.

There is, however, another method of increasing a nation's wealth, a method most strikingly illustrated in the case of the United States. Loans, plus technical assistance and grants (in the form of immigrants from the Old World), rendered the process of American economic growth smoother and simpler. . . .

Japan's economic growth, it may be observed, was the fruit of a combination of the three methods: low wages, a planned economy, plus technical assistance and foreign loans.

These historical experiences answer the question as to whether the underdeveloped countries can raise themselves from poverty unassisted. The misery of these lands is so acute and pervasive that economic development must be promptly accelerated. The English method of financing future prosperity by accepting a lower standard of living through several generations is out of the question. The standard of living in the underdeveloped countries is now so low that it would be impossible to depress it further in the hopes of accumulating a significant sum for investment. Moreover, to preach such a program in the face of the rising expectations of all mankind for a life of decency and dignity would provoke revolutionary resentment. We cannot in conscience accept the communist alternative. Some method must be found, then, to increase investment markedly without seriously reducing the meager consumption of the underdeveloped countries. This is possible only with help from abroad. The inability of the underdeveloped countries to aid themselves effectively indicates, therefore, a grave obligation falling on the wealthy nations.

2. The principle of relationship declares that *people who are nearer to us have a greater claim on our help than others.* . . .

A nation has, of course, the gravest obligations toward itself. It must help itself even before aiding those countries with which it is most closely associated by common interests or historical ties. In the light of this principle of relationship a nation has greater obligations toward its colonies or former colonies. Moreover, it is justified in extending larger assistance to those nations which have shown a willingness to oppose the expansion of Communism. It further follows that the obligation to help is reduced in proportion to the sacrifice required; that the obligation of richer countries is relatively greater; and, finally, that if the presumed obligation can be filled by either a loan or a grant, a loan is to be preferred. . . .

That the primary and gravest obligation to help underdeveloped countries rests on these nations themselves is an obvious conclusion of this principle of relationship. The examples of the means of economic growth illustrated by England, Russia, the United States, and Japan made no mention of the immense physical effort and the pioneering spirit displayed in these successes. To the extent that the underdeveloped countries fail to apply themselves to their proper task of raising standards of living — if the rich continue to live luxuriously, if order and justice are absent even for foreign investors — to that extent the obligation of other countries to aid them is reduced. We must not forget, however, that the lack of sound judgment in economic matters and even the presence of corruption and a self-conscious nationalism with overtones of xenophobia are part of the growing pains of developing countries. We must help them outgrow this awkward stage with patience and understanding.

3. The third principle of specification in determining obligations of social justice declares: *Help is to be proportioned to its usefulness*. . . .

Thus, when a country lacks the fundamental conditions for economic growth there is no use pumping in dollars. What is needed first is education, technical assistance, and perhaps even political reform. If such a country does not want this kind of assistance, the obligation to help it is diminished, since dollars are not a cure-all. For underdevelopment is also due to the character of the people, to local institutions and habits, to illiteracy and health conditions, and to the influence of religion. The principle of need may suggest prompt action. The principle of possibility, on the other hand, may in certain cases warn us to go slowly.

The principle of possibility comes into play again when an underdeveloped country is unwilling to accept bilateral help on the grounds that such assistance constitutes foreign interference and a new form of colonialism. Bilateral help can, to be sure, claim a certain priority under the principle of relationship, since this method seems generally speaking more profitable for the helping country. Even so, the need of the underdeveloped country may be so grave that richer nations may be obliged to participate in a form of multilateral aid, a method which they have already endorsed in signing the Charter of the United Nations.

So far our discussion has been concerned explicitly with moral principles and not with practical politics. Political policy is not exclusively determined by moral principles: these cannot do more than indicate certain directions and set certain limits within which a policy may be good or bad. When we come to concrete decisions, our answers will ultimately be determined not merely by moral principles but by the counsel of practical wisdom as well. This is particularly true when one considers the permissibility of attaching conditions to foreign aid.

The principle of possibility indicates that the help we are obliged to extend is determined by its expected effectiveness. It is not unethical, then, to promise greater help on condition that certain economic and political reforms be introduced which will increase the effectiveness of that aid. Whether in given circumstances such conditions should be announced is a matter for practical wisdom to decide. The same is true concerning the type of aid to be extended, whether it is to take the form of loans, grants-in-aid, technical assistance by governments or by private investment. The moral principle in question merely declares that, given serious need, we must do what we can, taking into account the expected results and legitimate self-interest. What in the concrete we are to do and how we are to do it falls within the scope of practical policy. . . .

A final observation: it is not sufficient to make aid to the under-developed countries a passing gesture. International social justice requires the establishing of institutions, the creation of a stable social order where justice is independent of the whims of individual nations.

The nineteenth century will again offer an illustration. At that time the consciousness of social obligations among members of the national community was so vague as to be properly described as inchoate. As the idea crystallized and the determination to see it realized developed, social justice began to be written into statutes, began to be incorporated into political and social institutions and into commercial practices. The same process is occurring in the international sphere. At present we are dimly conscious of some sort of a duty to aid underdeveloped countries, to foster their economic growth. The fulfillment of this obligation, how-ever, depends upon the good will of the rich nations and their unilateral decisions in the field of foreign policy. And yet it is certain that all the peoples of the underdeveloped countries have a clear right to a life of decency and dignity, a right which can be only tenuously achieved with-out a stable social world order. In the absence of treaties these rights are, to be sure, unenforceable today. But they exist nonetheless.

Foreign Aid Programs*

ALICE BOURNEUF

I believe that, from the point of view of an economist, the most im-portant basic notion in *Mater et Magistra* that is new in papal docu-

---

* From "Problems of Underdeveloped Countries," *Review of Social Economy*, Fall, 1962.

ments, and that underlies the various positions taken on domestic and international questions, is the notion that governments must play an active role in solving many of today's problems. The principle of subsidiarity is restated and reaffirmed, and there are many references to the virtues of private enterprise, to stimulating private enterprise and private initiative, and to promoting efforts at collaboration. However, there are also many explicit and implicit judgments in the encyclical on the necessity in present circumstances for governments to play an active role in domestic social affairs, in the development of programs for underdeveloped countries, and in international economic affairs. . . .

The specific statements on underdeveloped countries in *Mater et Magistra* do not emphasize the removal of government restrictions on the movements of labor, goods, and capital. There are parenthetical remarks implying that the elimination of restrictions is proper and desirable, but there is no tendency to make freedom from restrictions the beginning and end of morality in international economic affairs. Furthermore, cooperation is not advocated primarily to eliminate restrictions, as was so often implied in the early postwar years. The governments of both advanced and underdeveloped countries are urged to play a positive, active role; they are to supervise, stimulate, and assist progress and development. Justice in the international distribution of wealth and resources is not to be achieved by the mere operation of competitive forces, free of restrictions, any more than justice in the domestic distribution of wealth and income is to be achieved by letting market forces determine the rewards to factors of production.

The section on underdeveloped areas starts with the statement that even in cases of "differing progress of citizens in regions within one country, justice and equity demand that the government make efforts to remove or minimize imbalances." The government should "provide the principal public services" in these areas. In its efforts to remove the imbalances the government needs competent administration, and must take account of such factors as labor supply, internal migration, wages, taxes, interest rates, and "investments in industries that foster other skills and employments." Public policy should further not merely the "useful employment of workers and the stimulation of initiative, but also the exploitation of resources locally available." Also "it is precisely measures for advancement of the general welfare which civil authorities must undertake. Hence they should take steps, having regard for the needs of the whole community, that progress in agriculture, industry, and services be

made at the same time and in a balanced manner so far as possible."
Public authorities are also called upon to complement the efforts of the
farmers, to explore avenues to instruct citizens in the necessary skills,
and to explore avenues to help them procure capital. All of these statements imply that the free enterprise and free price system, by and of themselves, cannot be relied on to ensure adequate and appropriate progress
and development for any country or area, any more than they can be
relied on to ensure full employment or price stability.

These statements will probably be the subject of considerable discussion and controversy. While none of them imply approval of a type of
economic planning which relies permanently on direct controls or widespread public ownership, they do imply a type of planning. Underdeveloped countries and areas are told to survey their resources and prospects and to try to promote balanced development of various sectors.
Public investment in basic power projects, like the TVA, and public
undertakings in a strategic sector, such as steel or machinery, may well
stimulate and assist private producers to develop the resources of a country
and improve their techniques. Public transport facilities and government
banks for development loans, with priorities for certain types of loans,
and special credit facilities for farmers, also may meet these criteria. To
my mind such activities may be in line with action called for by the
encyclical. I would think even widespread direct controls for a short
period to help get a development program started may be justified. . . .

Another important position taken by the encyclical is that advanced
countries have an obligation to make economic aid, capital, and technical
assistance available to underdeveloped areas. It is not in accord with a
just distribution of the world's resources to have millions undernourished,
badly clothed, badly housed, and subject to chronic diseases. Few would
argue that this obligation does not exist but many — Catholics and non-
Catholics — in the United States violently oppose our current aid program, and there is little evidence that Catholics take the lead in the
annual struggle for its continued existence.

Many insist the trouble is that our present aid program is badly administered — that it is a giveaway program, will not really help, is not encouraging the poorer countries to help themselves, or is wasteful. These critics
will find some comfort in reading the passages in *Mater et Magistra*
which stress the necessity of efficient administration, and the idea that
underdeveloped countries must be encouraged and stimulated to help
themselves.

In my opinion, however, the United States aid programs have on the whole met these criteria. There have been, and no doubt will continue to be, instances of mistakes and bungling, and of some waste. During my five years in Europe working on the United States aid program, I encountered some such instances, or heard about them. But no informed person today is unaware of the outstanding success of the Marshall Plan. . . .

The problems of the underdeveloped countries are clearly more difficult than those of Europe after World War II. The political, cultural, educational, and technical problems are quite different. I am convinced, however, that the carping criticisms of the way the present program is being run are no more justified than were those in the Marshall Plan period. In the post World War II years the same arguments went on, and many Congressmen and others endlessly complained that the program was wasteful and inefficient.

Another line of attack on our present aid program is that the principle is fine but that the United States program is too big, or beyond our economic capabilities. There is no unequivocal and simple way of deciding how much aid we should be giving, or can afford to give. I personally find it difficult to believe that something in the neighborhood of $2 billion a year in economic aid is enough to meet the demands of justice and charity. The per capita income of the United States is in excess of $3,000 per year today. According to the best estimates available there are many countries in underdeveloped areas with per capita incomes ranging from $50 per year to $300 per year, measured in terms of the current purchasing power of the United States dollar. In view of the fact that we have an average annual income ranging from 10 to 30 times the average income in underdeveloped areas, I do not think it would be an excessive burden to give one percent a year of our income to these poorer countries. This would mean economic aid of over $5 billion a year, instead of around $2 billion. The actual amounts given must of course be geared to the ability of those receiving aid to make good use of it.

As far as the United States economic capabilities for foreign aid are concerned, at least two aspects must be considered. With the United States economy sluggish, and growing at a slower rate than most advanced countries, and with unemployment averaging around 5 percent, it is quite possible that substantial additional foreign aid would stimulate added output and in fact would not lead to a net reduction, but an increase, in the amount of goods and services consumed by the average

American family. Admittedly, if the aid is financed by added taxes there are offsets to its expansionary effects, but in times of large unemployment added taxes may not be called for.

The other aspect of the question of our economic capability for foreign aid is the balance of payments problem. Paul Samuelson has said that the relatively recent development of balance of payments deficits and gold outflows has resulted in the United States "rejoining the human race." Under present conditions the United States cannot run the risk of greater deficits, larger gold outflows, and the destruction of world confidence in the dollar. However, I agree with the basic position taken by the administration that every effort must be made to cut foreign military expenditures, to persuade others to bear more of the defense burden, and to cut tourist expenditures on luxuries abroad, rather than to cut economic aid. . . .

Another important principle stated in the new encyclical is that the more advanced countries should not undertake aid to underdeveloped countries unless they are assured that the benefits will accrue to all classes in the country, not to just a privileged few. The United States Alliance for Progress program in Latin America has wisely stressed this principle, difficult as it is to get the appropriate action and support from domestic authorities in some countries. The demands of justice alone would argue for this position; but there are also practical and realistic reasons for its adoption. The chances of an aid program leading to a country's continued progress and development are slight if only a few benefit from the beginnings of industrial and economic progress while the majority are in dire circumstances. Political stability is endangered, and economic progress may be hindered by the failure to develop domestic markets, skills, and initiative.

The encyclical stresses the importance of technical assistance, and of training programs for the people of the underdeveloped countries. Economic efficiency, as well as Christian charity, requires careful attention to the human beings, or human resources, in the area. The encyclical also insists that political domination, or a new form of colonialism, should not go along with foreign aid. . . . And the encyclical warns against the destruction of spiritual and cultural values in countries with strong traditions of respect for such values, and the substitution of pure materialism. It also insists that individual countries in underdeveloped areas have a right to their own forms of political and economic organization. All of these positions seem to me to be important and wise.

One of Pope John's statements on the problems of underdeveloped areas raises a question of interpretation in my mind. This is the statement that the governments should take steps to see that the various sectors — industrial, agricultural, and service sectors — should progress "at the same time and in a balanced manner as far as possible." I do not think the word "balance" means proportionate or equal rates of growth, for example; from a strictly economic point of view, since resources are unevenly distributed, it would seem quite unreasonable to interpret the word "balance" in this way. It would be foolish for Norway, with only 3 percent of its area cultivatable, and with vast unexploited hydroelectric power resources, to give equal weight to the development of agriculture and industry. My impression is that the word "balance" in the encyclical has more the connotation of proper, appropriate, or reasonable than of equal or proportionate.

In the economic journals today arguments for and against "balanced" economic development imply still a different meaning. A balanced program plans in advance for each sector's production of the goods required as inputs by other sectors. The word balance does not imply equal or proportionate development of sectors, but development with a total scheme of inputs and outputs in mind. Opponents of this type of program do not argue against any particular plan for the eventual rates of development of the various sectors. They argue that the best way to get the desired outputs is to let supply and demand, or competitive pressures, bring about the expansion in most sectors, while particular stimulus is given to development of certain sectors. I would be surprised if the encyclical had any intention of taking sides in this technical controversy.

I think the encyclical's emphasis on balance is closely related to its concern for the farmer, and the family farm in particular, and for the problems of population expansion at a rate in excess of the expansion of agricultural output. To an economist the emphasis on family farms for the United States must be justified on noneconomic grounds. From the point of view of economic efficiency, it seems clear that we should get many millions of families off small unprofitable farms. But the situation in many underdeveloped areas today appears to be different. Governments tend at times to give too much emphasis to steel plants or other major industrial projects. Even though there is a lot of underemployed labor on the farms, farming methods and outputs must be raised to improve the health, standard of living, and efficiency of the people. In many countries small family farms are bound to exist for some time to come. Also, the distribution of large land-holdings to landless peasants may be desirable as a first step in achieving a more equal distribution of resources. In these areas aid to small family farms, and efforts to stabilize farm prices and help the farmers in other ways, must be important in any development program.

On the whole I think Catholics should rejoice that the Vatican continues to take an active and inspired part in the social and economic discussions of our time. I heard one Catholic scholar say that if he ever had any doubts that the Holy Spirit was guiding the Church, the appearance of *Mater et Magistra* would suffice to dispel them. With this I heartily concur.

CHAPTER 9

UNFINISHED BUSINESS

> *To search for spiritual perfection and eternal salvation in the conduct of human affairs and institutions is not to rob these of the power to achieve their immediate, specific ends, but to enhance their power. The words of our divine Master are true for all time: "Seek ye, therefore, first the kingdom of God and His justice; and all these things shall be added unto you." The man who is, as it were, "a light in the Lord," and who walks as "a child of light," has a sure grasp of the fundamental demands of justice in all life's difficulties and complexities, obscured though they may be by so much individual, national and racial selfishness. Animated, too, by the charity of Christ, he finds it impossible not to love his fellow men. He makes his own their needs, their sufferings and their love.*
>
> Pope John XXIII in Mater et Magistra

From Woodrow Wilson's New Freedom, through the New and Fair Deals and the New Frontier, to Lyndon Johnson's Great Society, this nation has been trying to build a better social order, one truly responsive to the just aspirations of all the people. For the first time in history, the problem is no longer the old dismal one of parcelling out scarcity. We face the happier challenge of distributing abundance. President Johnson's war on poverty is no romantic crusade for a beautiful but hopeless goal. It is a realistic fight that can be won. Our farms and factories can produce enough — and more than enough — to provide every family in the land with an American standard of living. At the same time, we can improve the environment in which we live, by modernizing our transportation systems, beautifying our cities and countryside, raising the levels of art, education, and culture.

The antipoverty war will not be a summer campaign, however. The obstacles that must be overcome are old and formidable. Despite all the reforms of the past several decades, both income and wealth remain badly distributed. Our Negro citizens still find the bars of racial discrimination hard to hurdle, as do many of our Spanish-speaking brothers. Seventy-five years after the Sherman Antitrust Act, we continue to struggle with the vexing problems of competition and concentration of economic power. Unless mothers work outside the home, as a growing number do, families with more than a child or two are at a disadvantage in our society. The increasing efficiency of capital is creating an imbalance between gains in production and job creation. (According to a Brookings Institution study, one dollar of capital yielded ninety-two cents of output a year in 1962, compared with seventy-two cents in 1948.) Besides coping with fast technological change, with its strains on collective bargaining, employers and unions are being challenged to coordinate their wage, price, and investment decisions with public economic policy. In many cases, strikes seem as outdated as President McKinley's tariff policies. Yet there appears to be no democratic alternative to them.

We have the brains, resources, and, being a rich nation, the time to improve a system that is already giving a large majority of our people the material basis for a richly satisfying life. That is no small achievement. Although much of the recent ferment over morality in business, labor, and the professions has not been dramatically productive of higher standards, the ferment itself is encouraging. So is the concern over the individual's role in an increasingly organized society. So, finally, is the growing involvement of the nation's churches in the civil rights struggle and the antipoverty campaign. Measured by the criterion of justice, our economic system is a big improvement over the one we had two generations ago. We can with good reason look hopefully to the future.

The Christian Conscience and Economic Growth*

WILLIAM F. KENNEDY

A high rate of economic growth has characterized the American economy in recent years and the continuance of this development appears to be one of the most highly cherished aims of our society. Yet this aim has not received the attention its importance merits from intellectuals concerned with a sound Christian social order.

---

* From "The Christian Conscience and Economic Growth," Social Order, April, 1957.

The failure to see and focus upon the rapid rate of economic growth as a central concern of Christian economics is demonstrated in the generally excellent essay on ethics and economics by Professor John C. Bennett in the volume, *Christian Values and Economic Life*. To avoid misunderstanding, it should be noted that this essay is chosen, not so much because it exhibits this current failure of discernment, but because it typifies so well recent developments in social thought of many intellectuals, Catholic as well as Protestant, who are concerned with Christian ethics and economics.

Professor Bennett recounts that in the 1930's he felt that the capitalism of the times was on its last legs and that solutions to the grave economic problems of the day were to be sought in some alternative system, preferably a Christian socialism; but that now he finds himself in accord with the great bulk of professional economists who believe that the most satisfactory basic system is the fluid-type, "present-day" capitalism. As Bennett and many others concerned with Christian ethics now see, a free market economy which has solved the problems of severe depression and mass unemployment is preferable in a modern industrialized society to the planned economy of socialism. . . .

The compelling economic reason for economic growth is that it offers a good solution to the problem that in our time has engaged all social philosophers (naturalistic as well as Christian), the problem of poverty in the midst of plenty. A generation ago many Christian social philosophers could be accused of being overly devoted to a naive kind of social reform which would solve everything by dividing national income more equally. It is a gain that Christian social philosophers now recognize some of the complexities of a redistribution of income pointed out by the economists: that the economic status of those at the bottom of the income scale can be more rapidly improved by efforts to get a larger pie to divide than by endless squabbles over the sizes of the slices to be cut from a pie that always remains the same; and the fact that the size of the pie may be adversely affected by reforms directed against the more productive and better-paid members of society.

The period of rapid economic growth of the past twenty years brought not only great increases in real income but a more equal distribution of that income. Social legislation aiding the poorer members of society was more acceptable to the richer members who paid for it because their own real incomes were increasing more than the out-of-pocket costs of reforms. In other words, the costs of social reforms and of redistribution of income in favor of the poorer classes were met for the most part from a growth in national income rather than from a levy against the richer classes. With all that has been accomplished, the need continues for economic growth to provide the income required to raise living standards of the poorer members of society. . . .

Economic growth has accomplished much good in the social order and has promise of accomplishing more. As a result, in the framework of the Benthamite economism which is so much in favor with today's public opinion, a rapid rate of economic growth is placed in a high, if not the highest, place in the hierarchy of values.

It is precisely at this point that the social philosopher of a different persuasion can make his contribution by showing clearly a critical judgment. . . .

The rate of economic growth belongs in the realm of means, not ends. By itself, it should not be considered as a social aim at all. To the extent that a society adopts a conscious policy of an optimum rate of economic growth, the optimum should be a computation resulting from technical possibilities and the ordering of the particular aims of society, which, in turn, should be the result of a real discussion of values by its members. . . .

The high rate of economic growth, both past and prospective, in an advanced economy, points, therefore, to new areas of inquiry in a discussion of values, particularly those of Christian individuality and freedom.

While the social philosopher must still be concerned with the poverty-stricken, the problem of the laboring masses no longer has its former urgency. Six percent of nonfarm families received incomes under $2,000 in 1953, but ten percent received incomes of $10,000 and over, while 23 percent received incomes of $7,500 and over. One of the results of a high rate of economic growth will be to raise more families to higher economic levels. It is significant, therefore, for a discussion of the prospects for the survival of values of Christian individuality and freedom, to inquire how these values are faring within this group.

This higher income group includes the most productive members of society and, for society to maintain a high rate of economic growth, it is necessary to find ways to make these people continue to work hard. On this point economists stress economic motivation and the necessity of financial incentives if good men are to be kept in the more responsible and demanding jobs in business, government, and the professions. Avarice and greed are obvious dangers but I do not wish to stress this point so much as that of the dangers to the values of individuality and freedom.

An advanced economy dedicated to a high rate of economic growth must have rising levels of spending for consumption, investment, and government. This need has swept aside the traditional way of life of "plain living and high thinking" associated with an earlier New England society and often identified as the Puritan way of life. The breakup of this way of life, for more than New Englanders and Puritans, was vividly depicted in the novels of F. Scott Fitzgerald in the 1920's. Fitzgerald's was more than mere literary observation, for Keynes was making a similar diagnosis for England immediately after World War I.

Social pressure under these circumstances has been built up to a point where it is extremely difficult for the individual with above-average income to follow the way of plain living and high thinking. For the old ideal, an ubiquitous advertising has substituted "gracious living" — and even the Christian hardly notes the strange twist given here to an old word "grace." In deciding upon, acquiring, using, and tending a vast array of material goods, the whole process of "having" leaves the bewildered possessor little time for "being."

Social pressure is exerted against the most competent members of society as producers as well as consumers. If the economy is to forge rapidly ahead, it must get the most out of them. As a result these overwrought people, among the most intelligent members of society and capable of understanding the way of spiritual perfection, lack the time for, or in the hectic rush of their lives lose the spirit of, the solitude and silence emphasized in practically all the spiritual writings in the Christian tradition. Nor should we fail to note the generally bleak picture of frustration in these lives depicted by almost all contemporary poets and novelists. Social pressure leading to even more busyness only aggravates the condition.

This discussion has been necessarily negative in that its chief purpose was to show that the popular aim of a high rate of economic growth cannot serve as a foundation of a sound, Christian social order. It might be useful, therefore, to conclude with a brief account of a positive method of approach to a sound social order and, thus, to show how a policy of the rate of economic growth fits into the total picture.

To do this briefly, I am going to draw heavily upon an outstanding example of an economist's exploration of the fundamental methodological problems in designing an economic and social order in the humanistic, Christian traditions of the West: Professor Wilhelm Röpke's solid study, *The Social Crisis of Our Times.*

There are two important steps in his method that should be stressed for the Christian social philosopher and economist. The first is a thorough exploration of the values and meanings of our culture. . . . This kind of inquiry is vital to any social reform because our social crisis is marked by the weakening of the foundations of society through an acceptance of the predominant positivistic and scientific philosophy that dismisses all values as nonsense.

Once our values are made clear, the second step can be taken. This consists in the design of an economic and social organization that will preserve and promote these values. The point is that economic structure and organization *do* make a difference. The free market principle is taken as the core, but only the core, of this social order because it is the surest protection of the individual against the threatening power of the state. But economic structure and organization are important at even lower levels. For example, many of our values are dependent upon the institution of healthy family life and, consequently, in agriculture the social order built around the core of the free market principle must foster the family farm in preference to factories in the fields.

Röpke's method has the virtue of showing that a particular rate of progress is secondary. It only should enter into consideration after we know our purpose and the forms and methods of social institutions that are consistent with it. This does not mean an end to economic progress, for an economizing of resources would be enforced by free entry under the free market principle and better methods would supplant less efficient ways of doing things.

The rate of economic growth would be the resultant of individual evaluation of what was to be gained by a more vigorous pursuit of things economic as against what other values would thus be lost. This emphasis on individual evaluation is in contrast to a system where ideology enforces rapid progress as a social duty upon all. . . .

A program of high rate of economic growth has won popular acceptance on account of its simplicity as a political program and on account of the good it has clearly accomplished, but it is a deceptive force that, given free rein, will take us where we would not. George Orwell in his book, *1984*, depicts three world-states, the successors to Russian communism, British socialism, and American capitalism, all of them by that time amounting to pretty much the same thing. This nightmarish vision frightens the reader not by its fantasy but because it shows blown-up what the reader senses the future really portends. The identity I see among the three is a whirlwind of high rate of economic growth for its own sake threatening to toss aside all values and institutions that stand in its path.

Comments on Professor Kennedy's Thesis*

REV. JOHN C. BENNETT
JOSEPH P. McKENNA
VERNON J. BOURKE
JOHN C. CORT

Rev. John C. Bennett

I am much interested in Professor Kennedy's article on Economic Growth. He refers to an essay of mine as showing no concern about the effect of economic growth on our culture as a major ethical problem. I am sure that the essay in question did not do justice to this problem. I regard it as a most fateful and most baffling problem and one reason that I did not emphasize it is that I have so little to suggest about what we should do in regard to it.

I wrote an editorial in *Christianity and Crisis* (October 17, 1955) about this problem and called it "the next moral dilemma." I described the dilemma as the Christian attitude toward the ever-expanding economy with the pressure upon us to consume and consume and consume, whether we need or even desire the products almost forced upon us. The function of advertising is in large measure to make us artificially dissatisfied with what we have, to lead us to regard luxuries as necessities and to demand the latest model of the product most recently elevated to that position. The dynamics of the economic system require this continuous expansion until we find ourselves persuaded to consume to meet the needs of the productive process. A good case can be made for the idea that in the United States the most perplexing issue in economic life in emphasis is no longer the problem of justice in relation to elemental needs — but the problem created by an abundance of goods which threatens the quality of life on a quite different level.

The problem of justice remains central in the relationship between our standard of living and the poverty from which most of the world still suffers. It also remains in America in relation to various groups which

---

* From "Comments," *Social Order*, April, 1957.

are still at a disadvantage. Here there is no vast proletariat which is in need but there are particular "pockets of poverty." There are victims of racial discrimination, underpaid white collar workers, newcomers who have not yet been integrated into American life. There are blighted areas in cities and rural slums and there are many aged and many chronically ill who remind us that the basic problem of economic distribution has not been solved. But in principle it has long been faced and it creates no new dilemma.

The effect of this steadily rising standard of living on the culture, on the quality of life of those who are its beneficiaries has never been faced and the dilemma which it creates is new.

We cannot invoke the ascetic principles which have often governed Christian ethics, even the very moderate asceticism which insists on the moral and religious value of simple living, in order to oppose the whole conception of a dynamic economy. The freedom from depression and unemployment, which would bring back in acute form the problem of justice as the central problem, depends upon the continued expansion of the economy.

The reduction of the American standard of living in more than marginal ways would not increase the economic well-being of other nations. In fact, an American depression would bring disaster to many nations and would raise serious questions concerning the viability of democracy in the uncommitted areas of the world.

If we are to have an expanding economy based upon mass production, we cannot deny the necessity of mass consumption of new goods and, for this, advertising is obviously essential even though it often raises serious questions. We cannot say that any particular development of a product should be regarded as final or that some new "gadget" is really so unnecessary that it should not be made. The absurdity of the idea that we have reached the final invention that can be socially justified is clear when you apply it to an earlier period. This technological dynamism is here to stay. We cannot basically reject it without denying the goodness of creation, since technology is the elaboration of what is given in creation.

At the Amsterdam Assembly of the World Council of Churches there was a tendency on the part of many Westerners to be pessimistic about these technological developments but they were brought up sharp by the delegates from Asia, who told them that they still wanted more technology. It is true that what at first may be luxuries become necessities, and no one would want to see this process reversed in particular cases.

Electric refrigerators may once have been luxurious gadgets, but now the whole process of distributing food is dependent on them.

Only a sentimental nostaligia felt by the privileged can allow us to forget that, without the technological revolution and a dynamic economy, there would be no relief from poverty based upon scarcity or from long days of heavy labor as the expected human burden.

Yet, there is a dilemma. We are being carried along by a process that is becoming an end in itself and which threatens to overwhelm us. At present it is chiefly an American problem and for a long time one of its effects will be to separate us who live amidst such dazzling prosperity from the people who live in less favored countries. The advertising on which the process does depend appeals largely to pride and snobbishness, and in doing so increases both. There is a loss of sense of proportion in living when we become so quickly dissatisfied with last year's models. Our lives can easily be so cluttered with things that we have little time for anything else. There is something in the idea of simple living even though the content of such living cannot remain static. Our scale of values becomes terribly distorted when there is so much emphasis on the new, the ephemeral, the material.

This is not to criticize those who make the products in question, or those who promote and sell them. They, and all of us who consume them, are caught up in the same whirl. . . .

Joseph P. McKenna

We live in an imperfect world. The first step in its perfection is to determine why it is so. Our present concern is with economic growth. Dr. Kennedy sees in our modern passion for change the cause of our degradation; I see change as the cure.

Adam Smith described growth and capital formation as the cause of the wealth of nations. Far from being an end in itself, as Dr. Kennedy describes it, growth offers a palliative for many of the pressing problems of the family and the society. Family harmony is often strained by worry over finances, the cost of housing, medical care, education, and social status. Similarly, the social fabric is strained by the existence of low-income groups, subsistence farmers, the aged and the unemployables. For the family and the society, more money offers a way of escape. For the prospect of a life that was "nasty, brutish, and short," we have substituted "better things for better living through chemistry," metallurgy, and the other technologies of a growing economy.

To those who were too ineffectual to master the machine, it has always seemed that men were becoming enslaved. A cry of romantic nostalgia continues, with a call to return to an idyllic pastoral world that never was. The practical men, who were strong enough to use machines to their own ends, have always rebuffed these romantics in the curtest fashion.

This faith in the efficacy of growth has not been misplaced. Real income has grown and working hours have continually declined. In our own century, the average work week has fallen by a third, supplying that much more time to spend with the family. New appliances and products have returned the housewife to family membership, no longer a full-time drudge who was too busy doing for her family to do anything with them.

Even our problems are symbols of a better world and our frustrations at failing to make the most of it. Mother and father have found time to rejoin the family but have not yet learned how to make this new participation effective. Juvenile delinquency has become a problem, one that could be avoided when children went to work in mines and factories at twelve. Young people, who formerly had little choice of occupation, seem to find too few vocations to engineering, teaching, or the religious life.

We could make more of the opportunities which the modern world has given us but surely nothing is gained by destroying our opportunities to avoid misusing them. Even the problems which worry us most would have been incomprehensible to earlier generations. Imagine how ridiculous a nineteenth-century man would consider our complaint that working men do not use their leisure wisely; in his day they had no leisure to use.

Rather than complain about economic progress, one might with equal logic object to modern medicine, which prolongs a life which people often spend badly. But think how previous generations would have been delighted to worry about what to do after sixty-five.

Even in the list of missed opportunities are the hints of opportunities seized. The mass publishing industry which produced Mickey Spillane also sold a quarter million copies of the *Iliad* and made a book on child care the nonfiction best seller of all time. A record industry which spawns Elvis Presley also makes Toscanini available to every home, even after his death.

Even some of the perennial problems of mankind seem to become less acute in a society which has progressed enough. It has been 2000 years since Christ warned that "After all these things do the heathen seek" and we must admit that the heathen among us do so still. But big business leaders (a phrase which was a nineteenth-century synonym for black-guard) now expect to devote at least a quarter of their energy to public activities. . . .

All societies must depend very heavily on their most productive members and allow them less time, leisure, and freedom from care than the mass of the citizenry enjoys.

It is a current literary fashion to examine the tension-bound world in which modern executives live. Still one feels that the degradation forced upon the members of Morgan, Stanley, and Company is somewhat less than upon the partners of the earlier counting house of Scrooge and Marley.

In sum, then, growth is a necessary prerequisite for achieving the goals which Mr. Kennedy seeks. That we have not yet achieved them is a measure of the growth still required and of our failure to seize the opportunities which growth has provided.

Vernon J. Bourke

Professor Kennedy's article on the moral embarrassment occasioned by an economy of abundance points up several good questions. I should like to concentrate on four.

1. Is there an economic abundance in the United States today? This is a question of fact and philosophers are not always good at facts. I do not presume to deny that there is in America some sort of abundance. Concretely, of what is there an abundance? Is it of immediately useful goods, such as food and clothing; or is it more in the area of "goods" which do not satisfy any important human need? Is the gold at Fort Knox part of our real abundance?

There is a further subquestion: how much real abundance would there be if all our citizens' basic needs were adequately satisfied? A good portion of our people do not eat properly, cannot get satisfactory health care, and so on. The problem of distributing apparent excesses of goods is still not licked, even in this wonderful country.

Yet I cannot deny that Americans are better endowed with material goods than most other peoples. So, Professor Kennedy's fundamental problem is a real one.

2. What does a Christian conscience judge in regard to the disposition of excess goods? Many modern Christians think that having money in the bank is a mark of virtue. Weber and Tawney probably overstated their criticisms of one type of enterprising Christianity which found its fulfill-

ment in profitmaking. The truth of the matter is that some Christian consciences are very tender when it comes to judging the laziness of others and very tough in asserting that wealth is the reward of Christian diligence. Yet there are voices raised in criticism of such acquisitive Christianity.

I have written elsewhere about St. Thomas Aquinas' views on the use of excess material possessions. Briefly, while Aquinas favored individual initiative in the production and handling of such goods, he insisted that the right to use these goods is common to all men. This means, in practice, that a productive worker or manager may first concern himself with the satisfaction of all the reasonable needs of himself and his family. But, if his production exceeds these personal needs, the surplus should be distributed to other persons who can use such goods. Thus baldly stated, the Thomistic position may seem either very right — or very wrong.

There are difficulties in working out its practical details. Yet the main lines of a Christian attitude toward one's abundance of real goods seem to me to be covered in St. Thomas' position. What is needed now is a careful application to present circumstances. There is no point in trying to find this in the text of St. Thomas; he did not know our contemporary economic situation. Economists with a conscience might do well to study the Thomistic suggestions on the right to common use.

3. What does economic progress mean? Many terms used in economics are metaphorical. The main thing about metaphor is to know when you are using it. Growth, for instance, has a proper sense in reference to plants and animals. But what grows economically? Is simple quantitative increase growth? Similarly, progress implies movement toward a desired goal. Is this what economic progress is? If so, what is the goal? Consider a statistic: the circulation of comic books in the United States grew from ten million in 1940 to 1200 million in 1954. In some sense, this is an instance of economic progress: think of all the added work for new workers! Yet, is this an example of improvement and real abundance in our culture? . . .

4. How can we identify our values? This is the basic question. I am in perfect agreement with Professor Kennedy on this assertion. Christianity provides a hierarchy of values, of which too few contemporary Americans are aware. It is ironic to have a non-Christian, like A. K. Coomaraswamy, remind us of this in a Catholic magazine ("Am I My Brother's Keeper," Jubilee, January, 1957). We do not even share the same values as the Fathers who framed the Declaration of Independence.

Our ideals have become more and more material; our judgments more quantitative. We have been overcome by megalomania: everything that is bigger is better.

Economics *is* concerned with values; it is refreshing to read an economist who recognizes that it is. Kennedy is right: the economist must judge in terms of values of some sort. The big problem is to identify our values. And this is not merely a problem for economists.

John C. Cort

Like most professors, Professor Kennedy seems to me to be a little weak on specifics. What specifically does he want to push instead of economic growth? Stronger family life, yes. A return to "plain living and high thinking?" More contemplation among the captains of industry?

It seems to me that there are values within the economic order, or perhaps I should say evils, which might demand our attention before we start worrying about the higher levels of thought and contemplation, desirable as these may be.

Granted that Eric Gill, Peter Maurin, and the prophets and prophetesses of the *Catholic Worker* were frequently talking through their hats. Even so, they had some points. We have given little or no thought to the problems involved in reconciling mass production and the demands of human personality, the loss of interest in the job, of pride in craftsmanship, of even the most elementary identification with the whole act, and fact, of creation.

I would suggest to Professor Kennedy that he give some attention to the economic, as well as the spiritual, implications of that passage in *Quadragesimo Anno* wherein Pius XI urges that "the work-contract be somewhat modified by a partnership contract" so that "workers and other employees thus become sharers in ownership or management or participate in some fashion in the profits received."

I think it is possible to get quite starry-eyed over the vision of factories manned by men who are sometimes bored by the inevitable drudgery, like all of us, but nevertheless find a deep satisfaction in their work because it is not so mechanical that it makes automatons of them, or because they have worked out a relationship with management that makes it possible for them to identify themselves with the act of creation.

And I think there is a kind of economic growth to be considered in the dynamism of profit sharing and stock sharing. As Eric Gill once pointed out, men work best when they own and control their own tools and materials and when they are inspired by that kind of interest that can only come with self-interest.

Maybe we shall never be able to make contemplatives out of the captains of industry. But we might try making contemplatives out of the workers. Come to think of it, Christ did better with them than He ever did with the rich and brilliant.

Poverty in the United States*

DANIEL P. MOYNIHAN

If there are no other victories whatever — and there will be — in the war on poverty, at least it began with a notable advance for semantics. A nation that does dearly love nice things and soft words, that calls graveyards cemeteries and is now turning to "gardens of repose," was for once encouraged to call a particularly ugly fact by its rightful name.

At whatever point in recent history officialdom transformed the "poor" into the "disadvantaged," those who might have protested were apparently content to accept the change and drop the subject. American scholars contributed little either to the conception or the launching of the war on poverty. The impulse came from men of ideology such as Michael Harrington, responding in the face of unmistakable fact more from conviction than from analysis. Action came from the world of politics. The vast establishment of American learning, with its presumptive initiative in the qualitative concerns of American life, was passive if not inert in the face of the more elemental issue of want.

The universities turned their attention away from the problems of poverty in some degree because the problems were thought to have been solved, in the sense that the process of solution was well under way. . . .

We were wrong. At the pronouncement of the beginning of the end of historic inequalities of wealth, the distribution of income in the United States froze. In 1947 the 20 percent of the families with the lowest incomes received five percent of the national income. Fifteen years later it was still five percent.

We were wrong in supposing that anything happening generally in the United States would also be happening specifically. The nation is too

* From "Public Spending and Community Enterprise," *New City*, October 1–15, 1964.

vast and much too varied. And as it turned out, by the 1950's things were getting relatively worse, not better, for many specific groups of people. By the end of that decade Robert J. Lampman of the University of Wisconsin was able to show that income shares generally were not changing, and since then Oscar Ornati and Herman P. Miller have demonstrated that for persons with certain characteristics of age, color, sex, area, and occupation the situation was in fact deteriorating.

Because our statistics single them out, the experience of Negroes during this period is the one that can be seen most clearly. The majority of the poor are not Negro — four-fifths are white — but the majority of Negroes are poor. What has happened to them is probably not unrepresentative of the common experience of the poorest groups during the great postwar prosperity. And what happened was awful. Real incomes did rise, and opportunities for Negroes with education and training did open up as never in the past, but by and large things got worse. In the first place, Negro wages relative to white wages, after moving ahead at a very good pace during the 1940's, suddenly began to fall behind — possibly for the first time in history. In 1951 the average male Negro wage earner was receiving 62 percent of corresponding white earnings. By 1962 he had dropped back to 55 percent.

Simultaneously, Negro unemployment began its seemingly inexorable rise: 4.4 percent of Negro male workers were unemployed in 1951; by 1962 the rate had almost tripled to 11 percent. Unemployment among white men rose, but by 1962, at 4.6 percent, it was only two-tenths of a point higher than the Negro rates a decade earlier. . . .

The Negro family structure began to crumble under the impact of unemployment, dislocation, and the peculiarly savage welfare policies of the federal government, which practically required that families break up as a condition of welfare assistance. With the family base eroding, there was less and less to build on as the years went by.

The great upsurge of Negro militancy was an unavoidable fact that demanded and was entitled to a mature and generous response. But there was another factor: the stalemate of social progress as defined in the institutional terms of the 1930's and their aftermath. The New Frontier came to power with an impressive list of things-to-be-done, but most of them were defined as extensions of earlier programs or reassertions of earlier ideas. Many of these incremental battles had been fought and lost previously, and before long it became clear that they were being fought and lost again. . . . It was clear the nation urgently needed a new definition of the social problem that would unite rather than divide, and a tract from the distant and almost forgotten world of apocalyptic ideology provided it: the issue was poverty. When President Johnson proposed that we go to war against it, he added just that measure of activism that the proposition needed. The stalemate was broken. A whole spectrum of program ideas that individually were deadlocked and doomed were put together, added to, and, before anyone could have believed it, enacted by a coalition in Congress and a body of opinion in the nation that could not have been conceived a year earlier.

What we have had is a great stroke of luck. After two decades of immobility, the old rigidities are giving way and the nation is moving ahead in an area where deadlock was turning gangrenous. The object now must be to exploit the opportunity. Almost certainly this will require an intense effort of analysis to understand much more about what has been the trouble, and how the present effort must proceed if it is to achieve its objective — an effort which must now involve the world of scholarship.

The first question is, what is the nature of poverty in the United States. It is curiously not a simple question. The problem is that the normal, historical condition of human life is poverty. It has always been that way, and in terms of world averages, it still is. But certainly mass poverty — and we have that — is hardly the necessary condition of life in a nation whose wealth grows by $30 billion a year, whose economists routinely assume the economy will have grown another third by the end of the decade.

We are not far from the centenary of Henry George's *Progress and Poverty*, which put the matter in terms that still must be contended with: "The masses of men, who in the midst of abundance suffer want; who, clothed with political freedom, are condemned to the wages of slavery; to whose toil labor-saving inventions bring no relief, but rather seem to rob them of a privilege, instinctively feel that 'there is something wrong.' And they are right."

We must now talk not of the masses of men, but of the minority; but that does not alter the conditions of the individuals involved.

I will venture that there is something of this kind going on: that the "paradox" of poverty amidst plenty in the United States is in some important respects only a surface reality, that underneath, in a number of specific instances, the relationship is causal.

The most familiar fact is advancing technology. The source of our prosperity lies in the unsparing application of technology to the processes of production. The word is "unsparing," the effect is demonic when compared with the way other peoples, altogether as anxious to get rich as we are, nonetheless manage to restrain themselves. The new technology is fundamentally a creative process, but in that process it destroys communities, destroys jobs, and destroys people. These are the new poor.

The destruction of the American coal miners is a prime example. We have the cheapest coal in the world, and in measure just about the cheapest steel and the cheapest power. We also have the cheapest coal miners. In the 12 years from 1950 to 1962 almost 70 percent of the soft-coal mining jobs in the United States were eliminated, with such indifference to the effect on the lives of the miners and their families that it is hard to think of it as a contemporary event. . . .

A similar case is that of our agricultural workers. The United States has the cheapest food in the world. This has come about through the application of science and technology that in recent years has driven millions of farm families off the land, into the cities, with little or no preparation for the life they then have to lead.

Through all this there is a steady, if essentially impersonal, bias against the unskilled and the ill-equipped. There is evidence of a continually rising standard of minimum acceptable abilities, so that more and more those at the bottom are left out.

The bias is painfully evident in the area of job creation. From 1957 to 1963, when the population of the United States grew by 18,097,000, only 300,000 new full-time jobs were generated by private demand. Since 1957 almost half the jobs added to the American work force have been in state and local government positions that tend to be skilled and almost invariably require examinations and accreditations of various sorts.

This is a major explanation of the problem of youth unemployment. During 1963 every additional teen-ager entering the work force caused a net addition to the number of unemployed youth. At 15.7 percent in the second quarter of 1964, the unemployment rate for teen-agers was as high as in any year in the postwar period — nearly half again as high as during the comparable period in 1957.

This situation is clearly worse among the children of the poor. As late as 1947 unemployment among male Negro youth was actually *below* that of whites. Since then it has risen from 7.6 percent to 25.4 percent in 1963 and is now almost twice the rate of white youths.

It may be that the characteristic fault of modern society will not be the exploitation of the poor, but their exclusion, based upon means tests of ability and training. . . .

Industrial progress does not have to produce poverty, but with us it seems to be doing so, for some groups at least. By contrast, although returns are not altogether in, it appears very likely that the industrial democracies of northern and western Europe, without any particular travail, have in the course of the past 15 years quietly put an end to poverty in their own nations. It is as if it were too obvious a thing not to do if it could be done, and when the resources became available it was.

The American experience appears to be related to qualities that are peculiar to us. The most striking quality of the American nation is the size of the country and the diversity of its people. There is nothing in history to match the incredible mixing of "race, color, religion and national origin," superimposed on a continental territory that stretches up and down and across the globe. . . .

The advantages gained from this diversity in the population are real, because the differences are real. At the same time there are disadvantages, and these too are tangible. Because of them Americans have been unable to reach sufficient agreement on a whole range of issues involving "race, color, religion, and national origin," not to mention region, to the point that we are almost unique among modern nations in the absence of certain types of uniform public services. The most important of these is education. Are we not the only industrial democracy in the world that does not have a national system of support for elementary and secondary education? The result is that persons who live in the poorest states and communities in America get the poorest education, with the resultant tendency to perpetuate that system. Perhaps the major social discovery of the postwar period has been the work of men such as Theodore W. Schultz and Edward F. Denison, demonstrating that investment in human capital — not physical capital, not technology — is the major source of contemporary economic growth. That being the case, our inability to establish national minimum levels of support for education has very likely had the effect of accentuating the difference between investment in the human capital of the well-to-do communities as against the poor ones.

It is no answer that things are getting better for almost everyone, even if at differential rates which widen the gaps between top and bottom. Everyone is vastly better off today, but the inequalities that persist still offend against the light. So long as excessive disparities exist between those who inherit privilege and those who inherit disadvantage, the social order is out of balance.

It does not follow that the problem will be resolved when everyone is living in the style of white, middle-class America. Oscar Lewis has observed that the existentialist writers have been desperately trying to recapture in middle-class lives exactly the spontaneity and sense of the present which is the flower in the cap of poverty. Somehow, surely, people can be left alone, without being left to rot.

That is why unemployment for the moment is the master problem. The essential sin of which our society is capable is not that of allowing people to remain poor, but in making them useless. In an age of over-activity, to be unemployed is to be guilty. The evidence is strong that men on the margin of the work force, recurrently or even permanently out of work, suffer the worst kind of personal disintegration. The victims in the main of utterly impersonal forces, they nonetheless take it personally. Their families suffer and their children are deprived in ways unknown to the prospering majority.

If our society has any moral purpose, if we acknowledge any common responsibility for the minimum well-being of all, then surely our understanding of natural rights must extend to the subject of employment. Labor, in the words of Pope John XXIII, is "both a duty and a right of every human being." In an industrial world that has not yet come to terms with the question of leisure, men without work are deprived of an essential condition of human dignity, and there has not been a week in the past decade when by any counting there have been fewer than a million such in the United States. . . . We have not understood this clearly until now, and perhaps not even now. Full employment is an accepted ideal in our economy, much as perpetual motion would attract the managers of a generating plant, but the idea that it *must* be achieved, even at a price, because the cost of not doing so is intolerable, is not generally accepted. The very fact of unemployment, although it may involve relatively few, threatens many. It is the source of the untold rigidities and fears in the world of industrial and social relations.

Next to the problem of unemployment is that of low wages for men with large families. The United States is singular in the general absence of arrangements for adjusting income to family size. Except for assistant professors in small Catholic colleges, the number of children in a family has generally no relation to family income, save as an inducement to moonlighting. One can even detect a general assumption that families are smaller than they actually are. The City Worker's Budget prepared by the Bureau of Labor Statistics, and on which most conceptions of minimum living standards are based, assumes a family of mother, father and two children, which is somewhat below the national average of families with children anyway, and almost irrelevant for a family of ten, of which there are a good many.

In 1961, 24.5 million children, or 37 percent of all children under 18, were in families with four or more children. These constituted 11 percent of all families, and about 18 percent of all families with children. In 1961 nearly half (48 percent) of all children in families with incomes under $3,000 were in families of four or more.

One of the most disturbing indices of social disorganization in the nation are the Selective Service rejection rates. If all young men of 18 were called up for examination, a third would be rejected as unfit for military service. (In actual practice more than half are rejected, but not all are called.) Roughly one in six would fail the mental test, which measures minimum achievement at about the level of a 13-year-old school boy. Seventy percent who fall below the mental standards come from families with four or more children and about half come from families of six or more.

Clearly we require a strong wage system, and a strong trade union movement to maintain it. But it may also be that special adjustments should be made for family size at low income levels.

At this point a warning is in order. Although it is no problem to describe in general terms what needs to be done, it is essential to emphasize that these simplicities are turning out to be difficult of achievement, and that in fact most "natural" forces seem to run contrary. The overwhelming danger we face in the area of poverty is that we will not have the energy and social creativity to make our system run properly, but will instead settle for making up for its shortcomings by massive programs of public assistance. Despite all of those who sincerely feel these programs are already too large, the plain fact is that they exist, and the course of least resistance is to let them go on getting bigger. It would be disgracefully expensive to do so, but also, somehow, easier. Life surely provides examples of how often people individually and collectively will pay a price for not having to change their ways.

The American welfare system is one of the proudest achievements of a generous and compassionate people. But it must not be allowed to become the economic system of a permanent subculture. Men need jobs, families need fathers, communities need independence. This must be our objective, and it is an objective entirely compatible with the fullest care for those individuals who find themselves temporarily or even permanently unable to look after themselves.

This is the object of the President's war on poverty, with its emphasis on jobs and job training, education, and community action. It is within our power to change the course of recent events.

Racial Discrimination*

MOST REVEREND ANDREW G. GRUTKA

The record of oppression due to racial prejudice is shamefully long. Its blot smears the pages of history. Each wave of immigrants to our country experienced the sting of prejudice. They were poor, unskilled, uneducated, and unable to communicate. Many were forced because of social and economic necessity to segregate themselves. Their efforts to improve their status were often met with scorn and contempt. Gradually the "foreigners" gained acceptance. This acceptance came about not so much by change of attitude based on Christian justice and charity as by natural assimilation. Second and third generations could not readily be recognized as a distinct ethnic group.

The Negro is faced with similar challenges in housing, employment, education, and political denomination. From him, however, the challenge is intensified and perpetuated by the high visibility of his darker skin. Regardless of his personal qualifications, he is seldom, if ever, acceptable without reservation in the dominant white society. He is not free to live where he chooses in accordance with his economic status. He is often thwarted in his employment and educational aspirations. He is politically restricted, religiously frustrated, socially ostracized, and individually demoralized. So consistent has this pattern of discrimination against him been that today the United States as a nation is being accused of hypocrisy in view of the glaring discrepancies between principle and practice.

Prejudice, segregation, and discrimination defile every thing they touch but their effect on housing, employment, education, religion, and associations are especially deplorable.

* From "The Divine Mosaic of Mankind," Catholic Mind, October, 1964.

The evidences of segregation in housing are strikingly acute. So is the evidence that this is deliberate. This containment implies that one race is not fit to live with another. This is immoral. Some of our cities and all of our suburban areas are virtually devoid of Negro homes. This condition is far from a matter of choice on the part of the Negro. Christian doctrine and democratic principles affirm the right of all persons to live where they choose and in homes in which their economic position permits them to live.

Segregated housing inevitably leads to overcrowded housing. This in turn gives rise to slum conditions and the consequent problems of physical, social, and spiritual deterioration. It is cruel to advertise the benefits of good housing and then tolerate slums in which culture and the practice of virtue are practically impossible. At the root of discrimination in housing lies the ugliness of personal prejudice against darker-skinned people constantly generating feverish suspicions, hatred, distrust, and unwillingness to behave as a neighbor. Realtors, property owners, and prospective buyers and sellers who resort to unwritten restrictive covenants and rely on the feebleness of law enforcement against discriminatory selling are guilty of perpetuating segregation.

While legislation in itself cannot directly destroy prejudice, its influence is important in the combating of discrimination. Good legislation can become a potent educational force, giving support to the timid and prodding the conscience of the indifferent. Legislators and government officials are obliged to conscientiously strive for laws aimed at preventing or eliminating racial discrimination in housing. The votes of citizens should approve and accept these laws with the firm resolve to abide by them. . . .

Closely aligned with the housing problem is inequality of economic opportunity. Significant gain has been made in diminishing racial discrimination in hiring but much more remains to be accomplished. Insufficient is the concern given to the flagrant discrepancies evident in upgrading and promotion practices. Granted that race should be no criterion for promotion, neither should it be a barrier to advancement. Promotion on the basis of talent and achievement is an honorable and just claim which deserves unbiased recognition. . . .

Discrimination in professions, crafts, and trades discourages the acquisition of proficiency and skill. No one gives his best where his talents are not appreciated. Because the Negro has been hindered in his preparations for occupations requiring special skills, justice calls for special efforts in the behalf of his training. Restricting the Negro to unskilled tasks not only checks his progress but works to the detriment of the nation's labor force. Proper motivation and equal opportunity can provide the Negro youth with solid confidence which will strengthen his faith in himself and brighten his outlook in the future. Equal opportunity for employment can prevent despair, overcome racism, and curb the spirit of rebellion.

In furthering the best interests of Negro youth and the future of America, the racial segregation of schools can no longer be tolerated. It is hypocrisy to teach democracy in segregated schools. Segregated schools exist because there is segregation in housing. Eliminate the one and the other will soon vanish. It is irony to educate for democracy with all its implied rights and freedoms in deliberately segregated institutions of learning. How cruel to open classroom doors and reveal opportunities for a better way of life — to awaken desires for nobler goals and then to close a gate of constraint on neighborhoods where real culture and virtue are hardly possible, and where dreams turn into nightmares. Catholic parochial schools should be outstanding examples of the unity and equality of all human beings which Christian doctrine demands.

Our hospitals have made praiseworthy strides in the integration of patients and personnel. They should be on constant alert to eliminate any vestiges of discrimination. Physicians, nurses, and hospital personnel are offered numerous opportunities for the practice of the corporal works of mercy. Any bias in the performance of these works would tend to retard recovery and add to the physical and mental discomfort of the patient.

Organizations bearing the name "Catholic" or associated with Catholic causes ought to have qualifications for membership which are identical in every respect for any sincere applicant. Everything else being equal, our Negro brothers should be extended invitations and welcomes into our associations in ways that show more finely our delight in having them. Past negligences can be atoned for by heartwarming examples of Christian brotherly love. "Charity" says St. Peter, "covers a multitude of sins" (1 Pt 4:8).

The Common Good*

MOST REVEREND JOHN J. WRIGHT

Moral and legal philosophies at the moment tend to polarize around one or the other of two seemingly contrary, and sometimes conflicting, goods: the good of the individual and the good of the collectivity. Those who are preoccupied with the primacy of individual good tend to take their stand or find themselves accounted with the parties of the Right in our era of state socialism. Those who tend toward the collective good, and consequently give place of primacy to the rights of the state, turn up in our day in the ranks of the Left.

Unfortunately the social philosophies to the Left and those to the Right have polarized at their extremes, with a consequent bitter antagonism between those in both camps who might normally be moderate. This antagonism is reflected in the spirit of suspicion with which men approach those who disagree with them, however slightly, on social legislation. It is reflected also in the intemperate name-calling by which men of "conservative" instinct or judgment increasingly find themselves dismissed as Fascists or reactionaries, while those of more "liberal" impulse or vision find themselves decried as if they were revolutionaries or anarchists.

Even more disastrous is the manner in which extremists on every side become symbols and spokesmen of the camps with which they are identified, even when they are neither typical nor worthy representatives of these camps but, more often than not, unwelcome nuisances to their own side of Center.

Unfortunate, too, is the resultant "guilt by association" among sincere political "conservatives" and honest social "liberals" who find themselves cut off from equally honorable and sincere citizens in the opposite political or social camp because of the sharply polarized divisions of contemporary opinion. This paralyzing sense of guilt is intensified, to the great hurt of all concerned, by the embarrassment these same good men find in the intellectual and moral company they must keep on their own side as a result of this same polarized condition of political thought. And so, high-minded "liberals" are too often associated with actual or po-

* From "The Common Good," *Commonweal*, December 26, 1952. Also in *Catholic Mind*, March, 1953.

tential traitors; while great-hearted "conservatives" are frequently distressed to find themselves tarred with the same stick at bigots, misanthropes, and the hard-of-heart generally.

What to do? The time-tested philosophy of Christendom, blending the hope of Hebrew prophecy, the wisdom of Greek speculation, the sanity of Roman law, and the charity of Christian Revelation, had a phrase which provides the saving word. That philosophy spoke of a third good, with richly personal elements, yet truly public in its nature. That third good, conciliating and unifying, is more humane than the mere good of the State; it is more generous than the mere good of the individual. It is what the scholastic philosophers of Christendom and the Founding Fathers of America called the "common good."

Devotion to the "common good" may yet rally in a single cooperative effort generous "conservatives" and thoughtful "liberals." That which constitutes the "common good" of political society, Jacques Maritain reminds us, is not only the collection of public commodities and services — the roads, ports, schools, etc., which the organization of common life presupposes; it is not merely a sound fiscal condition of the state and its military power; it includes also the body of just laws, good customs, and wise institutions which provides the nation with its structure; the heritage of its great historical remembrances, its symbols and glories, its living traditions and cultural treasures. The "common good" includes all of these and something more besides — something more profound, more concrete, and more human. It includes, above all, the whole sum of these: a sum which is quite different from a simple collection of juxtaposed units. Even in the mathematical order, as Aristotle pointed out, 6 is not the same as 3 plus 3. A victorious army is immeasurably more than the mere physical total of the strength or even the valor of the individuals who compose it. . . .

The "common good" so conceived is not only a collection of advantages and utilities; it is strongly moral and ethical in its content. It includes elements of rectitude and honor, of morality and justice. Only on condition that it embrace these is the "common good" truly such: the good of a people living in a community, the good of an organized human city, rather than the booty of a pack of thieves or common hoard of a mob of gangsters. . . .

Here again M. Maritain is our guide: the "common good" is always ethically good. Included in it, as an essential element, is the maximum possible development, here and now, of the persons making up the united multitude, to the end of forming a people organized not by force alone but by justice. Historical conditions and the still inferior development of human society make difficult the full achievement of the ends of social life. But the end to which it tends is to procure the common good of the multitude in such a way that the individual as a person gains the greatest possible measure compatible with the good of the whole. The economic guarantees of labor and capital, political rights, the moral virtues, and the culture of the mind, all contribute, through the "common good," to the realization of this individual independence. . . .

So the "common good" is all the heritage from the past and all the hope for the future which good men share under God. Common to many, it is therefore *public*; perfective of the individual, it remains somehow *personal*. It calls the individual out of himself to share things with the general community, but it puts the resources of the general community at the service of the things closest to the person of the individual. . . .

The "common good" is preserved and promoted by the nurse who braves the danger of personal infection in order to serve that good; by the scientist who forfeits individual convenience in order to increase it; by the parent who forgoes individual advantage in order to rear future citizens to enhance it; by the saint who renounces individual pleasure in order to sanctify it; by the soldier who disciplines individual preference in order to defend it; by the party or regime or even the national state which abdicates particular claims or narrow prerogatives in order to conciliate those who share it. . . .

Out of a reaffirmation of the reality and claims of the "common good" there would come many results greatly to be desired. A quickened appreciation of the "common good" would turn the tide against the reckless setting of class against class, the irresponsible incitement of group against group. It would coordinate anew the interests and the efforts of labor *plus* management, tradesmen *plus* intellectuals, statesmen *plus* generals, as against the present so frequent pitting of good men against other good men in the conflicts of labor *versus* management, intellectuals *versus* tradesmen, statesmen *versus* generals within the same nation and presumably seeking the same good.

Such an appreciation of the "common good" which unites, as against — or, rather, as *above* — particular or factional or partisan goods which divide, would make possible the "Vital Center" for which certain political philosophers are pleading, a "Vital Center" which can exist only when honorable moderates of "Right" and "Left" prefer working with each other in behalf of the "common good" to working with extremists of their own respective camps, extremists who seek only the particular good after which their side aspires.

The conscientious citizen who walks a little left of center, freed from the embarrassment of constant association with senseless revolutionaries, should be able to make common cause in the quest for the common good with the no less honorable citizen who steers his course a little right of center and is too often condemned as the friend of soulless reaction.

A clearer concept of the reality and the rights of the "common good" may suggest a formula for planning a better international order, to conserve the value of the established nations, but also to be enriched by other, perhaps more basic and humane supranational values, as little by little we come to appreciate how much of our heritage out of the past and our hopes for the future are shared within all nations.

Finally, a new emphasis on the nature of the "common good" will reorient the minds of men toward other goods, higher goods which transcend mere private advantage or even temporal common weal. The longer men meditate on the nature and the notion of the "common good," the more surely will they come to understand that there is no true good so secular, so of the earth and earthy, but that it comes from God, has been hallowed by His Christ and, by its consecrated use, can be a means to Heaven.

There is no "common good," no truly human heritage or valid hope of any people, which lies outside God's Providence, is not bound up with His purposes, is not somehow predestined, however natural it be in itself, to find its place in the supernatural order that God has revealed, and through which all things created are finally brought back to Him.

CHAPTER 10

THE SOCIAL APOSTOLATE

We reaffirm at the outset that Christian social doctrine is an integral part of the Christian conception of life.

On this account, We ardently desire that more and more attention be given to the study of this doctrine. While We note with satisfaction that in some schools it has been taught with success for years, We strongly urge that it be included as an item in the required curriculum in Catholic schools of every kind, particularly in seminaries. It is to be inserted into the religious instruction programs of parishes and of associations of the lay apostolate. It should be publicized by every modern means of mass communications. . . .

In this task of communication, Our beloved sons of the laity can make a great contribution. They can do this by acquainting themselves with this doctrine, by making their actions conform to it and by zealously striving to make others understand its significance.

Pope John XXIII in *Mater et Magistra*

The most moving sections of the social encyclicals are the appeals for a return to integral religious practice. All the Popes were convinced that the gross abuses which marred the Industrial Revolution could have been avoided, or at least mitigated, if men had lived as Christians in their public as well as their private lives. One after another, from Leo XIII to John XXIII, they elaborated the social implications of Sacred Scripture, insisting that these, too, are part of the Christian commitment. In fact, they saw no lasting resolution of the conflicts in society until men who believe in God brought their working lives and their economic institutions into conformity with the divine plan for the use and development of nature's resources.

It is in this context that the Popes assert, as Leo said, that there can be no satisfactory solution of the social problem apart from religion. For not only does religion enlighten minds, with its insights and moral guidelines; it also strengthens wills by its appeal to the social virtues of charity, temperance, and justice. Such is the force of man's acquisitive instinct that it will wreck, unless controlled by a superior force, the most perfect socioeconomic system ever devised. To some extent, human law can be relied on to curb the unlimited thirst for riches and power, but human law, as the communists are discovering, can never be an adequate substitute for religious motivation. It is significant that only in communist countries is the death penalty imposed today for "economic crimes."

Although the Popes have been solicitous about the social formation of the clergy, the main thrust of their message is aimed at the laity. The apostles to the workers, wrote Pius XI, ought to be fellow workers, and apostles to business men ought themselves to be business men. Laymen are present where the problem exists; they are active agents in the economic process. Only the exceptional cleric has the necessary experience and technical competence for an intelligent and effective social apostolate. Furthermore, many social questions now become the subject of legislation, and are, therefore, involved in some way in politics. Only in rare cases — such as the civil rights question or the migrant farm labor problem — where the moral issue is clear and predominant, can the clergy appropriately exercise an active leadership role. For the rest, the field of practical social reform belongs by vocation to laymen.

To play his part effectively, the layman must be familiar with the Church's social doctrine. "It is indispensable, today more than ever," as Pope John said, "that this doctrine be known and assimilated. . . ." In this respect the room for improvement is vast and challenging. Until the Popes cease to be, in social matters, consistently far in advance of most Catholics (not excluding the clergy), the task of social formation will remain urgent, unfinished business. Too many Catholics will continue to be, not heralds of a brighter age, but pillars of the status quo.

Catholic Social Doctrine and the Layman*

ED MARCINIAK

Speaking of the Church, an historian has described the present century as the "age of the layman," likening it to the age of the cathedrals or the

* From "Catholic Social Doctrine and the Layman," *America*, February 7, 1959.

age of martyrs. What he meant was that all over the world, from Nome to Santiago, an increasing number of Catholic laymen recognize more clearly their place in Christ's Mystical Body and His place in their daily lives. More and more, fathers and mothers, farmers and tradesmen, public and private officials, regard their daily work in the Church and in the world as a vocation.

Nourishing this deepening sense of a vocation is the social doctrine of the Church. Truly, this social teaching is the layman's doctrine — reminding them that they are, in the words of the first Pope, "a chosen race, a royal priesthood," called to exercise their lay responsibility in the workaday world. The Church's social doctrine was not promulgated to guide priests in their daily sacerdotal work. It was designed preeminently to answer the questions: "How would Christ act were He a banker, a baker, a broker or a bartender?" What meaning does the gospel have for a man's working life, for his school, for his neighborhood, for his family, for his government?

In modern times the Church has elaborated this teaching and made it available to laymen through papal letters and addresses. For this guidance and direction many lay Catholics have proclaimed publicly their gratitude to the Holy See.

Regrettably, this has not always been the layman's reaction. Some have actually resisted papal teaching, arguing that the Popes were meddling in matters that there none of their business. In our country some laymen have publicly tried to undermine the Church's teachings on interracial justice, the right of workingmen to organize, and the need for world organization to help secure peace with justice.

Such men reluctantly, if at all, acknowledge the right of the Holy Father to teach and lead. They misunderstand not only what papal social doctrine is but also what place it ought to occupy in the life of a layman. . . .

Frequently it is said that if Catholic people only knew the Church's social doctrine, the social problem would be solved. Hence laymen are admonished to read the encyclicals. But is mere knowledge enough? Today millions of Catholics, graduates of Catholic schools, readers of the Catholic press, and active members of Catholic organizations, no longer suffer from a dearth of knowledge. For them the question is whether they will or will not give the Church's social teaching the respect it deserves in their daily lives. . . . You may persuade men to read the papal encyclicals on peace and on the need of world organization to secure international justice. Such reading will never guarantee wholehearted assent. Instead it may lead to adroit rationalizations by which a Catholic layman thinks he can avoid supporting a world organization for international justice without jettisoning the Church's social teaching. . . .

Take an issue like Pius XI's recommendation that employees share in profits, management, and ownership. The layman may dismiss the Holy Father's positive recommendation as advisory and expendable — and do nothing about it. On the other hand, having drunk heartily of the Church's social doctrine, the layman may become intoxicated by its vision of man and society. He becomes a man with a cause. As a government official, an employer, a sales manager, a workingman, or a union leader, he sets out to discover ways and means of realizing Pius XI's ideal for employer-employee cooperation.

In some quarters the social doctrine is distorted by confining it to those great encyclicals, *The Condition of Labor* by Leo XIII and *Reconstructing the Social Order* by Pius XI. This is not a small mistake. For the Church's social doctrine was designed to help the layman transform all of his life. To gain the full social doctrine of the Church, one must range through encyclicals on *The Mystical Body of Christ, The Sacred Liturgy, Christian Education of Youth, Christian Marriage, The Function of the Church in the Modern World,* the *Sacred Heart and World Distress* and many others. . . .

Some Catholics speak as if the social doctrine of the Church was limited to the field of labor, management, property, unions, prices, profit sharing, the living wage, and social legislation. This is another mistake. As a matter of fact, the layman in the United States may daily face far more important moral issues in his home, office, or neighborhood. What does he do about family life under the rhythm of urban living? The duty of stewardship in an age of abundance? The importance of freer world trade? The conditions of migratory labor? The hiring of Negroes in white collar jobs? The impact of advertising upon family values, the role of credit and installment buying? The march of monopoly in the media of mass communication? The privileged position of insurance in our economy? Who would dare to say that these are not social institutions to be transformed by laymen in the image and likeness of God?

The headline of a recent article in a New York newspaper was "Only Squirrels Save." When President Eisenhower, early in 1956, recommended that the American public save and be careful about spending its money, one labor leader excoriated the President, saying: "Do you want to throw men out of work?" When a member of the President's Cabinet prepared a speech in 1956, he referred to thrift as an old-fashioned virtue — no longer practical. When a man refused to spend his savings during a recession, some regarded him as a traitor to the American way of life. How sound are such opinions about thrift and saving? . . .

It would be a mistake to look upon the Church's social doctrine as nothing more than a set of tools handed to laymen. The fact that an apprentice has a chest of tools does not endow him with the skill of a carpenter. To qualify as a journeyman, an apprentice must learn how to use the tools of the trade. Exactly the same problem exists with the Church's social doctrine. There are men who know the doctrine but do not know how to use it. They don't have what could be called the "engineering" virtue, the habit of social justice. Without this skill they can never turn the Church's social teaching into a living doctrine. It remains a mere handbook of "do's and don'ts." Let me cite one specific example.

In 1957 the Cardinal Archbishop of Chicago issued a pastoral letter admonishing his faithful against Sunday shopping and selling. A perplexed baker called upon his pastor to ask whether, in view of the Cardinal's strong language, he was morally obliged to close his bakery on Sunday morning. In the typical parish he would have received either one of two answers:

(1) "You have to close, no matter what the consequences. You're selling on Sunday, the Lord's Day."

(2) "In your special circumstances the Sunday rule against selling wasn't intended to apply to you."

Instead, the baker received a third reply, which revealed that the pastor not only knew his social doctrine but also was skilled in the virtue of social justice. He asked the baker, "Why is it that you can't close your store on Sunday?" The baker replied: "If I shut my doors three blocks down there's another baker who'll get part of my Sunday business, and in the opposite direction another baker will get the rest. Financially I can't afford to lose this business to my competition."

The priest continued: "Why don't you talk to the other bakers about all three of you closing down on Sunday? Then none of you would profit on the other's observance of Sunday." That made sense to the baker. As a result, the baker and his pastor visited the other two bakers who, not surprisingly, were also eager to close but feared their competition. Today all three are shut on Sunday morning.

The moral is clear. These men did more than know the Church's social doctrine. They knew what to do with it. In short, the pastor and his baker-parishioner were practicing the virtue of social justice.

Finally, the Church's social doctrine is not a handbook to which a layman can refer for a solution whenever he is confronted by a problem. The social doctrine is but a starting point, better still, a vantage point from which he can regard his vocation as a layman. The social doctrine is less a set of moral rules and more a Christian vision of man and his many works. . . .

There is a profound paradox about the layman's handling of papal social doctrine: only by withdrawing from the Pope can the layman actually come close to him. The social doctrine may not be left to the general principles outlined in an encyclical. It must be incorporated, by laymen, in the meat-and-potatoes immediacy of human existence. On this level the layman who has absorbed the teachings of the Church must carry on — but on his own responsibility, in his own name, and within the social conditions in which God places him. In such circumstances, as he invokes the aid of the Holy Spirit, he dare not speak with the authority of the Church. . . . But transformed by Christ and His vision of society, the layman will, in turn, transform the world into Christ's image.

Social Formation of Catholics*

LOUIS J. TWOMEY, S.J.

"In my lifetime the issue would most probably be resolved one way or the other (in favor of) Christianity or communism. . . . The job, I felt, was first and foremost to get Christians moving, not just because they were anti-Communist but because they had been made to see that their actions . . . would decide the course of history for centuries ahead."

Thus spoke one of the Catholic world's most distinguished laymen, Douglas Hyde. He made the statement in 1950, two years after his conversion from twenty years of top-rank leadership in the British Communist party (cf. *I Believed*, G. P. Putnam's Sons, New York, 1950, p. 305).

---

* From "Social Formation: The Forgotten Imperative," *Catholic Mind*, May–June, 1961.

All available evidence today points to the urgency of taking at face value Hyde's summing up of the supreme crisis of our times. . . .

By the nature of their commitment, Catholics are anticommunist. But many, perhaps even most, are purely negative in their confrontation with communism. They seem unwilling to admit that communism is an effect, not a cause; that the worldwide, and now the spatial, threat of communism would never have been possible had it not been for the religious, political, economic, and social failures of the West. By the West, I mean that grouping of nations whose guiding principles are derived, professedly at least, from Judeo-Christian teachings.

It is these failures of the West which have created the conditions in which communism took root on November 7, 1917, and thereafter flourished as no other movement in history, not excluding Christianity. For communism is dynamic negativism. It is rushing to fill the voids created in men's souls as well as their stomachs by the unwillingness or inability of so-called Christian nations to measure up to their profession. It should be obvious, then, that communism will be withstood and eventually rolled back not merely by damning it, but by the dedicated implementation of the imperatives of Christian justice and Christian charity.

But this approach will become actual only when we Catholics, and particularly we Catholic educators, have the humility to admit our own large share of responsibility for communism. In this regard let me suggest by way of a series of questions some possible leads to what, in my opinion, is a long overdue examination of conscience.

Why in the minds of uncounted millions of little people everywhere is the Church conceived in the image of the upper classes only? . . .

How is it that Pius XI in 1925 could say to that tremendous social apostle and founder of the Young Christian Workers, Canon [now Cardinal] Joseph Cardijn: "The greatest scandal of the 19th century was the loss of the workers to the Church"? . . .

How explain the fact that in the Western world communism has made its deepest inroads in those nations with Catholic foundations and traditions? I refer to Italy, with the largest Communist party outside of Soviet Russia and Red China; to France, with the strongest Communist party in the free world and where less than two percent of the workers are practicing Catholics; to Spain, which tore itself apart on this issue of communism from 1936 to 1939 in one of the bloodiest of civil wars; and to most of the republics in Latin America, where communism is an imminent threat.

Where were the priests and the nuns and the educated laity during the agonizing decades when the little people of Cuba were either forgotten or deplorably ground down as virtual slaves for the rich land owners, the cattle ranchers, the American corporations, and for the well-scrubbed, well-heeled elite in Havana? Why was it left to a wild man like Fidel Castro to capture the imagination of, in his language, "the humble people," to win their loyalty, and then stand by the side of Nikita Khrushchev to hold out to them his perverted type of salvation?

Why among the newly-emerging African nations does the Church find itself in a precarious situation mainly in areas formerly the colonial possessions of countries with Catholic culture? And this after decades of missionary effort.

But it is easy to spotlight the real or imaginary sins of others. To turn the light in on ourselves is quite a different matter. And yet who of us can deny the serious deficiencies in our own record? In the perspective, for example, of the cold, calculated overriding of the God-given rights of our Negro fellow citizens, what American can rightly question the tragic truth of the indictment of former Secretary of State, John Foster Dulles, that "racial discrimination in the United States is our greatest national scandal and our most dangerous international hazard"?

What American Catholic can deny that many Catholic schools, on every level of the educational hierarchy, will accept atheists, agnostics, Protestants, and Jews who are white, but not even the most highly qualified Catholics who are Negro?

How explain that some Catholic hospitals receive white patients, however complex their ethnic composition, but not Negro patients, however grave their ailment?

Why is it that, although Negroes may be members of so-called "white" parishes, they are rarely allowed to participate in integral parochial life?

How account for the dismal truth that graduates of our Catholic schools are, by and large, as racially prejudiced as those who have been educated in secular institutions? . . .

And in other fields of human relations, the picture is hardly more encouraging. Why is it, for instance, that very many graduates of our Catholic schools, priests and religious included, have what almost amounts to an instinctive prejudice against organized labor and seemingly accept the proposition that labor unions are somehow inherently suspect and a threat to "the great American way of doing business"? How the laboring masses were lost to the Church in Europe and Latin America becomes less puzzling as we examine the lack of interest in, and sometimes the positive antagonism toward, the organized labor movement on the part of large numbers of priests and religious and laymen, most of whom are descendants of the banana peddlers, the ditch diggers, the railroad workers, and the coal miners of a generation or two ago. . . .

And in still another vastly important field, that of international relations, we discover large numbers of Catholics who look with suspicion, not to say hostility, on any effort to build up a world order that would demand the slightest surrendering of absolute sovereignty on the part of the United States. How can they maintain this rigid isolationism in the face of the often repeated pleadings of Pope Pius XII, the greatest and most genuine of all internationalists? It was he who said: "Nothing is more in conformity with the traditional doctrine of the Church . . . [than] an effective political organization of the world" (cf. address to the Fourth Congress of the World Movement for World Federal Government, April 6, 1951). Again, how can a not inconsiderable number of prominent Catholic newspapers and editors, priests and religious, laymen and laywomen keep up a constant harassment of the United Nations Educational, Scientific and Cultural Organization? And this despite the fact that our present Holy Father has often praised UNESCO and maintains permanent observers there. . . .

This brief and certainly incomplete probing into our deficiencies is a painful process. Assuredly, I do not relish it. But, in my opinion, it is necessary if we would come to know something of the reasons why within forty-three years communism has extended its land-spread to almost one-third of the earth's surface and its tyranny over 37 of every 100 of the earth's population. It will also give us an insight into the shoreless tragedy of why millions of the racially and economically exploited look elsewhere for deliverance than to the institution founded by the poor Christ. Moreover, through this probing, we can, if only we will, alert ourselves and our students to the demands of "the revolution of rising expectations" in the Far East, the Near East, the continent of Africa, Latin America, and even here at home. Upon the outcome of this revolution will depend the survival of all that we have known and loved. . . .

We sincerely believe that Catholic education has gone far, very far indeed, in getting men and women ready to evaluate the things of time in the perspective of eternity and to live accordingly. But, as we see it, it has not gone far enough. Until we are willing to recognize social formation as a functional and integral part of the educational process, we will continue to turn out graduates who, although they may be exemplary individuals and family members, will never come to know the true richness of the Faith as it applies not only to personal and family living, but to the right ordering of political, economic, and social life.

Under our present handicap of failing to make social formation a principal objective in our several curricula, we cannot hope that later on our graduates will be able to make any significant contribution to the Christian reconstruction of society which all the modern Popes, from Leo XIII down to and including our present Holy Father, have said is a dire necessity. . . .

The Zeal of Marxists*

RALPH GORMAN, C.P.

Near the middle of the nineteenth century two men, unknown to each other, spent several years at Brussels in Belgium. Both were passionately interested in social questions and both observed at firsthand the terrible evils of laissez-faire capitalism in that small but highly industrialized country. One was Karl Marx. His program of reform was embodied in the *Communist Manifesto* and in *Das Kapital*. The other became pope under the name of Leo XIII. His program was proclaimed to the world on May 15, 1891, in an encyclical called *The Condition of Labor*. . . .

The reception afforded the widely divergent social doctrines of Marx and Leo is a sad commentary on human nature and the faith of Catholics. The teachings of Marx have been adopted as the Communist bible; they have been studied, analyzed, and applied; they have been spread over the earth with a fanatical and violent zeal.

The teachings of Leo, like those of his successors, have had a mixed reception. They are little known outside the Church. An elite few among Catholics have received them with enthusiasm and have tried to apply their principles to the solution of the pressing problems of our modern industrial society. Some Catholics have opposed them as the unauthoritative pronouncements of an ecclesiastic who knows little about the

* From "Two Great Documents," *Sign*, May, 1951.

economic laws that rule our industrial world. The average Catholic, if he has heard of them at all, has only the faintest idea of what they are about.

Many Catholics were scandalized at the bold teachings of Leo XIII. After sixty years and added papal pronouncements on social questions, a large percentage of Catholics are as reactionary as their grandparents in 1891. They feel that in her social teachings the Church is leaving her altars to descend into the marketplace, that she is involving herself in matters that are not her concern.

The fact is, of course, that the Church is entirely within her sphere in interesting herself in the moral aspects of our industrial problems. She cannot admit a divorce between business and morality; she does not teach a religion restricted to Sundays or by the four walls of the church; she does not propound a code of morality that affects a man's private life but overlooks his business and public life. The Church has a place — and by divine right — wherever human beings think and live and act.

And the Church has an interest too in worldly goods. She recommends detachment, but she is an enemy of poverty — at least of a poverty so great that it forces a man to neglect the spiritual in order to concentrate all his efforts on obtaining the bare necessities of life. She is an enemy of the poverty that creates slums, that forces women and children into factories, that contracts the whole horizon of life to the absolute essentials of food, clothing, and shelter. The Church knows that people ground down by such poverty too often turn a deaf ear to her spiritual message while they listen to the siren voices of false saviors.

In the areas of social justice and social charity there are grave deficiences in our American industrial life. The encyclicals provide the remedies — but they do not provide them ready-made. They offer a guide, a set of principles, a beacon light, a philosophy rather than a detailed, concrete program. Application of these principles here and now to our particular problems requires study, intelligence, prudence, and a never-flagging enthusiasm. Perhaps it would not be invidious to recommend that for this anniversary of *Rerum Novarum* we resolve to learn a lesson of zeal from the followers of Marx.

Profit Motive Isn't Enough*

ROBERT C. HARTNETT, S.J.

What is regarded as the fourth part of *Quadragesimo Anno* is devoted to the "renewal of the Christian spirit," without which Pope Pius XI said social peace could never be established. The central message of the encyclical is largely based on "reason," enriched by the Church's 1900 years of experience. The last part is devoted, one might say, to *motivation*. Those who regard the "profit motive" as the all-sufficient "incentive" in economic life would do well to ponder Pope Pius XI's substantially different teaching.

1. First of all, we must substitute a Christian perspective for "that excessive care for passing things that is the origin of all vices. . . ." Our Divine Lord taught us that "the cares and riches and pleasures of life" choked the good seed He spread among souls. How true this is of the social teaching of Christ's Spouse, the Catholic Church! What good, asks the Holy Father, are "sound principles of economic life" if men's passions are swept away "in unbridled and sordid greed"? The Pope is addressing Catholics. He deplores the extent to which they have fallen victims of "greed for gain." "The sordid love of wealth" is labeled by Pope Pius XI "the shame and great sin of our age." The great Christian virtue which should control this passion, of course, is *temperance*, or "Christian moderation." How many Catholics are there who think this virtue applies only to indulgence in food and drink?

2. "Social justice" is the virtue around which, one could almost say, Catholic social doctrine is built. Ordinary justice, as between individuals, requires honesty and fair-dealing, such as the payment of a living wage and an "honest day's work" for it. "Now it is of the very essence of social justice to demand from each individual [and "each single part"] all that is necessary for the common good" declared Pope Pius XI in 1937.

Most people realize what is meant by the term *maldistribution of wealth*. They instinctively know that some kind of *proportion* should exist in the possession of worldly goods. This is the sort of equality the virtue of social justice looks to — an equality of proper proportion in the distribution of wealth, based on people's human needs and their social contributions.

---

*From "Catholics and the Social Encyclicals," *America*, May 12, 1951. Also in *Catholic Mind*, October, 1951.

The *test* of whether a Catholic's thinking is permeated by this virtue is simple. When you are discussing social problems with non-Catholics (at least with *some* non-Catholics), do they interrupt you and say: "Of course, you are looking at this problem from the point of view of social justice. I suppose I am not. That is the difference between us"? If you do not think in terms of social justice, you hardly possess the virtues the Church expects of you.

This virtue applies, not only to industrial relations, but to housing, racial discrimination, and all similar problems directly affecting the common welfare. A day hardly passes when an ordinary citizen does not discuss a question involving social justice. . . .

3. "Charity," or what Pope Pius XI also calls "social charity," which is "universal," must always take a "leading role" in effecting social reconstruction. Justice, whether "strict" or "social," can more easily measure out what is due to the respective partners in any social economy — local, regional, national, or international. But the spirit of Christian love is needed to inspire us to carry out the demands of justice. It is true, "no vicarious charity can substitute for justice. . . ." But the attitude of Christian brotherhood can and must incline us to be generous in fulfilling the requirements of justice. Besides, there are many occasions in which social virtues closely associated with charity, such as mercy, supply what is wanting in the demands of justice.

The Holy Father deplores the number of those "who, professing to be Catholics, are almost completely unmindful of the sublime law of justice and charity. . . ." The encyclical is, therefore, pointedly addressed even to "good" Catholics. If they wonder whether they are carrying out the heavy obligations Pope Pius XI has set forth as binding upon them, they might simply ask themselves: "How much is it *costing me*, in terms of dollars and cents, to be a *socially* practicing Catholic?" If the very query seems strange, that only shows how far we have left the Church's social doctrines on the margins of our daily thinking.

"Catholics," declares the Boston *Pilot*, diocesan weekly, for April 28, 1951,

> especially have a reputation for conservatism which some of us would like to think is undeserved. . . . The great pity here is that we have not been wanting in leadership, but simply reluctant in responding to its demands.

We are *against* a lot of things. But what do we stand *for*? There isn't the slightest excuse for our not knowing what the Church expects us to stand for. It is not enough to blame our schools. We can read.

The Liturgy and Social Reform*

PAUL MARX, O.S.B.

"No folly is more characteristic of the modern era," writes Pope John in *Mater et Magistra*, "than the absurd attempt to reconstruct a solid and prosperous temporal order while prescinding from God, the only foundation on which it can endure." In his introduction to the fourth part of the encyclical he insists:

> Whatever the technical and economic progress, there will be neither justice nor peace in this world until men return to a sense of their dignity as creatures and sons of God. . . . Man separated from God becomes inhuman to himself and to those about him, because the proper ordering of social relations presupposes the proper ordering of one's conscience to God, the source of all truth, justice, and love. . . .

In emphasizing the need of Christian spiritual regeneration as an absolute essential for genuine social reconstruction, the Holy Father is repeating the convictions of the other Popes who wrote on social problems of the world. In 1901 Pope Leo XIII observed in *Graves de communi*:

> It is the opinion of some . . . that the social question . . . is exclusively economic. The precise opposite is the truth. It is first of all moral and religious, and for that reason its solution is to be expected mainly from the moral law and the pronouncements of religion.

His successor, St. Pius X, initiated a liturgical renaissance, which he hoped would inspire apostolic men to set things aright in God's world.

In *Quadragesimo Anno*, Pius XI declared, after his analysis of socio-economic life, that "two things are most necessary: reform of institutions and reform of morals." Indeed, he added later, "if we examine matters diligently and thoroughly, we shall see clearly that this longed-for social reconstruction must be preceded by a renewal of the Christian spirit, from which so many persons, far and wide, devoted entirely to business, have unfortunately departed. Else all endeavors will be vain. . . ."

One need only to remind himself of Pius XII's strong condemnation of materialism and his frequent appeals for liturgical restoration, an active lay apostolate, and a return to human and spiritual values to see how much he was in rapport with the thinking of his predecessors in their plans of restoring society to Christ.

---

* From "Spiritual Renewal and Social Reform," *Social Order*, October, 1962. Also in *Catholic Mind*, April, 1963.

In the fourth part of *Mater et Magistra*, Pope John assures us that Christian social doctrine is "an integral part of the Christian conception of life." But knowing and asserting this doctrine is not enough. It must be, he insists, "translated into action," a commission which he admits is freighted with difficulties because of the "deep-rooted selfishness of human beings, the materialism that pervades so much of modern society and the difficulty of determining the demands of justice in particular cases."

The Holy Father speaks of the necessity of testing and strengthening one's intellectual, spiritual, and apostolic formation in the crucible of daily apostolic experience and effort. He approves and commends the use of the Cardijn formula — observe, judge, and act — in the organization of apostolic movements. In a hedonistic world that reduces "the whole meaning of life to a panting search after pleasure and the gratification of all desires," he bluntly informs Christians that they must be ready to face their obligations with an heroic "spirit of moderation" and a "willingness to suffer with the help of God.". . .

Again and again one meets the words *action* and *practice* in his references to the laity's role in implementing Christian social principles and directives in a world of gigantic and spectacular scientific and technical achievements. While toiling unremittingly at such wonders, men face a real danger of "sapping the forces of . . . soul and body," of losing sight of their supernatural goals and coming to admire their own products "to the point of idolatry". . . .

Pope John, while realistically appraising our era as one "penetrated and shot through by radical errors" and "torn and convulsed by deep disorders," is nevertheless cautiously optimistic, for he realizes the immense possibilities for good that are now opened to the Church — provided the lay followers of Christ "renew and increase" their "personal Christian commitment to the shifting affairs of this world."

The Pope finds this commitment delineated in three basic and related ideas: the Mystical Body, the apostolic life, and the liturgy. The doctrine of the Mystical Body is the very core-idea of the liturgy, and apostolic action is the fruit of genuine liturgical living. These are the ideas that create an apostolic and world vision and produce the needed motivation for apostolic charity, qualities so important that without them there will be no permanent social reform. . . .

The supernatural community of the Mystical Body is the God-given model and inspiration of all right social living. Since Catholics understand that God established a supernatural community in harmony with social human nature as the necessary means for salvation, they should have a better idea and guide than other people on how to form the natural world-community of mankind. If each member of the Mystical Body is in some way responsible for the welfare of the whole Body of Christ, so too in the natural order is each one in some way responsible for the whole family of mankind.

In today's shrinking world, men must relearn the truth the Church has always taught: the doctrine of human interdependence and solidarity is based on the Christian brotherhood of man under the Fatherhood of God. Only when this teaching is activated will the "universal common good" Pope John talks about be realized. Christians who have a thorough grasp of the doctrine of the Mystical Body and sincerely apply its directives find monstrous any acts of racial discrimination and economic injustice. . . .

As the Holy Father notes: "Today, the Church is confronted with the immense task of giving a human and Christian tone to modern civilization." In the fulfillment of this mission the Church turns "especially to her lay sons." One reason why the role of the laity is still so little understood in our time is the failure of the lay people to understand the organic life of the Church as the Mystical Body of Christ. Failure to think of the Church as Christ extended in space and time explains, too, why long pleas for, and accounts of, the lay apostolate have been written up without even a hint of its sacramental basis. True Catholic Action is not Catholic "busyness," but Christ acting through men whose lives are the prolongation and the unfolding of the Incarnation by virtue of the sacramental characters of baptism and confirmation, through which each member shares in Christ as priest, ruler, and teacher. Undoubtedly such a failure to grasp essentials made it necessary for the Pope to warn us "not [to] foolishly dream up an artificial opposition — where none really exists — between one's own spiritual perfection and one's active contact with the everyday world." On the contrary, in reference to the Mystical Body, the Pope emphasizes:

> When Christians put themselves to work — even if it be in a task of a temporal nature — in conscious union with the divine Redeemer, every effort becomes a continuation of the effort of Jesus Christ and is penetrated with redemptive power: "He who abides in Me, and I in him, he bears much fruit." It thus becomes a more exalted and more noble labor, one which contributes to a man's personal spiritual perfection, helps to

reach out and impart to others on all sides the fruits of Christian redemption. It further follows that the Christian message leavens, as it were, with the ferment of the gospel the civilization in which one lives and works.

What the Pope pleads for is an apostolic, incarnational Catholicism. But such is not to be had without an understanding of the liturgy and its central idea, the Mystical Body of Christ. For the liturgy has a double outlet — Godward in worship and manward in apostolic action and charity. Therefore, in connection with the sanctification of holydays John XXIII speaks of "the proper and fitting worship of the eternal Godhead" and "participation in the Holy Sacrifice of the Mass, a memorial and application of the redemptive work of Christ for souls". . . .

In his encyclical on Africa, Pius XII explained how the first intentions of the Holy Sacrifice are social, apostolic, and missionary. How many at Sunday Mass pray and offer themselves with such vision, mindful of the needs of the world? And because so many do not, the everyday life and work of too many Catholics are anything but an unfolding of what they should have done at the corporate worship and common Sacrifice of the Mystical Body. "Is there any wonder," the organizer of the American liturgical apostolate, Father Virgil Michel, asked, "that the life of many Christians is made up of a minimum of passive submission to rules and formulas in matters religious, and a maximum of activities outside the Church in matters secular? . . . If he is predominantly a passive Christian at Mass, can we expect him to be an active Christian in his daily life out in the world?". . .

Today it is sometimes said that the job of the layman is to apply Catholic social principles to life in the secular order. While this is true, it does not state the whole truth. Christianity is infinitely more than a doctrine — a set of truths or a code of ethics. So, too, Catholic social action is infinitely more than the application of social doctrine, ethics, and moral theology to a secularized social fabric — tacked on, as it were, from the outside. Catholicism is human life supernaturalized in Christ. Christian life means living every moment of the day in and for Christ, who incorporates mankind into Himself, is active through His living members, and supernaturalizes all their life and activities. Catholic laymen, then, must bring to bear on the temporal order not only religious truths, Catholic social principles, and social ethics, but also the redemptive powers of Christ. . . .

"Catholic action," Dom Aelred Graham has written, "is largely a waste of time when it is not the fruit of Catholic thought." There is a sense in which one can strongly object to his statement: Catholic action is not just the fruit of Catholic thought but rather also of Catholic life. The thoughts of many Catholics on major world problems may be entirely Catholic while the same persons do not act in a Catholic way. It is one thing to know one's social and apostolic duties; it is quite another to perform them. Men must also be inspired to want to do them in our cold and indifferent world. In brief, the heart must be influenced, the will must be strengthened, the inner life touched. Men must be saved from self-conceit, weakness, selfishness, limitations; disorderly appetites must be restrained — and all of this entails much more than Catholic thought, important and essential as this is. Hence we have Pope John's insistence that, after knowing the Church's social doctrine, it must be "translated into action." And apostolic action is the fruit of thorough, uncompromising Catholic living, the overflow of intense life in Christ, the external operation of the spirit of Christ within us.

This reminds one of the integral vision of Father Michel, for whom the liturgical was always the primary apostolate. Philosophy (thought), he said, clarifies the ends of Catholic social action and gives it direction. Social science puts us into contact with the existential, factual world and works out possible empirical means to realize these ends. Vigorous sacramental living — the liturgy — gives such a movement the vitality of men who continue the life and work of Christ in God's world.

List of Authors

Becker, Joseph M., S.J., Cambridge Center for Social Studies, Cambridge, Massachusetts.

Bennett, John C., President, Union Theological Seminary, New York, New York.

Bourke, Vernon J., Professor of Philosophy, St. Louis University, St. Louis, Missouri.

Bourneuf, Alice, Professor of Economics, Boston College, Chestnut Hill, Massachusetts.

Brown, Leo C., S.J., Member of the National Academy of Arbitrators and former Director of the Institute of Social Order.

Buckley, Louis F., Regional Director of the Bureau of Employment Security, U. S. Department of Labor, New York, New York.

Corley, Francis, S.J., Professor of History, St. Louis University, St. Louis, Missouri, formerly Editor of *Social Order*.

Cort, John, American Newspaper Guild, on leave with the Peace Corps in the Philippines.

Cronin, John F., S.S., Assistant Director of the Social Action Department, NCWC, Washington, D. C.

Davis, William J., S.J., Regis College, Willowdale, Ontario.

Dunne, George H., S.J., Assistant to the President, Georgetown University, Washington, D. C.

Fitzgerald, Mark J., C.S.C., Professor of Economics, University of Notre Dame, Notre Dame, Indiana.

Gorman, Ralph, C.P., Editor of *Sign*.

Grond, Linus, O.F.M., Director, International Federation of Catholic Institutes for Social Research, Fribourg, Switzerland.

Grutka, Andrew G., Most Rev., Bishop of Gary, Indiana.

Hartnett, Robert C., S.J., Professor of Political Science, Loyola University, Chicago, Illinois, and formerly Editor of *America* and *Catholic Mind*.

Higgins, George G., Msgr., Director, Social Action Department, NCWC.

Janssen, Leon H., S.J., Member of Katholiek Sociaal Centrum, Schiedam, the Netherlands.

Kennedy, William F., Chairman, Department of Economics, University of California, Santa Barbara, California.

Kenney, James E., Professor of Economics, Le Moyne College, Syracuse, New York.

Lercaro, Giacomo Cardinal, Archbishop of Bologna, Italy.

Le Roy, Albert, S.J., for many years a member of the secretariat of the International Labour Organization. Father Le Roy died in March, 1963.

Marciniak, Ed, Executive Director, Chicago Commission on Human Relations.

Marx, Paul, O.S.B., Professor of Sociology, St. John's University, Collegeville, Minnesota.

Masse, Benjamin L., S.J., Associate Editor of *America*.

McCarthy, Eugene J., Hon., U. S. Senator from Minnesota.

McGinley, Laurence J., S.J., Former President of Fordham University, New York, New York. Director, Center for Intercultural Formation, Cuernavaca, Mexico.

McHugh, L. C., S.J., Professor of Ethics, Georgetown University, Washington, D. C.

McKenna, Joseph P., Professor of Economics, Boston College, Chestnut Hill, Massachusetts.

McKeon Richard, S.J., Director, Industrial Relations Association, Le Moyne College, Syracuse, New York.

Metzger, B. L., Director, Profit Sharing Research Foundation, Evanston, Illinois.

Moynihan, Daniel P., former Assistant Secretary of Labor.

Mueller, Franz H., Professor of Economics, St. Thomas College, St. Paul, Minnesota.

Murtagh, James G., Rev., former Editor of the *Advocate*, Melbourne, Australia.

Neill, Thomas P., Professor of History, St. Louis University, St. Louis, Missouri.

Newman, Jeremiah, Rev., Professor of Sociology, St. Patrick's College, Maynooth.

O'Boyle, Patrick A., Most Rev., Archbishop of Washington, D. C.

Offerman, Bernard J., Associate Director, Institute of Industrial Relations, Loyola University of the South, New Orleans, Louisiana.

Orazem, Frank, Professor of Agricultural Economics, Kansas State University, Manhattan, Kansas.

Quinn, Francis X., S.J., Georgetown University, Washington, D. C.

Raftis, J. A., C.S.B., Member of the Pontifical Institute of Medieval Studies, Toronto, Canada.

Smith, W. J., S.J., Editor of *20th Century*, Kew, Australia.

Smith, William J., S.J., Director, St. Peter's Institute of Industrial Relations, Jersey City, New Jersey.

Somerville, Henry, an editor of the *Canadian Register*. Mr. Somerville died in 1957.

Taft, Philip, Professor of Economics, Brown University, Providence, Rhode Island.

Thau, Theodore L., Secretary, Business Ethics Advisory Council, U. S. Department of Commerce.

Thomas, John L., S.J., Cambridge Center for Social Studies, Cambridge, Massachusetts.

Timasheff, Nicholas S., Professor Emeritus of Sociology, Fordham University, New York, New York.

Twomey, Louis J., S.J., Director, Institute of Industrial Relations, Loyola University of the South.

Vizzard, James L., S.J., Director, Washington Office, National Catholic Rural Life Conference.

Watt, Lewis, S.J., Long-time Professor of Ethics at Heythrop College and a leading English social thinker. Father Watt died in 1965.

Wright, John J., Most Rev., Bishop of Pittsburgh, Pennsylvania.

List of Sources

Advocate 143–151 a'Beckett Street, Melbourne C. 1, Australia
Aggiornamenti Sociali, Piazza S. Fedele 4, Milan, Italy
America, 106 West 56th Street, New York, New York 10019
Catholic Mind, 106 West 56th Street, New York, New York 10019
Christus Rex, Main Street, Naas, Ireland
Commonweal, 232 Madison Avenue, New York, New York 10016
International Labour Review, Geneva, Switzerland
Le Moyne College, Industrial Relations Association, Syracuse, New York 13214
Messenger, 68 Broadview Avenue, Toronto 8, Ontario, Canada
Month, 31 Farm Street, London W. 1, England
New City, 21 West Superior Street, Chicago, Illinois 60610
Pax Romana Journal, Route du Jura, Fribourg, Switzerland
Review of Social Economy, De Paul University, Chicago, Illinois 60604.
St. Joseph's College, Council on Business Ethics, Philadelphia, Pennsylvania 19131
Sign, Monastery Place, Union City, New Jersey
Social Order (Discontinued publication in December, 1963)

Index